TRANSFORM YOUR FUTURE & WELLBEING

AN ESSENTIAL AND EMPOWERING GUIDE TO EDUCATE
AND INSPIRE YOU TO REACH YOUR TRUE POTENTIAL

RICHARD S. OLIN

Includes the Building Blocks of
Achievement and Prosperity

BENEFITS OF UTILIZING THIS GUIDE:

- Inspire you to uncover your passions, vision, and mission and realize personal and professional success through self-reflection, planning, and implementation.

- Document through journaling prompts what is evident and important to you in your life and challenge you to adapt and overcome life's adversities.

- Provide an illustrative Diamond Cycle of Achievement as a transformative strategy to apply to your individual beliefs, mindset and behaviors to gain a more positive participative approach. Convey the Structure and Building Blocks of Achievement and Prosperity that provides a blueprint of life changing competencies to foster your ongoing achievements and prosperity.

- Motivate you to build your brand and career vision and a supportive inner core circle as a Board of Advocates and Advisors to help you realize personal and professional success.

- Empower you to take control of your focus, beliefs and attitudes and utilize emotional hygiene techniques to elevate your emotional wellbeing. Help you become more positive, confident, compassionate, and build higher emotional intelligence and self-concept skills.

- Challenge you to be a growth-minded participant versus a fixed-minded spectator in life and continue to learn, explore, and transform routines into productive habits.

- Convey the importance of continuing to search out new social connections and groups.

- Assist in planning your next steps for success related to most aspects of your life.

- Learn to create a comprehensive financial plan and take control of your cash flow, investments, and retirement strategies for your prosperity.

- Complete an essential life directory and organizer of all your personal, emergency and financial information.

- Challenge you to volunteer, mentor, and give back to your community as a generous attempt to become more involved and live a more fulfilled life.

- Create a healthier, grateful, more positive mindful lifestyle and a balanced harmonic wellbeing.

- Help you plan well, live well, get well, adapt well, and grow well!

- Instill the importance of treating every day as a gift and not a given.

OWNERSHIP INFORMATION

Your Name _____

Contact information _____

_____

_____

To be kept at home in a safe secure place with other important documents.

If you are interested in ordering in bulk or require additional information, please visit Richard at:

www.HarmonicWE.com
Or
www.RichardOlin.com
HarmonicWE@gmail.com

A portion of all proceeds of this book will be donated to the following Non-Profit Organizations that my wife and I have been a part of:

St. Jude Children's Hospital

The Valerie Fund of NJ

Limit of Liability/Disclaimer of Warranty: This book is for informational purposes only. While the author and publisher have used their best efforts in preparing this work, they make no representations or warranties. The advice, methods, and strategies contained herein can and do work but may not be suitable for your situation. It is not intended to serve as a substitute for professional assistance. If professional assistance is required, the services of a competent professional should be sought. A health care professional should be consulted regarding your specific medical situation. This work is sold with the understanding that the author and publisher are not engaged in rendering medical, legal, financial or other professional advice or services. The author and publisher specifically disclaim any and all liability arising directly or indirectly from the use of any information contained in this book. The fact that an individual, organization, or website is referred to in this work as a citation, example and/or potential source of further information does not mean that the author or the publisher endorses the information or products the individual, organization, or website may provide or recommendations they/it may make. Readers should note that websites and other entities may no longer exist.

Copyright © 2020 by Richard S. Olin

All rights reserved. No part of this publication may be reproduced, stored in a retrieval system, or transmitted in any form or by any means, electronic, mechanical, photocopying, recording, scanning, or otherwise, except as permitted under Section 107 or 108 of the 1976 United States Copyright Act, without prior written permission of the author or Publisher.

First Edition November 2020

Library of Congress Cataloging-in-Publication Data is available upon request.

IBSN   978-0-578-80425-5

Editing by Elise Gallagher

Cover and layout design by My 2 Cents Design

Illustrations by Richard S. Olin

Printed in United States of America

AN IMPORTANT NOTE TO THE READER:

Thank you for allowing me to come into your life. My hope is that this guide empowers and helps you and your loved ones. I am grateful for the opportunity to provide direction and assistance with meaningful transformative changes that will help you achieve your desired potential in life.

> *"You are the architect of your future and wellbeing."*
> — Richard S. Olin

CONTENTS

INTRODUCTION.. i

PART I: THE DIAMOND CYCLE OF ACHIEVEMENT

CHAPTER 1: THE DIAMOND CYCLE OF ACHIEVEMENT 1

CHAPTER 2: VISION PLANNING 11

CHAPTER 3: POSITIVE BELIEFS..23

CHAPTER 4: PRODUCTIVE ACTIONS..37

CHAPTER 5: CELEBRATING YOUR ACHIEVEMENTS...............49

PART II: THE STRUCTURE & BUILDING BLOCKS OF ACHIEVEMENT & PROSPERITY

CHAPTER 6: FOUNDATIONAL COMPETENCIES 59

CHAPTER 7: BALANCED HARMONIC WE WELLNESS ENVIRONMENT 153

CHAPTER 8: CORE COMPETENCIES 157

CHAPTER 9: HIGH LEVEL COMPETENCIES 217

CHAPTER 10: PEAK COMPETENCIES..239

CHAPTER 11: CONCLUSION..261

PART III: YOUR JOURNALING WORKBOOK

ESSENTIAL LIFE DIRECTORY & ORGANIZER 271

ACKNOWLEDGMENTS 337

NOTES...339

Welcome

The older I get the more I realize how difficult change is for many of us. We are often set in our ways and it becomes increasingly difficult to pivot and adapt to change even though change is the "law of life." As the world and environment that surrounds us impacts our lives by triggering situations and events, our ability to adapt to these changes becomes increasingly and critically important.

When I was left without work as a real estate appraiser after the financial crisis of 2008, I witnessed this difficulty firsthand by having to adapt and change careers very quickly. I then realized that there are resources, information, and strategies devoted to assisting with certain elements of personal and professional life changes. However, I could not find a cohesive resource that effectively consolidated and simplified these illusive strategies. Herein lies my attempt to convey some of the most important elements and competencies to facilitate our ability to adapt, change, design and achieve the things we desire in order to inevitably prosper.

I have always been intrigued and focused on how to effectively make change occur and ask myself questions related to certain life elements. What are my visions, passions, routines, beliefs, and mission, and what will my legacy be? What are the best strategies, resources and proven techniques available to assist in becoming successful and reaching one's desired potential? How can I be a good mentor for my children based on my own unique experiences by consolidating, simplifying, and sharing many of these elements? What is true success?

I wondered why there wasn't a guide for these questions and elements that was similar to how champion athletes, successful businesses, and franchises have their own playbooks, business plans, and financial plans. It would be great if there was a more precise process to follow to assist in expediting these goals and achievements. How can each of us utilize the expertise of a well-versed coach, mentor, or Board of Directors in our lives similar to how these same athletes and organizations have theirs to assist and expedite their success and prosperity?

If we could take a page out of the playbooks of the New England Patriots, Olympic Champion Michael Phelps's conditioning regiment, or the business plans of Berkshire Hathaway, Bridgewater Associates, or Blackstone Corporation it would lead us to the knowledge and specific elements needed to be more successful. One of my missions is to share a comprehensive guide, plan, and blueprint of these strategies and competencies to assist in your pursuit of success and prosperity.

The guide is your opportunity to personalize your approach to different aspects of your life. It is an invitation to inspire you to dream big. My hope is that these pages will encourage you to self-reflect and focus on some of the important missing elements in your life. You will gain better insight and be well-positioned to make the necessary changes that you want to become successful.

I have used this guide as a visualization tool to keep important passions and achievements in front of me for positive reinforcement. There are prompts and projects in each chapter to facilitate your self-reflective thoughts and beliefs surrounding the subject matter.

The act of documenting and memorializing these events, activities, and challenges afford you the ability to review these later so you can change and refine as opposed to letting them slip away undocumented. This structured guide will effectively assist with the gathering, planning, implementing, evaluating, and revising of your most important missions and goals. I also provide examples of how other successful individuals use these same strategies and techniques to their benefit and advantage.

These techniques will empower you to adapt to life's endless array of distractions and interruptions. Avoiding and/or learning how to manage these distractions, problems, and adversities will help you toward a more successful outcome. I provide specific examples of challenges that have derailed and detoured my success during my life using only trial and error, and detailing potential strategies as a better alternative. Adjust, adjust, adjust will be a mantra that will flow/persist.

We will explore the notion that your beliefs and attitudes significantly affect your future and wellbeing. A portion of the guide is dedicated/intended for you to review and reflect upon if you are more of a growth minded person who is continually looking to learn, experience, and advance yourself or more of a fixed minded person who feels that things are the way they are and shouldn't be changed.

I will share a target of beliefs and self-concept that is provided as a visualization tool for you to better understand where you think you land in relation to either a positive growth mindset versus having more negative reactive thoughts. Sections of the guide share/illustrate the importance of conditioning yourself using mindfulness and other techniques to focus your energy on more positive beliefs and thoughts. It is intended to empower you to practice and condition your mind with simple steps and strategies through many mediums serving as your personal emotional hygiene to build your positive self-esteem and self-image. Many examples and studies will be provided and reviewed to illustrate how simple conditioning, planning, documenting, revising, and persistence will help with your overall happiness and wellbeing.

My hope is that you will be inspired to focus on investing in yourself as opposed to spending your gifted time on distractions. It will convey a focused initiative to motivate you to take on small actions that can grow into more productive routines and habits. We will analyze if you are a participant that is actively engaged in life or have similar characteristics of a spectator who is more prone to be a viewer. This helps formulate a key point that I try and impart as a critical determinant and effect on one's true success. It also ties into the question of; do you take a proactive approach to life or more of a reactive approach? Time management skills and considerations will be reviewed for you to think about your daily habits and routines in a unique way.

I encourage you to create plans that include a budget, cash flow analysis, net worth statement, and financial plan similar to how businesses and successful individuals have their own detailed plans. I have continually assisted in developing these detailed plans and blueprints for my clients as a Financial Advisor.

We will design an achievement collage, which I have also completed that hangs over my desk to reinforce positive achievements and admire. This project will facilitate mentally rewarding yourself with consistent and repetitive review of successes and achievements as they are accomplished.

The middle of the guide is dedicated to reviewing all six wellness components that ultimately create a balanced and harmonic wellness environment. This review assists in isolating what areas are strengths and what areas are weaknesses, thus creating a more balanced wellness approach.

We will look at/review who is in your inner core social circle, who is an advocate, and who may be a detractor of your success. This will allow you to make some tough decisions regarding who you truly want to surround you as an advocate moving forward.

Building a brand and developing your career are important elements to focus on in creating your career roadmap for success and will be discussed in detail. Sections on networking, volunteering, and mentoring will provide you with strategies to help drive the connections needed to build your personal brand, mission statement, career vision, and Board of Advisors similar to those of successful individuals and organizations.

The final section of the guide is a workbook that is set up as an organizational tool and directory that enables you to reference and document important personal information. This includes your personal passwords, PIN numbers, medical information and providers, financial statements with account documentation, beneficiary and legacy information. There are sections in the workbook for your family tree, a bucket list, list of character traits, and general questions along with your mission statement and other thought-provoking prompts. My vision is to facilitate and inspire you to be the architect of your destiny with a focused approach on the strategies and competencies needed to help you pave your path to prosperity. My hope is that the journal will inspire, educate, and empower you to plan well, live well, get well, adapt well, and grow well.

The foundation and growth of this project not only came alive from researching and writing, but also from my years of assisting clients in creating, evaluating, implementing, and revising their own personal investment, retirement, protection and estate plans. Working with individuals on developing their personal financial priorities and goals allowed me to see firsthand the expectations, concerns, understanding, and interest level of the process and its multitude of ramifications for my clients and their family's financial wellbeing. I soon began to realize that I could share these same strategies and competencies with a much broader audience.

The focus of this project, emerged out of a recent downsizing from a successful career as a market sales manager and Supervisory Principal at a large financial services firm. Coincidentally, while driving home the morning I was downsized, I got the call that my dad had passed away. This is one unique example of a situation of how life threw me a knuckleball. While managing, training, and developing my former team of financial advisors on their own business, career growth, and developmental plans I came to the same realization that I could impart these same resources, strategies and techniques to another audience.

The benefit of managing diverse teams of advisors, relationship managers, as well as a market of retail banking centers, has allowed me to have a broader understanding of how to manage, train, and coach for successful outcomes. Each of these associates and clients have their own set of unique needs, concerns, skills, strengths and weaknesses and it afforded me the opportunity to provide them guidance on their individual development and financial plans.

As a prior small business owner, I was fortunate enough to be able to learn, sometimes the hard way, how to build a brand and a company from an idea into a thriving business, delivering and executing on a specific business plan and associated strategies. The totality of my unique career path (that has also included decades as a real estate appraiser, recruiting consultant, and bartender) has provided me the foundation needed to communicate to you what I think are the most productive and beneficial tools, competencies, and strategies to assist in your unique journey. My hope is that you will use it to inevitably pivot to invest in yourself to reach your desired visions and potential.

"The greater danger for most of us lies not in setting our aim to high and falling short, but in setting our aim to low and achieving our mark." — Michelangelo

Michelangelo is regarded as one of the greatest artists of all time as a painter, sculptor, designer, and architect. By sharing these words above he challenges us to reach our true potential. Where have you set your aim in life; high, low, at the bullseye, or have you not given it much thought? What's your plan to get there? How can you refocus your attention and aim for the bullseye?

"You are the designer and architect of your future, destiny and wellbeing." — Richard S. Olin

Just as Michelangelo painstakingly painted the Sistine Chapel, sculpted his "David," and designed numerous buildings, so to can you craft, transform, and fully design your own journey and way of life. This moment is a great time to devote and focus your attention on your situation — where you are in life, how you got there, and what you can do to change things for the better. It is also an opportunity to better understand why you believe the things you do and have the thoughts, attitudes, and habits that are inherently yours.

I encourage you to take a moment and write down a brief description of where you have set your aim: high, low, at the middle and WHY you think it is there?

_____

_____

_____

_____

_____

Please make it a point to fill in the prompts with a response and not move forward without adding ink on the pages. Part of the benefit from reading this is to have a better understanding of the true you. Include the WHY in your responses when prompted as it will add context and detail and hopefully provide you a better understanding of the full situation and your own rationale.

Two of the big questions we seem to continually ask are — what success is and how do we attain it? There are so many differing opinions of the answers. Some of us think it is about material wealth due to our world of enhanced social media, celebrity, and fame. That was my definition as a younger adult in addition to becoming an Olympic ski champion. Many of us think it is primarily about being in good physical shape and eating healthy foods. Others, many whom I have worked with and associate with, think it's a combination of their career aspirations to becoming a managing partner or corporate executive who is wealthy. As I get older, my definition of success changes. The impact of having two of my best friends pass away unexpectedly at a very young age effected my definition at that point in time. It morphed into living a longer life from the prior definition of attaining material wealth. As I got older, it seemed to encompass a combination of several components of being healthier, wealthier and wise, as the saying goes.

When I started to do a considerable amount of research for this project several years ago, I reread a book: The 100: A Ranking of the Most Influential Persons in History by Michael H. Hart. Aristotle was ranked fourteenth in the book behind all of the great religious organizers, world explorers, and accomplished scientists. He is considered a great philosopher, scientist, educator, and ultimately an influencer of his time in history, very much different than the influencers of today.

Aristotle was an historical figure who had great insight into what is and should truly be important to us all. His teachings resonated with me as a teenager and then those studies and days faded away. However, when I began to recently study his teachings about "taking the time to self-reflect and take a logical approach; on wellbeing and being prosperous"; this activity resulted in a real benefit for me. I had a clearer understanding of myself and my situation. As I read and learned more about what he had been taught by Plato and imparted to Alexander the Great as a mentor, I began to quantify and write down my own personal take on these impactful concepts and grandiose ideas. My limited understanding of his notion of true wellbeing, prosperity and "living the good life," as he called it, was that each of us should have balance between our physical, emotional, intellectual, and political or social wellbeing. This was my "ah ha" moment.

As I embarked upon a renewed effort to write down and consolidate the most important factors one should consider when traversing their complicated lives for my children, I kept these concepts and ideas in mind. This guide expands these into more detailed competencies. When I was a real estate appraiser early on in my career, I analyzed and quantified a properties Highest and Best Use. In life I think it is important to be able to quantify our own highest and best use taking into consideration Aristotle's enlightening teachings.

I encourage you to take a moment to write down a brief description of what success, and more importantly what "prosperity and wellbeing," means to you and WHY.

_____

_____

_____

_____

_____

Once we dig into the details, it may be interesting to see if what you documented above differs from your later definition. Please include the WHY response as well.

When my father passed away a few years ago around the same time I was beginning to formulate this project, I wrote a eulogy for his funeral about his storied, energetic, and diverse life. I began reflecting upon his life and it gave me pause and became an awakening moment in my life. As I wrote specific details about his life regarding his career, military and civic service, relationships, challenges, problems, business ventures I also began self-reflecting and journaling about my own.

Two themes emerged from this task. The first was that this was my rocking chair moment. This happens when we sit back for a moment and think or reflect upon what our lives have consisted of to date and what we can make of the remaining time we have here on Earth. Imagine yourself sitting in your rocking chair on the front porch of your home gazing out at the landscape of your property and more importantly the landscape of your life. This is exactly what I think Aristotle was trying to impart to us millenniums ago.

The second is what I found to be beneficially important to me in journaling these close personal thoughts, ideas, visions, passions, and goals. For me, documenting, and in some way memorializing these ideas, was critical to my broader understanding of my situation. It also afforded me the ability to design, review, revise, and implement the important elements of what my future potentially holds for me. It has morphed into an organizational tool for my life's priorities, passions, positive beliefs, productive behaviors, and lasting achievements.

So, let's get it started! Get comfy, and put on your creative vision thinking cap!

Prompt: Take some time to think about what passions and overall goals and interests you have. This is your own rocking chair moment on your front porch. Place yourself in a comfortable chair, maybe even a rocking chair if you have one, and be mindful of your past and how you would like to see your future play out. Keep in mind how you may want to be viewed or remembered when you are no longer around. It is similar to writing your own biography, mission and/or eulogy. Throughout my life, I always wrote down many passions and goals that I had not yet started or achieved using many different formats. One of these goals was to create the Structure and Building Blocks of Achievement and Prosperity provided later in the guide. Another was to volunteer and mentor others and take control of my own destiny.

The goals that you should include are ones that you want to define your life and legacy. They may be related to your personal brand, potential intellectual accomplishments, career goals and financial goals, exploring something new, how you will overcome an adversity you may be going through currently, etc. Write down at least 4 to 5 to review later while creating your passion and vision collage. What are the main things that you want to accomplish in your life? Include the WHY as to what the IMPACT BENEFIT will be to you and your life by accomplishing it/them! This relates to the beneficial end result of completing the task and its positive impact on your life. Be creative and think of potential stretch goals and passions you may have related to your own personal growth regarding your physical, emotional, intellectual, financial, social as well as occupational components.

1 _____

_____

_____

2 _____

_____

_____

3 _____

_____

_____

4 _____

_____

_____

5 _____

_____

_____

    Approximately two years ago, my wife and I were walking through Quincey Market in Boston while my daughter was attending her college orientation. There were a few people gathered around a table where some musicians were playing and teaching a group of onlookers how to play simple notes on the harmonica. These Horner representatives were very adept at playing blues and rock and roll riffs that piqued my interest. I always loved music since I was a kid. However, other than a brief lame attempt at guitar and piano lessons as a child, it was more about concerts, listening, and enjoying the music. I decided to sit down and give it my best shot with the lesson they were providing while blowing air, spit and ear piercing sounds out of the harp.

Two years and ten harmonicas later, I have been able to play multiple songs in several genres with my wife banishing me mostly to the basement. Here's a tip, if you like to whistle, you will probably enjoy playing the harmonica and it should make it easier for you to play as it was for me. Also, when learning the harmonica, find a place away from your partner to preserve his/her wellbeing! More recently, I decided to pull out my guitar from the 1970's, restring it, and learn cords and songs. It has been another recent turning point in my life as I have a renewed appreciation for this art form and musicians' talents.

I always strive to be a participant in life taking on new challenges whether it's playing an instrument, skiing down an expert slope at 12,000 feet, snorkeling a reef, learning an investment and planning strategy, or performing magic. This is an important factor in becoming successful as we challenge ourselves to take on new experiences and have a growth mindset.

The older I get the more I realize the importance of taking the time to invest in myself as opposed to spending my gifted time on needless and benefit-less distractions. Life has a way of offering us opportunities to grow. Sometimes, things that have significance aren't directly in our focus and it takes a random encounter to unlock their importance and benefits. The passion of playing a harmonica or guitar was not on my priority list or radar a few years ago or even more recently, but it eventually rose to the top of that list and has been a huge impact benefit on my wellbeing and life.

It has been noted that people don't plan to fail, most just fail to plan. Studies consistently document that by writing down goals, you are much more likely to reach them, than if they're not written down. Do you have your own written plan? Are you interested in attaining a higher level of achievement, organization, success and prosperity? Then you are in the right place at the right time in your life. The best time to get started is yesterday and the next best time is today.

Designing your future destiny begins with blueprints and their revisions that are the basis of this guide. With the initial self-reflective phase complete, we can begin to dig into the details and layout the cornerstones.

The structure needs to have solid footings for stability to anchor and ground us to stay strong, last and endure. They include visions, having positive beliefs that feed productive actions, and the eventual celebration of ongoing achievements. As we cycle through them they will create meaningful results and lead to new personal growth. This is the strategy and competencies that successful individuals and businesses utilize in their planning and execution.

Once we have laid out these cornerstones and the strategy of the Diamond Cycle of Achievement, to be reviewed in detail, it is time to build a strong and solid foundation. These may incorporate some of the same materials and similarities of the cornerstones, but with a different composition and features to make them secure. This will be accomplished using other tools, resources, and techniques like utilizing a coach or mentor to simplify the process and making sure the project is financially sound and solvent while always learning while we continue to grow.

As we complete the foundational work and competencies, we can continue to focus the cornerstone strategies on certain core level competencies that will provide additional stability and support for the higher levels and peak. Some of these include: conditioning your mind and body, creating your brand, developing your career, and continuing to overcome life's distractions and adversities.

Higher level competencies that are layered on top of the core levels include: exhibiting motivation, confidence, generosity, and high emotional intelligence EQ among others. These enhance stability of our character traits, while allowing us increased flexibility. They grow out of and tie back into the foundational and cornerstone competencies. The peak competencies include having high self-concept, persistence, and being adaptable. They round out the structure, allow additional flexibility, and help us reach our true potential.

This completes the construction of the Structure and Building Blocks of Achievement and Prosperity that is the basis for the blueprint strategy and competencies. The flow and design of this guide grows and builds from each level of competencies similar to how your own personal growth may evolve.

In addition to self-reflecting and understanding what our passions and visions are, it's important for each of us to understand what our mission is in life. This will be reviewed in detail in the brand and career development section. This ties in well to the notion of having a growth mindset. We are often asked especially in interviews, what is it that you're focused on or pursuing currently?

I am always intrigued by people's answers as it speaks volumes about their focus, what's important to them, and have they taken the time to think about or self-reflect upon their answers. Most of the time when asked these questions or something similar, the answers are primarily focused upon our occupation and associated tasks. Often, many of us quickly dive into the details and/or avoid it if we are not engaged in meaningful employment or a career.

I used to respond accordingly, with the usual; I am a financial advisor that assists individuals with their planning…. Now that I am more self-aware and realize that my occupation does not solely define me, my response is closer to: I am a proud family man, mentor, and volunteer who tries to live life to its fullest through traveling and skiing, writing, performing, a collector and creator of art; who assists clients with their life's focus and financial planning by implementing strategies for success. A big pivot from the prior and one that better describes my mission and what I am focused on and am pursuing. Take a moment to think about how you answered this question in the past and how you may want to pivot to another more detailed response.

Prompt: Write down your prior response to: What is it that you are pursuing or are focused on?

_____

_____

_____

_____

_____

Now, document a potential new response or mission statement to this question with more detail._____

_____

_____

_____

Why should you care about taking the time to write a mission statement, build your brand or reinvent yourself, and why is it more important now than ever before?

There are several paradigm shifts that continue to take place within our society that will greatly affect our futures; some more than others. Some of these paradigms have changed my life over the past few years and led me to where I am today. One of the greatest of which involves Artificial Intelligence, which affects our lives in so many ways.

As I read and learn more and more about AI's affects, it becomes evident that outside forces have the ability to affect many of our own personal choices and focus areas in our lives. This inevitably involves controlling our eyeballs in a way to influence and determine things like what we may focus on daily in our spare time, read and in turn feel about many topics in addition to what we may want to buy. The collection of our personal data in conjunction with social media is a critical element of AI. AI may know more about us than our own partners or family members as big tech tracks our interests, searches, needs, and wants.

Social media companies collect our information, compete for our attention and finite time. This affects the daily choices we make. Although not a primary focus of this project, it appears more and more relevant that these elements are competing forces for our limited resources that should be dedicated to our balanced wellness. We will later explore how much time and energy you focus on your social construct versus the other wellness components described and its potential longer-term effects.

Over the past few decades, there has been a significant shift related to hiring and consulting practices regarding the US workforce. This has led to a more competitive white-collar workforce that includes labor outsourcing and the hiring of foreign contractors on H1-B and L-1 Visas as a corporate strategy to contain labor costs and attract the highest qualified employees. The continued introduction of Robotics technology will also have far reaching affects for the future of many jobs increasingly related to low tech, transportation and retail positions within certain industries and the economy. The ability to earn a higher degree, certificate, change between career paths and the transfer of skills as we get older will be more critical to our overall success and prosperity than ever before.

The third paradigm shift that is worth noting for all of us to consider has been the process of transitioning the burden of saving and investing for retirement and health care needs squarely on the shoulders of the employee. In the past, there was a three-legged stool for retirement (as we called it in the industry). This included a combination of three income streams that retirees would access for retirement income and included: social security benefits, corporate and government pensions, and retirement savings in tax deferred plans. Based upon several factors that include freezing and closing a large portion of these institutional pension plans and potential reduction of social security benefits, there is significant responsibility for the employee to account for his/her own retirement income needs. It is now often an unbalanced two-legged stool.

Gig workers and self-employed individuals are in this same situation. Health Savings Accounts (HSAs) and Flexible Spending Accounts (FSAs) are other financial offerings that many of us will need to better understand and manage. The implications of these changing trends are that each of us has a greater responsibility to learn, understand, and manage our financial future by planning appropriately. No longer can an employee work for one company for a career lifetime and depend on his/her pension plan to send them a monthly check. We each need to take responsibility for our financial wellbeing during our careers and retirement.

These paradigms will be touched upon later in the financial, occupational, social, and emotional wellness sections of the guide. These changes, along with other factors like younger adults and millennials only staying at jobs on average for 3.5 years, and this new era of entitlement are creating a challenging environment for many of us to adapt, change, and prosper.

Here, you will learn helpful tips and techniques to document your planning process and encourage you to think differently about these paradigm shifts. Empowerment is a powerful feeling that will boost your energy level to focus on investing in yourself and your brand to help overcome future challenges.

Please note that I am not a doctor, psychologist or psychiatrist. My intention is to provide a summary of the details, resources, studies, techniques, and next steps we can utilize to help us grow. This guide is the place to bring this all together in a simple cohesive fashion, so that you can learn, analyze, plan, reevaluate, and document your hard work. This will enable you to build a strong and solid foundation to assist with your personal and professional growth.

I can appreciate that we all go through struggles at different points in our lives. You may feel as though this is not a good time to change the direction of your compass or path. Often, no time feels like a good time or the best time. My recommendation is to not think about making every change necessary right away or it will become very overwhelming. This guide is an opportunity to help you better understand yourself first and foremost. It is a resource to inspire and challenge you by coaching and mentoring you to tackle the most critical gaps and areas of your life where there are structural deficiencies. Providing the most beneficial competencies to focus on will help position you to begin to incorporate other strategies provided.

Thereafter, it may afford you the ability to develop and grow from some or several of the other higher-level competencies where there may be smaller gaps to close. This is about challenging you and motivating you to begin a brief or more significant detour depending upon what your individual needs are now and in the future. We just need to take that first step and much of the rest will follow.

Thank you for purchasing my work and allowing me the opportunity to come into your life in a positive, productive, and collaborative way. I am hopeful that this work will have an impact benefit on your life and those close to you that rely on you.

TEN TENET'S OF THE GUIDE

1. Inspire you to uncover your passions, vision, and mission and realize personal and professional success through self-reflection, planning, and implementation.

2. Document through journaling prompts what is evident and important to you in your life and challenge you to adapt and overcome life's adversities.

3. Motivate you to build your brand and career vision and a supportive inner core circle as a Board of Advocates and Advisors.

4. Empower you to take control of your focus, beliefs and attitudes and utilize emotional hygiene conditioning and techniques to elevate your positive emotional wellbeing and self-image.

5. Challenge you to be a growth-minded participant versus a fixed-minded spectator in life and continue to learn and explore and transform routines into productive habits.

6. Share strategies, resources, and competencies to help you design and transform your future and wellbeing.

7. Empower you to invest in yourself and not spend your gifted time on life's distractions.

8. Create a healthier, grateful, more positive mindful lifestyle and a balanced harmonic wellness environment.

9. Help you plan well, live well, get well, adapt well and grow well!

10. Instill the importance of mentoring and volunteering and treating every day as a gift and not a given and live a more fulfilled life.

HOW TO BENEFIT FROM THE GUIDE

- Complete all prompts and projects on each page.
- Self-reflect and be honest with your answers.
- Review and/or rethink prior subject matter and responses.
- Add phone reminders and calendar updates as you progress.
- Gather and organize required documents that include receipts, personal information, medical, financial, legal, etc.
- Document any other needed information in the Workbook and additional space at the end.
- Review and discuss important considerations and feelings, beliefs, goals, next steps with a partner, confidant, friend, inner core circle and Board of Advisors.
- Spend time during your quiet time/stretching/yoga/meditation/mindfulness and/or exercise to visualize certain elements and achievements and reward yourself emotionally.
- Link each of the competencies that you are primarily focusing on to your daily routine.
- Retain and use 4x6 index cards to reinforce certain competencies that become relevant and create a daily review process.
- Pullout the Workbook pages on positive self-esteem, strategies, and gratitude affirmations and place them in well trafficked locations like a desk, mirror and computer.
- Use the additional space provided to begin or continue your scheduled journaling routine.
- Share by giving the guide as a gift to a family member or someone close to you that you think would benefit.

PART ONE

The Diamond Cycle of Achievement

CHAPTER 1

The Diamond Cycle of Achievement

Successful individuals and teams always have a formula for success. It may incorporate one or multiple strategies. However, there is always a foundational component. While studying and learning about financial competencies for my securities exams to become an advisor, I read a great deal about John Bogle's investment strategy of buying low cost index funds and how this was the basis for the Vanguard Corporation's incredible growth and success, which will be touched upon in Chapter 6.

Thomas Edison, one of the greatest inventors of all time, used a strategy of persistence and knowledge to continue to experiment until he got the beneficial results desired. Jeff Bezos, founder of Amazon, used a simple strategy of providing a wider selection of lower cost products that were easier to purchase online. History is inked with so many athletes and professional franchises that have made their mark by incorporating a specific strategy into a wider game plan to excel.

That is why I am beginning this guide with the Diamond Cycle of

Achievement; the simplified strategy that can act as the guide for your future achievements. That does not mean that utilizing some of its parts will not create success, as it will. But taken as a whole, it is a complete formula for success by focusing all the components on a particular competency or challenge.

Let's break it down into the initial three competencies with the fourth one at the center creating the diamond configuration. Much has been written and detailed about the importance of each of these components separately and to a certain degree in combination with one or another. The premise of my updated approach that I am advising is the combination of all four. Again, I want to emphasize that each separately is effective. However, the power and veracity of the whole diamond, having a better understanding of the WHY impact benefit and process, and utilizing the available tools will create faster, more significant changes and long lasting achievements. It has worked for me and it will work for you. So, what is the meaningful formula or strategy for success and prosperity that is simple enough yet cohesive enough to endure and stand the test of time?

The Diamond Cycle strategy begins with having a vision, passion and/or goal planning. This component coupled with positive beliefs will feed into actions and habits that will create results. If we were to place a coach or mentor in the center to simplify and expedite the process of each of these three components, then we have the diamond configuration. It has been said that every achievement that ever was began with a dream. Visions borne out of dreams that have follow through with a plan lead to accomplishments. The critical element often missing from this process of success is having true belief.

We will spend a significant amount of time analyzing and cultivating a better understanding of our own beliefs to see where we are in relation to a focused target that is provided. Without the belief that we are capable and worthy of this goal or achievement, we often are overcome with fear and doubt and fall short of our intended vision.

As I sit here today working diligently on the remainder of this guide with a goal of helping and sharing my thoughts, strategies and tools with you, I am often clouded with the thoughts of: Will anyone really care; will it be received in a good way or will I be faced with critical responses since I am not a career writer among my other doubts and concerns. It is my ability to use the techniques provided and persistently trudge forward that will see this project through to fruition with the assistance of the other three components.

I have always been good at goal planning and writing down lists of things I need to accomplish; I am okay at the action planning and forming good habits at times, but I often struggle with having the beliefs that I can get it done. (More to come in Chapter 3).

The third component of taking action and creating behaviors productive to moving the process and strategy forward is critical and often cited as being the key element. The wildcard, that I term it, is the help and assistance of a coach or mentor that will inevitably simplify and expedite this process and strategy. This is the one that is positioned at the center of the strategy since the mentor can play a pivotal role regarding all three aspects of the strategy — vision planning, positive beliefs, and action planning. A primary focus is for you to search out these coaches and mentors and think about becoming a mentor for someone else. We can all play a part here in some fashion.

Prompt: Take a moment to review the Diamond Cycle of Achievement that follows and take note of all four components of this strategy. Rank each component in the order of how you think you are utilizing their benefit toward your success (visions, beliefs, habits, mentors). Start with 1 being assigned to your strongest component and 4 for your weakest. Include a note as to the WHY, why you feel it is more a strength and focus or a weakness and not as much in focus or in your "wheelhouse." **Please spend a sufficient** amount of time on each of the prompts provided in this guide and not rush through them. It's a marathon, not a sprint.

1_____

2_____

3_____

4_____

Diamond Cycle of Achievement

As we move forward you will gain a better understanding of the components and subsets of each of these competencies. You should think about focusing your time and energy on the weakest link noted above. We are only as good as our weakest link in the strategy. A colleague of mine once imparted to me that he had learned from his mentor or Hagie that you need to make your good better, before you make your better best. It's great to have endless lists of visions and tasks, but with no belief or action plan in place or a mentor to assist, it may be fleeting dreams or hopes.

This strategy also illustrates how a mentor at the center acts like the coach and/or pitcher of a baseball team orchestrating the strategies, timing, and pitch. The coach and pitcher are pivotal and work closely with the other important position players to assist with the goal of execution of strategies. The more adept the pitcher and his/her ability to change, throw different types of pitches and options at different velocities and directions, the more effective result attained.

These same abilities and strategies work very similarly in our lives. The trainer or mentor may work with you on a single competency like physical exercise and wellness or as a financial advisor with your financial wellbeing. He/she may be a member of the clergy that assists with your spiritual or emotional wellbeing. The mentor may work on multiple competencies similar to how a professor may be teaching you to set specific goals and then assisting with your career development offering options for you to incorporate certain behaviors and routines into your schedule. They can assist in helping to find the coop program or business connection you need to secure that important interview. The end game of the strategy is to pursue the desired results, both positive and negative, that will again feed new visions, actions, habits and achievements.

The final output and component of the cycle strategy are the results or achievements. Consistent review of achievements either on a daily or less often basis feed into the cycle's new visions, desires, beliefs, and actions. Although not a competency itself like the others, it is itself often overlooked regarding its importance as a focus for each of us. What I mean by this is that for myself, I know that I didn't take enough time in the past to reflect on what I have been able to accomplish until recently since it was not a focus and there was not a similar guide.

There are a lot of studies that describe the benefits regarding our emotional wellbeing when we take this time to self-reflect on these important confidence and motivational building achievements attained. We will explore this in more detail in Chapter 5. If there is only one project in this guide that you are going to complete (I advise completing all), I highly recommend the Achievement collage described in Chapter 5. It has afforded me a lot of pleasure being able to look at a piece of artwork on my wall, but also as a visualization tool to motivate me to add to it, build my brand, expand my dreams and desires, and provide additional confidence to pursue my desired goals and wellbeing.

Prompt: Take a moment to think about your life's achievements to date. What would you consider to be your biggest or most important or impactful accomplishment(s)? It may not refer back to your career or graduation completion; it may be a circumstance where you helped someone through a difficult time or situation, raising your children, a long journey that was successful or a difficult career change similar to what I endured.

Include WHY you consider it to be among your top achievements.

_____

_____

_____

_____

_____

_____

_____

Even though I have presented the cycle strategy in a linear and/or a clockwise configuration, it has been noted that it does not have to exclusively go in that one direction. William James, the distinguished psychologist in the 1880's published an article titled: *"What is an Emotion?"* In the article, James theorized that it is our actions that guide our emotions and behavior. This was groundbreaking new territory and contrary to the common notion of the time, where it was hypothesized that our feelings will guide our actions. He conceived of an emotion in terms of a sequence of events that starts with the occurrence of an arousing stimulus (the sympathetic nervous system) and ends with a passionate feeling, a conscious emotional experience. He set out to answer his question by asking another question: Do we run from a bear because we are afraid or are we afraid because we run? He proposed that the obvious answer, that we run because we are afraid, was incorrect, and instead argued that we are afraid because we run.

James also hypothesized that "emotion is the minds perception of physiological conditions that result from some stimulus". He cited as an example that, it is not that we see a bear, fear it, and run; we see a bear and run; consequently, we fear the bear. Our mind's perception of the higher adrenaline level and heartbeat is the emotion. The essence of James's theory or proposal was simple. It was premised on the fact that emotions are often accompanied by bodily responses (racing heart, sweaty palms, and tense muscles) and that we can sense what is going on inside our body much the same as we can sense what is going on in the outside world.

James' alternative path also shows a strategy to produce similar quality end results and achievements. Acting "as if" we are happy will create a happier being. William James and other modern theorists and studies have also shown that the more we act as if we are already what we desire to be, the more this will expedite these desired results. A good example of this is that when we dress up, we generally feel more important and perceive ourselves to be more successful. That is why you should always overdress for the occasion including interviews and meetings. If you want to have more willpower, act by pushing the object away from you or clinch your muscle to remind you to have willpower. Another example of how his theory takes shape and assists is when we laugh, we feel happy, and when we smile, we feel happy. To summarize, not only can an action follow a belief, but an action can also precede a belief.

Do you think you see the bear, get nervous, and run; or see the bear, run, and then get nervous? _____

Incidentally, a few years ago, I was inspecting a property for an appraisal in a northern New Jersey suburb and taking pictures of the house with the owner when all of the sudden the owner starts running back to the rear deck of his house. After putting down my camera and observing him, I asked what was going on. He then motioned and pointed over to the neighbor's yard where there stood a big black bear! I did a double take and then quickly ran back to his deck with my heart in my throat. I still wonder to this day what my answer is to this question above.

No matter what direction you proceed through the cycle, all directions lead toward progress, results, and achievements. You may want to take the strategy out of the workbook at the end and hang it up somewhere for you to review moving forward as its intended purpose.

As we move forward in the chapters, we will begin to review each cornerstone footing within this cycle and how it factors into the strategy and overall results. All four are critical elements of the strategy and progress. Some of us are planners, some of us are believers, and others are doers. It is the complete cycle continuum that you will ultimately benefit from. The longer the timeframe or gap between planning and action, the more likely it won't happen. Our environment can intrude and distract our focus, energy, and ability to achieve results, so take action now. It's all about dreaming, designing, believing, and executing with a little help from your advocate friends and mentors. To summarize, it is widely noted that visions and goals coupled with beliefs feed actions and create results or achievements.

Let's begin to set and review these cornerstone competencies and lay the groundwork for future add-on attributes and tie in competencies. They exhibit a golden color noted on the cover in the Structure as they are the keys to your overall growth, success, and prosperity!

CHAPTER 2

Vision Planning

"The best way to predict your future is to create it."
— Abe Lincoln

Based on this quote, I begin with vision planning as the first component or competency of the Diamond Cycle of Achievement and the first cornerstone footing in the Structure and Building Blocks of Achievement and Prosperity to follow. Having clear cut visions and goals is the keystone or first step toward creating a growth minded successful you. These visions and goals throughout our lives give us purpose, drive us and provide us with challenges. They should be what I refer to as SWWAT goals (Specific, Written, Why, Actionable, Timeframe).

Let's begin with specific goals. If they are not detailed and are too broad and unattainable, then you most likely won't see them through to fruition. They should not encompass several goals in one. An example of this may be a goal to do better in school or be financially independent or be the best player on your team. What needs to be noted first is to break this down into more manageable sized parts to potentially accomplish the whole.

Take for instance doing better in school. First, we need to break this down into which classes you need better grades in to raise your GPA. Then, you may focus on some of the others that are lacking, and after that you may need to adjust your curriculum to a more suitable class load to help you or seek out a tutor or go for after school help. These more specific goals combined with smaller actionable steps will assist in helping you reach the end result. Let's take the goal of being financially independent: successful and wealthy individuals have broken this down into more manageable and attainable smaller portions of working harder, budgeting, saving, and then investing these savings strategically.

The next letter in SWWAT and what I would consider to be the most important factors in vision planning (as a double W) are making sure you know the WHY or what the impact benefit is that you want to achieve. You should be WRITING these down and getting them in front of you using multiple formats!

Studies show that by writing down one's goals, you are 63% more likely to reach them than if they are not written down. You are additionally 76% more likely to reach the goal if you tell friends and close confidants in addition to writing them down!

Let's start with writing these goals down and then we can dissect and discuss the WHY. I have provided prompts so you can do this in one organized location for further action planning. It has often been noted that if goals are not in writing they don't exist. As an example, I have a written list of goals on my desk as general life visions; I have a list of specific business goals written on a sheet that I review daily and/or weekly; I have my financial goals on a spreadsheet and software program that I review monthly or quarterly, and I have other vision planning tools and resources in other formats described in detail within. This is and should not be for you a one and done. It is up to you and only you to determine how far you want to take this. It becomes even more challenging for us to write things down on paper due to our smart phones being the primary tool used for our calendars. We are moving away as a society from writing things down on paper to creating tasks or reminders on our phones or on our email calendars. More to come on this as an opportunity with a later prompt.

The other W includes the WHY you want to achieve these goals or passions. It is a critical element of success since you want to understand the IMPACT BENEFIT or end-result of how you will feel when this particular goal is completed. With the result and benefit comes the reward. By introducing visualization techniques into this mix, you will enhance your ability to understand the WHY for each goal. Understanding the WHY as the impact benefit will be discussed throughout the guide as it is a central theme for most prompts and used often by successful individuals.

It is important to note that these goals need to be attainable, realistic, and specific. There may be a need to break some of them down into more manageable options.

The T in SWWAT pertains to having a timeframe for completion and certain checkpoints for each goal. The timeline associated with each goal in terms of days, weeks, or months is critical to seeing these through to fruition. Without a timeframe and potentially broken down into smaller trackable checkpoints, there is a lack of framework or necessary structure. Set reasonable timelines for each and adjust, adjust, adjust if necessary.

Let's review some of your visions and passions and write down the rest of the SWWAT portion for each goal. Take some time to make sure that each of these are specific, attainable, and have a timeframe associated. You also need to explore the WHY surrounding each of these goals as the impact benefit for you to realize upon its completion.

In addition, provide some details as to how you will go about accomplishing each of them. If we visualize the result and even (as William James contends) act, "as if" we have already accomplished it, it is much more likely that we will successfully complete the goal. If, however, they are merely words on paper that are not specific, attainable, have no timeline or reasoning as to the why, then good luck accomplishing them.

Refer back to the introduction for the list you made but add stretch goals and think outside the box. This is another rocking chair moment.

Prompt: Write down a specific attainable shorter-term goal (7 days or less).

_____

_____

_____

Timeframe for next steps _____

WHY impact benefit to you?

_____

_____

Second vision shorter-term goal (7 days or less).

_____

_____

Timeframe and next steps

_____

WHY impact benefit to you?

_____

_____

Third vision mid-term goal (30-60 days).

_____

_____

Timeframe and next steps

_____

WHY impact benefit to you?

_____
_____

Fourth vision longer-term goal (90 days or more).

_____
_____

Timeframe and next steps

_____

WHY impact benefit to you?

_____
_____

Fifth vision or longer-term goal.

_____
_____

Timeframe and next steps

_____

WHY impact benefit to you?

_____
_____

Please make sure that you include the WHY in your responses when prompted as it will add context, detail, and provide you with a better understanding of the end result benefit and your own rationale.

Throughout recent history, there are great examples of how individuals utilized visualization techniques described earlier while conditioning themselves to be successful. These techniques are used by top athletes that need to use any edge available to succeed and win. One of the best examples of the use of visualization comes from Michael Phelps, the great Olympic swimmer who won 23 gold medals. He described his pre-meet and race visualization routine by sitting at the edge of the pool and closing his eyes and envisioning each and every stroke, kick and breath he would take prior to each race he swam. This provided him a sense of calm and helped him remove the unknown from each race. When things did not go the way they should have or how he had planned each one out, he relied on this visualization technique to help him cope with the situation and not overthink things in that moment.

Alex Hannold used visualization to prepare for his epic free climb of El Capitan in Yosemite Valley, as well as to execute each individual move and hold on the rock face of this 3,200 foot mammoth. If you have not seen the footage of this awesome and dangerous feat, I highly recommend viewing it. It speaks to our need to not only challenge ourselves as to what is possible or attainable but to set new goals and always move forward in a growth minded continuum.

There are many examples of how visualization techniques were utilized to assist and guide people toward greater success and prosperity. The important factor to consider and incorporate into your routine is to use this technique and others like it to help you succeed. I consistently use visualization techniques to prepare me for my next presentation, the next bend and drop of a steep downhill run, and next chapter in my life and so should you.

Prompt: Take a moment now and then do so every day moving forward. Lie on the floor or bed and think about visualizing something of benefit in your life that you have written down as a prior goal. Go through the motions and steps necessary to complete it and the aftermath of what it would feel like to accomplish it. Write down which one and try it for 5-10 minutes.

_____

I see myself doing this!

_____

The impact benefit of this is _____

Make it a point to repeatedly drive this activity to create a routine.

Vision Collage
IF YOU WANT IT, PUT IT IN FRONT OF YOU

One way to visualize your success is to make a Vision collage or passion board. Putting your visions, passions, and goals in front of you to review daily will keep them fresh and top of mind. This is a project that I have completed many times during my life and one that should be an enjoyable project. Part of my inspiration for this was when I started putting up single pictures of things that I wanted in my life that included artwork by Peter Max and Victor Vasarely, ski mountains to conquer, cars that appealed to me, and places that I wanted to venture to. I eventually completed several of these collaging projects, some of which will be reviewed later.

Completing this project and using it to help you visualize and understand the impact benefit and keep these passions top of mind are the true benefit. I have heard that there are vision collaging parties where groups complete these collages as a party theme. Get creative and enjoy.

Project: Create your own Vision collage and think about your primary passions, goals, and interests that you have provided in the previous prompts. Begin the project by getting a large backer board and gather pictures of these interests preferably in color. Think about the details which may include hobbies, groups, artistic endeavors, vacation locations, future alma maters and career paths by mind bending anything and everything. Be creative with your collage and try and think outside the box. For instance, incorporating a competition you may want to enter or a volunteer initiative or second career to start part-time. Maybe its gardening, learning magic, or an instrument or writing. A roadmap or picture as a background glued and framed will help guide you and can provide a timeline as well. Words, titles, and clipart options can help define and fill in the collage. A nice frame completes the project. Make sure to hang the collage in a place that you can view and enjoy the journey.

Remember that if you want and desire it, put it in front of you to visualize.

Having long-term career, family, financial, and intellectual goals are the backbone of our future destiny and legacy. However, this book is intended for you to make changes and accomplish goals starting today. In Chapter 4, we will review how small changes today can make a lasting difference for tomorrow.

Let's start to consider a few smaller more easily attainable goals you can start today and that may be accomplished over the course of the next few days or weeks. Take a look at your time management situation, your spending habits, maybe it's a hobby or class you wanted to sign up for, a group to join, reducing your social media usage, or how much time each day you are investing in yourself.

Prompt: What 3 smaller elements should you change now regarding your life that you wished were different? Are there any shorter-term goals you have not noted that you want to focus on today and WHY are they important to your success? Once you write these down, take some time to take that next small step needed to change them.

Do not go forward without taking these necessary smaller steps. You should also consider a 5-10 minute daily or weekly review of some or all these smaller goals in addition to the larger legacy goals you wrote down in the introduction.

Goal 1 and timeline _____

WHY impact benefit is _____

_____

Goal 2 and timeline _____

Impact benefit is _____

_____

Goal 3 and timeline _____

Impact benefit is _____

_____

If you are constantly attached to your phone, then you will benefit from setting up phone reminders with the goals above and throughout this book. Please take the time NOW, not later, to add these as phone reminders and/or on your calendars. Continue to drive this activity as we move forward with each prompt.

As noted, if you want something, put a reminder in front of you.

Memorialize it by getting it out there in front of you to focus on…

Vision Planning

My primary passion and goals are _____

My mission is to _____

Today I will invest in myself by _____ and

not waste my gifted time by _____ .

I will begin visualizing myself _____ .

In the next 30 days I have decided to learn more about and become adept at _

_____ .

I will focus on more productive tasks and routines early in the day.

I have decided to become more of a participant regarding _____ _____ and will drive this activity moving forward.

My balanced health and wellbeing are critical to my success and I have determined that changing my _____ will begin today and become a routine each day for the better.

I decided that I am motivated and enthusiastic to join _____ as I intend to meet and learn and/or accomplish_____ .

I am committed to saving more, spending less on unnecessary items, and beginning a thorough investment planning strategy.

Setbacks and challenges are part of life, and I am committed to not let them get in my way.

My career vision currently is _____

Carpe Diem – seize the day!

In an effort to help you make these more visible, I have included the Vision Plan in the Workbook for you to utilize/duplicate and eventually post somewhere in a high traffic area. This could be placed on a mirror, desk and/or a wall.

Note the statistic I provided in the beginning of the chapter that conveys if you tell someone your intentions, you are much more likely to see it through to completion. Make the effort now to schedule this discussion. Take a moment and discuss these visions and smaller goals with your partner, coach, advocate, or close confidant.

Who is the person best suited for this and what day and time have you scheduled this for if not now? _____

_____

Place your three most important goals on an index card or sticky notes with the timeline and the WHY and place in a visible location in your home, in your car or at your desk as a reminder.

Vision planning and self-reflection of your dreams and aspirations is the first cornerstone in the strategy of success and achievement. Take the time to figure out what makes you tick and what aspects of life you enjoy most. If you are interested in creating your own future and destiny, then use these prompts and projects to begin to define and frame up what that may eventually look like as long as they meet the SWWAT criteria. We can always add and revise as we move forward. The time to begin is now, not later! Once we have this preliminary list, we need to add a timeframe for each and understand their future potential impact benefit. **Visualization of the WHY or the goals impact benefit to you is critical to helping you succeed.** If you want and desire it, put the Vision Plan and collage in front of you to consistently focus on and memorialize. Make sure to include your partner, friend, advocate, or coach to discuss and help keep you accountable as it's more likely you will be successful in completing them.

We can utilize several different formats noted including lists, pictures, visualization techniques, a vision plan or collage, phone, and calendar reminders and journaling to assist with this step. I have several different places that I keep these in front of me on a daily, weekly, and monthly basis and you may want to as well. Life is a continuum where we grow, transform, and adjust our visions, goals and aspirations.

CHAPTER 3

Positive Beliefs

"What we feel we attract and what we think about we become." — Buddha

This old proverb from Buddha challenges us to better understand that if we consume self-compassionate thoughts and positive beliefs and keep them in focus then there is a good chance that we will feel more positive, relaxed, and at ease. In turn, we will attract positivity and become more positive.

It is one thing to create a plan as we have embarked upon and another to believe in yourself and its outcome and see it through to fruition. Your personal beliefs with their many elements, subconscious thoughts, feelings, attitudes, and self-concepts are part of the internal makeup that defines everyone. This subject matter alone can fill the pages of countless books and library sections.

As noted in the Introduction, this is the one component of the cycle strategy that has often been overlooked or eludes many of us. I have spent very little time in my life up until now working on this competency primarily because until recently, I did not understand its importance or know of the tools and techniques available. My aim is to motivate you and foster some awareness of your beliefs, attitudes, and thoughts and try and gauge if they are positive or negative and self-compassionate or self-deprecating. Then, I will share some simple techniques to help foster more positive self-talk and optimism for your improved health and wellbeing.

Prompt: What do you focus your thoughts on often, hourly, and daily? If you were to boil down your most time-consuming thoughts on a daily or weekly basis, what would they be and are they generally positive and optimistic or negative and pessimistic? Write down WHY you think you focus on these so often and if they truly warrant your focus, time, and attention?

_____

_____

_____

_____

_____

WHY _____

_____

_____

_____

    The power of our beliefs, thoughts, and attitudes have a profound effect on our lives. They cause us to do certain things and not others. They can either afford us the ability to reach for the attainable or hinder us from ever trying something new. Do you think that your life is yours to design, mold, and build within your control, or are you of the belief that you don't have this ability? Maybe you're conditioned to think that your life has been predetermined by your place within society and that in reality, life and your environment control you and your destiny.

Successful people like Thomas Edison, Andrew Carnegie, Michael Jordan, Tom Brady, and countless others like them have the belief that they can and will achieve the goals they set utilizing a positive enthusiastic proactive growth mindset. Example after example shows that it is this belief coupled with one's goal planning and drive that creates successful people. If Thomas Edison did not have the belief that he could harness the power of electricity into a glass cylinder to effectively provide light to the world, it would have taken a lot longer to discover his improved version of the light bulb.

I am reminded of a story I once read about a railroad construction worker named Nick Sitzman who, prior to the time of cell phones, had unfortunately locked himself inside a refrigerated railroad car at the end of his daily shift. As Nick desperately shouted and pounded his fists on the door and sides of the car, his thoughts lead him to believe that he would freeze to death if he was not freed. The next day, Nick was found lying on the floor of the car motionless beside carved writings etched in the soft flooring that read: I love my family. It turned out that he had died. When the investigation and autopsy were done, it was determined that the refrigeration for the freight car was not on and the temperature within the car never got below 52 degrees. Ironically, Nick had not died from freezing to death but the emotional trauma from the belief that he was going to freeze to death.

"Believe you can and you're halfway there."
— Theodore Roosevelt

You can control and design your life, future, and prosperity with positive beliefs and thoughts. It is our ability to overcome difficult events and challenges that sets us apart as successful or unsuccessful.

Aristotle in 350 AD noted in one of his many journals that every aspect of human life and society may be an appropriate object of thought and analysis. He provided the ancient world with a new logical approach where he went on to discuss the belief that it is worthwhile and valuable for human beings to conduct a systematic inquiry into every aspect of the natural world and thus…of their lives. He also noted that all humans seek to, "flourish as it is the proper and desired end of all of our actions." The accurate translation of this is wellbeing and we can ascertain that someone who is flourishing is living the good life.

Considered the father of modern education, Aristotle shared this logical approach to self-evaluation and self-reflection. It is from his methods that we can self-analyze our own lives to discover elements that will guide us toward future potential transformation and change.

From these teachings, we need to take the opportunity to self-analyze if we are of a fixed or growth mindset. This one belief can be a significant factor in either helping you toward success or being a determinant to who you become. Those of us who have a fixed mindset are significantly more likely to be content with the status quo and not be proactive and those of us with a growth mindset are more likely to be successful.

Those who have a growth mindset embrace new challenges and don't give up easily. They try to overcome life's adversities and practice self-compassion. They are helpful and not spiteful and tend to mentor and volunteer.

Fixed mindset individuals tend to criticize and have a hard time accepting criticism. They will quit easily and avoid change and challenges. They are highly self-critical, unforgiving, and often blame others. They use phrases like: "I can't do this since I'm… There is no point in doing this… I always struggle with this … It's because of them or it that I can't …" Be a good friend to yourself and begin to move toward a growth compassionate mindset.

The growth mindset is based on the belief that your basic qualities and competencies can grow and develop through your efforts, learning, resources, strategies, and additional assistance from mentors and coaches. Those that adhere to this thinking are proactively seeing endless possibilities versus limitations and roadblocks for the fixed minded ones.

The growth minded individuals view successes of others as inspiration rather than discouragement.

There are significant advantages for those who are willing to adopt a growth mindset versus a fixed one. It is our choice in life and the decision to transition from a fixed mindset to a growth mindset is ours to make. However, this change is easier said than done. Many with a fixed mindset have been this way for quite some time and are reactive to what life and their environment throw at them.

Although next to impossible to be proactive when it comes to all aspects of life, by being fix minded and reactive, we are back on our heels and not on our toes. In sports as it is in life, this creates disappointing and less than preferred outcomes. We will review in a later section on conditioning our mind ways to move from the fixed to a growth mindset. Appraise your current mindset.

Prompt: Do you have a growth mindset or a fixed mindset and WHY?

_____
_____
_____

Provide some benefits by making a change.

_____
_____
_____

Do you feel you control your own growth trajectory and destiny or is it based on external forces, life events, and circumstances and WHY?

_____
_____
_____

Do you consider yourself an optimist where the glass is half-full or a pessimist where the glass is generally half-empty? _____

Why do you think that is?

_____

_____

"Keep your thoughts positive, because your thoughts become your words. Keep your words positive, because your words become your behaviors. Keep your behaviors positive, because your behaviors become your habits. Keep your habits positive, because your habits become your values. Keep your values positive, because your values become your destiny." — Mahatma Gandhi

Having positive emotional wellbeing is a key factor to becoming successful. Our ability to utilize available emotional hygiene tools and techniques are critical to overcoming many of the issues, problems, and potential emotional trauma we need to endure at times. Every day we are bombarded with negativity that we need to combat. We need to offset these negative elements by keeping positive vibes and reinforcement in front of us, similar to how we go about offsetting the calories we ingest with exercise.

The more compassionate we are to ourselves with small doses of positivity, gratitude, compassion, love, faith, and reassurance, the stronger we will be to reach a more positive and optimistic self. What are the best available strategies to use to improve our positive beliefs and thoughts? The one I tend to use often is positive affirmations and self-talk conditioning. The list below hangs on my bathroom mirror. The notion of putting this in front of us to focus on reappears as being a critical element and central theme.

Positive Affirmations

I have integrity and will begin to love myself more.

I will begin today by being a more positive and optimistic person.

I believe in having a positive attitude and will reject the negative.

I decided that today I will be more grateful, happier and smile more.

I decided that I am capable of loving, giving and forgiving.

I believe in my ability to grow, prosper, and create my own destiny.

I am working on being self-compassionate and _____

I am confident in my ability to be mindful of the beauty of things.

I am generous and will look to be thankful and pay it forward or volunteer.

I believe in my ability to have a positive growth mindset and become successful, healthy, and well!

I won't let negative situations and problems ruin my day.

Prompt: In the Journal Workbook I have included a larger pullout page of these positive affirmations to assist with your conditioning by placing it in a visible spot to utilize daily or whenever you see fit. I find one of the most visible areas is my bathroom or sanctuary as I like to think of it now. I recite it as my morning mantra and ritual.

Some other techniques that we can use as emotional hygiene techniques include:
- Positive self-talk and self-compassion journaling
- A gratitude affirmations list or jar on the kitchen table
- Mindfulness review
- Meditation
- Faith and prayer

- Practicing forgiveness
- Achievement journaling and collaging
- Hygge and Ikigai

We will spend some time reviewing these emotional hygiene tools and conditioning methods in more detail in Chapter 8. For now, I think it is valuable to understand the importance of incorporating some form of positive reinforcement into your daily or weekly routine to counter and ward off the negatives. We will also provide details on how to link or pair up these routines with some of your other personal hygiene routines. It makes for an easy transition and one that I have smoothly incorporated into my daily routines.

I always thought this was very poignant and illustrative.... Our lives have often been compared to a car windshield as it travels through the roadmap of life…

When it is new, it is clean and pristine without any blemishes. As we begin the journey of life, we begin to encounter some minor elements coming at us from all directions in the form of problems and disappointments. As we move up the road, we may encounter some inclement weather with clouds and rain in the form of a job displacement, setbacks, challenges, and tearful emotions.

We may need to take a detour and find ourselves off road in unfamiliar territory where conditions may worsen. Snowy and icy elements may surface with a failed relationship, financial hardship, or outright rejection.

As we emerge from this rocky terrain, things may settle down for a bit when out of nowhere, a deer jumps in front of the car and we need to take quick and decisive action to swerve out of the way to avoid other similar life events like a chance theft, an unexpected situation, or illness.

The journey continues as we move further up the road where we may face a hail storm or a projected rock that scratches or cracks the glass when a marriage fails, your career position is eliminated, or a bankruptcy or addiction in the family occurs. Often, we tend to look through that rearview mirror and review the disappointment and carnage behind us.

As we move up the road of life, hopefully we are able to avoid the impactful crashes and devastating accidents that are all too common with a sudden premature passing or other significant event. It is our ability to turn on the wipers by utilizing these emotional hygiene tools to wipe away and clean the windshield continuously to counteract these events. We learn to wipe them away from our focus so they don't take over our lives and destiny. It is also important not to look through that rear windshield and focus on these negative events and baggage so we don't lose focus on our intended forward destination. It's time to clean your windshield and refocus your attention and aim.

Prompt: Take some time to self-reflect on your life's journey to date. What events and situations have taken place that you have not sufficiently wiped away and cleared from your focus of the past? Do you look through that rear windshield often and focus on certain negative disappointments? Provide some detail on each.

_____

_____

_____

_____

_____

_____

_____

_____

_____

_____

_____

It has been helpful for me to refocus my attention to get to a more positive and healthy emotional wellbeing. Now is the time for you to figure out what you are often focused on and adjust, adjust, adjust. Energy flows where your focus and attention go. You can't reach your destination if your attention is on "what is." If your energy and thoughts are on making excuses and blaming others, then you will not be focusing on positive thoughts and beliefs. In later sections, we will review how certain beliefs and attitudes factor into your daily actions and habits.

Prompt: Do your mind and thoughts focus more on the rear windshield making excuses and blaming problems and setbacks on someone or something else? Do your mind and thoughts focus on the road ahead and its potential optimistic positive forces and future potential opportunities?

_____

_____

_____

_____

_____

Take some time and review your browsing history on your phone and on your laptop and list out all the things through both Google and Safari, etc. that you have searched for and viewed recently.

_____

_____

_____

_____

_____

_____

List out what shows or things that you view on your TV/phone and computer

_____

_____

_____

_____

_____

_____

For now, let's focus on the topics and focal points of what your viewing resembles: is it sports/celebrity/shows/series/news/shopping/educational/financial or intellectual? How positively or negatively focused and driven are these posts, sites, podcasts and shows? How often are they educationally or intellectually driven, financially driven, or socially driven? Later, we will focus on the time management aspect of these same activities.

_____

_____

_____

_____

_____

_____

  How can you adjust your focus during your downtime from these to more positive uplifting and beneficial subject matter? Adding a note on your laptop can go a long way to remind you to focus on the positive and growth minded aspects of what you should be focused on.

  Aristotle put it this way regarding aiming for prosperity and wellbeing, "a clumsy archer may indeed get better with practice, so long as he keeps aiming for the target. Training through education and a constant aim to perfect virtue."

Target of Beliefs & Self-Concept

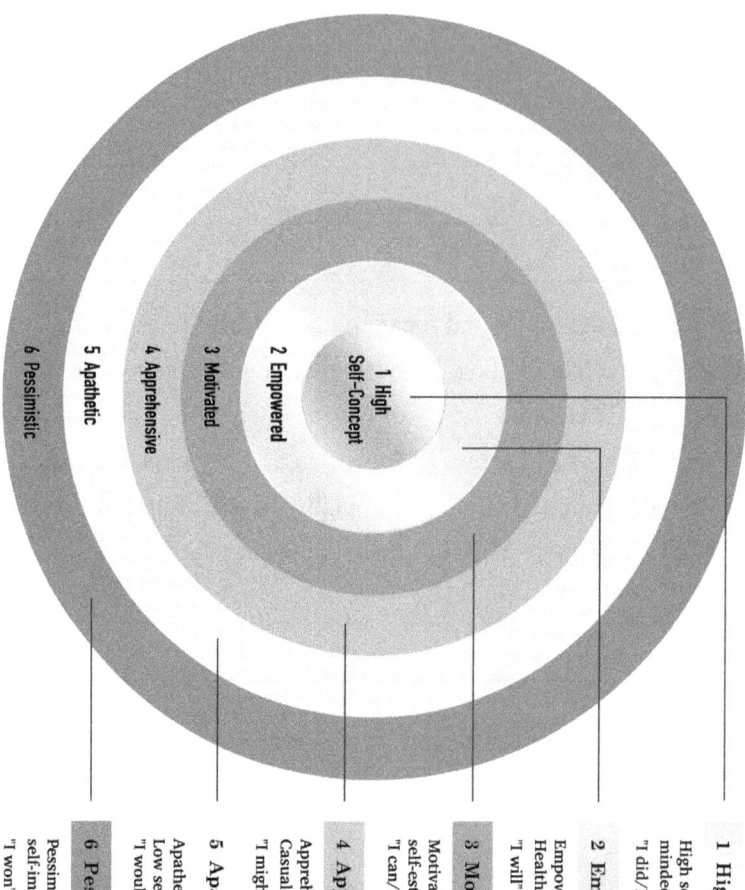

1 High Self-Concept
High self-concept: Balanced wellness, Growth minded, Optimistic, Confident;
"I did/I must"

2 Empowered
Empowered: Positive, Proactive participant, Healthy, Grateful, Invested in yourself;
"I will"

3 Motivated
Motivated: Generous, Above average self-esteem & image, Focused;
"I can/I should"

4 Apprehensive
Apprehensive: Doubtful, Skeptical, Status quo, Casual participant, Insecure;
"I might/I could"

5 Apathetic
Apathetic: Spectator, Reactive, Procrastinator, Low self-concept, Disempowered;
"I would/I can't"

6 Pessimistic
Pessimistic: Fixed minded, Unhealthy, Negative self-image, Resentful, Not invested in yourself;
"I won't"

34 | Transform Your Future & Wellbeing

Target of Beliefs and Self-Concept

Where on the target best describes you currently? # _____

Prompt: Its great practice to include in your positive affirmations beginning with "I decided to be ..."

Insert some of the descriptions in the three following prompts.

I decided to be more ... _____ compassionate and confident.

I decided to be ... _____

I decided to be more ..._____

We should strive to be at or near the bullseye with having positive beliefs and a high self-concept. The more growth minded and self-compassionate and better self-image that we have, the closer we are to the bullseye. Proactive participants in life that are confident healthy individuals with a balanced approach are prone to be near the bullseye. This is where Aristotle teaches us to move towards and where Michelangelo challenges us to "set our aim." Transform your future and wellbeing by setting your aim and focus at the bullseye! Move from the outside negative danger zone toward the bullseye and success and prosperity are within your grasp.

If you truly want something, then you must give up the fixed minded false belief that you cannot have it. Many of us hold these false beliefs with us as fact and circumstance. They hold us back from our true potential and having a more positive growth mindset. Are your thoughts and attitudes generally empowering, apathetic or disempowering based on the target?

We all have beliefs that are at times empowering and at times disempowering. It seems apparent that what we focus on often tends to blur these beliefs to be more positive or negative. Buddha conveys the importance of what we think about and what we feel.

There are resources and strategies available for each of us to clean our windshields of life and adjust our focus by consistent review and use of emotional hygiene techniques. I have provided some basic options so far and will highlight additional strategies and resources in the section on conditioning mind and body. We will review attitude, gratitude, mindfulness, and conditioning routines in more detail. Consider using the positive affirmations pullout provided in the Workbook to assist with these important conditioning routines. We will also review how to pair these routines in your sanctuary with other daily personal hygiene routines to simplify this process. These negative beliefs, thoughts and attitudes can become the cause of decay and lead to a lack of structural integrity of your whole. You don't want to undermine this critical support element that is central to your ability to grow, prosper and be healthy.

Please seek the guidance of a competent health care professional, to address any medical illnesses, concerns and/or issues.

"The ancestor to every action is a thought."
— Ralph Waldo Emerson

CHAPTER 4

Productive Actions

I once noticed a sign that I felt was very apropos as it said:

Life has no remote. Get up and change it yourself!

You are the only one that can act and change your life. Few people, if any, have a vested interest in helping you. Would you consider yourself a participant in life or more of a spectator? _____

Do you generally watch things happen before you or take action in completing tasks besides work, school, and your necessary responsibilities? Are you a player, athlete, competitor in the game, or bystander watching from the stands? Participants step up to the plate every day. They set their aim and take their swings and shots. They take a proactive approach to try new things and succeed or fail and learn from their mistakes. They volunteer and mentor to help others, donating their time and resources toward a greater good.

On the opposite side of the spectrum, spectators or bystanders sit idle on their sedentary laurels like a couch potato with their energy displaced into anxiety. They often take a reactive approach and quickly play the blame game as expert critics, pointing fingers that can manifest itself into blaming the world and others for everything that is wrong with it and them. It's easy to be a spectator and tough to be the participant.

When you hold the TV remote in your hand for hours, no good will come of it. Clients of mine reinforce the notion that hard work wards off the behavior of constantly eating and picking. They noted that when they begin retirement, it is often a tough transition and they gain a good amount of weight due to sitting around and not physically working out like they used to.

We should all strive to be participants or contenders in our lives and futures. Trying new things and taking risks along the way toward our greater success is important to our growth. Participants are proactively invested in their current and future design by mapping out their desires and vision. Our motivation as a participant plays an important factor in our overall outcome.

Participants change and adapt to circumstances as they present themselves because they are focused and engaged. The participant or competitor gets involved, sets goals, practices, and repetitively conditions their mind and body. They become more disciplined and motivated, meet new people, and may become more persistent.

These differences are made even more divergent with the advent of fantasy sports and online gambling. They provide additional platforms and reasons to keep spectators engaged in a meaningless or blowout game and financially destructive behaviors that our government needs to perpetuate for the tax revenue it generates. I encourage you to be a participant and challenge yourself to reflect, adjust, and not get seduced by these destructive habits. Get up and hide the remote!

Prompt: WHY do you consider yourself a participant or a spectator? _____

_____

_____

_____

What activities do you engage in that make you a participant and which activities do you involve yourself with that make you a spectator? List them (other than necessary daily activities). Think about your screen time activities related to shows, online surfing, sports, and social media.

_____
_____
_____
_____
_____
_____
_____
_____
_____
_____

Which of the above spectator activities should you work on removing or reducing from your routine immediately and what is the impact hindrance to your growth?

_____
_____
_____
_____
_____

    Recent studies indicate that approximately 40% of our daily routines are in the form of habits. These include daily routines of buying and/or preparing and eating meals, commuting to and from school or work, many tasks associated with school or work, morning hygiene routines, and evening rituals. Take some time to think about your daily routines and habits and how you may want to adjust some of these for the better. Time is a finite resource that we must use wisely.

Proper time management skills are an extremely important component for success. Successful people rank it as one of their top attributes for helping them toward becoming successful. Studies show that American's spend on average over 7 hours per day of screen time in front of the TV, computer and phone (non-work related). By contrast, successful people that I interact with consistently note that they watch less than an hour or two of non-educational TV or screen time surfing per day. The rest of their daily downtime was spent on educational, career, financial, and other personal growth and wellness activities.

Prompt: How many hours per day do you spend on non-educational screen time on your phone, TV, and computer? Track your prior week's consumption._____

_____

_____

Carpe Diem — Seize the day is the mantra I try and adhere to. I personally have been adhering to a mantra of: Accept every day as a gift and not a promise. I have been trying to limit my non-educational or non-financially related viewing to just 2 hours per day or less. If you want to be successful, one of my main pieces of wisdom is to also limit your leisure screen time to less than 2 hours per day.

This will afford you the opportunity to use this additional time more effectively toward other competencies that can advance your intellectual, occupational, financial, emotional and/or physical wellbeing. Ironically, Steve Jobs was quoted as saying, "Your time is limited, so don't waste it living someone else's life." This resonates more than ever at a time when many of us can't get enough screen time of celebrity and influencers.

So how do we adjust, adjust, adjust to changing our time management strategy? How do we effectively change our behaviors and routines? If it was that easy, everyone would make the adjustment. I have posted on my computer the following: Status quo is often the symptom, procrastination the disease. The forerunner of procrastination is complacency. We all become complacent at times and accept the status quo, but how do we avoid procrastination? Our time is so valuable, and we often discount this value daily.

"The man who moves mountains begins by carrying small stones." — Confucius

Taking small steps and making small adjustments can proactively assist with avoiding or minimizing complacency, status quo, and procrastination. They can become the building blocks to form a beneficial routine, behavior, and ultimately a habit. They can also have a profound effect on your overall results over time. This can be related to just about anything and everything. These small steps and changes in one's focus and direction can at times set off a chain reaction that lead to a better more productive environment.

An example of this in my life is how I approached this huge undertaking of writing this guide. As I sit here today, it seems like a formidable task that often discourages me into thoughts and ways to procrastinate. I will also describe in a later chapter on opportunistic timing and risk, how I have tried to carpe diem – seize the moment. Recently, I have challenged myself to write the guide within three months and have it ready to edit. My daily commitment is to take these small steps and write or gather 4-5 pages of material daily. Separating and breaking down these daily smaller tasks afford me the ability to see past the huge undertaking and piece things together. This smaller task has now become a daily routine and behavior that after a while has morphed into a habit.

> **"Commitment is what transforms a promise into a reality."**
> — Abe Lincoln

Another example of taking small steps to progress was when I began to learn how to play the harmonica and guitar. Without the ability to position standard lessons into my weekly routine due to time and responsibility constraints, I committed to learning and playing for at least 30-60 minutes every day, unless there were extenuating circumstances.

It has been this commitment that has driven the behaviors and routines to make it a specific part of my day. Instead of sitting on the Lazboy pre or post dinner and surfing the limited quality of shows on television, I remove myself from this environment and sit at my desk and practice. The fact that I love music and have a vision of being able to play some songs that I have listened to for decades also helps motivate me.

There are several elements at play here to help with changing a sedentary situation into a habit that emerged from my passion. First, I set out to journal the visions, put a timeframe on both, and put them in front of me so I could visualize a place in the future with success. Then, I formed the belief and attitude that I could accomplish them (even with doubt floating around in the back of my head); I changed my routine, linked up the new routines with another daily habit, and took small steps in the beginning to form new daily habits. I also discussed my commitments with my family and have sought out the assistance of mentors and coaches. This is the strategy and the individual components of the Diamond Cycle of Achievement.

If gaining commitment is an issue for you, then there are several commitment devices or behavioral change triggers that you can utilize in your daily life, similar to how we all use an alarm clock to wake up. Here are some potential options. The vision board, gratitude jar, and college contract for my kids have been a big benefit for me personally. My wife has requested a swear jar for some time now…

- Vision board for goal planning
- Phone screen time app tracker with limits
- Step tracker in phone health app
- Achievement collage for appreciation and fulfillment
- Gratitude jar for your table
- Swear jar for money as a deterrent
- Piggy bank for a savings plan
- College contract for students with minimum grade standards
- Fitbit for tracking your health
- Brushing teeth early evening as to avoid eating any more at night
- Email people in your core circle to mention changes you're going to make

There are some online sites that act like commitment devices. Acorn.com allows you to bank and save the change on every purchase to encourage you to save more as part of your financial commitment. More detail is provided on the phone screen time app tracker and limits in the section on habits.

 Each of our behaviors cause outcomes. The small changes in my behavior each day noted above had a significant effect on my life. When I began to analyze more deeply my routines and habits, I was dumbfounded as to why I was doing certain routines continually and not doing other more productive tasks. This is by definition a habit — when you don't even think about doing something and end up doing it. I realized that by introducing and linking new routines and tasks to certain daily necessary routines, I was able to make significant changes to my life.

 Examples include: during my morning bathroom routine, I now link up or pair certain emotional hygiene routines noted prior. Reflective positive affirmations or completing a simple breathing exercise while in the shower or brushing my teeth creates consistency. While commuting to work, I listen to books on tape or a financial podcast. Linking or pairing these routines, as twofers as I like to call them, with others creates the association that I need to drive these new habits. It has expedited superior results for me and should do the same for you.

Prompt: What is one (or two) daily habit(s) or routine(s) that are most detrimental to you? What are they and WHY? Maybe it is spending too much time binge watching shows or sports, time with someone who provides little benefit or value, time on your phone, gambling, or other destructive behavior.

_____
_____
_____
_____
_____
_____
_____

Think about a more productive routine that you can begin to invest in yourself and incorporate into your daily routines to replace the ones noted above and WHY should you make the switch. Maybe you have been meaning to sign up for that course, class, or certification, or start an investment plan by listening to podcasts or books on tape. Maybe you have been meaning to spend more time with someone and need to reconnect with them. It could be related to your physical wellbeing and exercising daily by taking a walk with a friend in the park while talking instead of connecting by phone. If you have not been getting the grades you desire, then commit to challenging yourself to get to the library directly after class instead of procrastinating. Maybe you have been thinking of making a career change and need to set aside some time researching how to make this happen. Take the first small step necessary by also noting it below to effectuate this change today.

_____
_____
_____

_____
_____
_____
_____
_____
_____
_____

What are some current necessary daily habits and routines that you can link up and pair with these new tasks and routines noted above? This pairing of twofers is an important step as a reminder or trigger in taking a task and creating a routine and habit. You may be able to utilize one of the commitment devices or behavioral change triggers to assist with this process.

_____
_____
_____
_____
_____
_____
_____
_____
_____

Please take the time now, not later, to add these as phone reminders and/or on your calendar. Continue to drive this activity if you will benefit from these phone alerts and reminders as the trigger needed.

What follows is a simple daily routine that I have incorporated for some time now. This daily ritual allows me to focus on my wellbeing. It may be a routine that you can benefit from.

My Daily Ritual

Most Important 30-minute Refresh of My Day Every Day!

- 10 minute morning refresh routine: includes a positive affirmation and gratitude review while getting ready; several minutes on the floor stretching/yoga, breathing exercises, and a minute or two to goal plan the most important tasks for the day.

- 10 minutes at lunch to: take a walk and be mindful of breathing and nature or listen to a wellness podcast; check on your vitals and trackers; read an article that is wellness related, or thank someone for his/her help and pay it forward. Grab a piece of fruit. An alternative is to connect with a mentor, coach, Board of Advisors, or someone within your Sphere of Influence (SOI) to review next steps or strategies.

- 10 minute pre or post dinner to: take the walk that you didn't at lunch and/or spend some time stretching, slow breathing, and meditating. Take a few minutes to review small and large achievements completed during the day and think about a few items that need to be cultivated for tomorrow. End with a few minutes of gratitude and self-confidence and compassionate self-esteem affirmations.

This is 30 minutes that you will not be distracted from any form of technology (other than wellness based) or social media. You will not allow negativity into your life, and you will create routines to bring positivity, gratitude, and generosity into your life. 30 minutes is 2% of your day! Try and make it 60 minutes.

We all should be proactive participants in life taking our shots, swings and avoid complacency. As an advisor, I consistently communicate to clients that no decision is a decision and, in this vein, no action is an action or lack thereof. Hold yourself accountable by reflecting on your routines and habits. The more unproductive time we spend in front of the screen instead of pursuing other wellness competencies, the further away we will be from our transformation to success. Reduce your unproductive time to under 2 hours per workday. Time management skills are critical to our success. Use Saturdays as your wildcard days to focus on your deficient productive behaviors and exercises related to your less focused wellness routines. Utilize some noted commitment devices and behavioral change triggers as tools in your toolbox for assistance. Link up and pair new routines with existing daily productive habits. Rome wasn't built in a day. Be mindful that it is important to start some of these, but not take all of them on at once. Appraise the situation and focus on the necessary and more destructive behaviors first, then move on.

"Conceive it and believe it, ignite it with action and you will achieve it." — Richard S. Olin

CHAPTER 5

Celebrating your Achievements

My father shared this with me many years ago. A friend gave it to him when he fell on more difficult circumstances and I think it speaks volumes.

A Choice

"I have a choice today. I can choose to do whatever it takes, no matter how uncomfortable, to have a productive day and feel good about myself, or, I can let outside circumstances control me, choose to do what is pleasant but unproductive and end my day feeling dissatisfied. It is up to me! There are no shortcuts. I am responsible for my own attitudes, habits, behaviors and results. I am responsible for my own success!"—Anonymous

This quote truly sums up how we need to approach every day.

It conveys the importance and difference between being a proactive productive participant and the reactive spectator that allows the external circumstances of life to control us. It conveys the importance of the three critical competencies that comprise the Cycle of Achievement. The results and achievements are the byproduct, but can also inspire and encourage each of us to pursue new and potentially related tasks, skills, honors, and accomplishments that we can build upon to grow.

The path to achievement is finding a strategy that works for you and developing a process that is repeatable. This will inevitably simplify the process and allow you to use the strategy and techniques at your own pace. It will provide you the consistency needed in this simplified manner to achieve results. It will also allow you to measure your results and success once you implement this repeatable process where it would be much harder to measure without a process. Find your zone, focus in on the Diamond Cycle of Achievement, create a repeatable process for each competency and the strategy and be consistent. I am honored to be connected to your meaningful and measurable results!

Achievements are the concrete end of our output. They are an opportunity for us to celebrate our accomplishments. Our ability to document and memorialize these successes in one format or another is an important element and theme of this guide. It will allow you the opportunity to review these positive results and garner more self-confidence and higher self-esteem and counteract the negative influences thrown at you. This chapter is dedicated to inspiring and empowering you to use these platforms as another emotional wellness hygiene tool to reinforce these positives.

Prompt: What is your proudest moment or moments to date (may not be a high achievement)? _____

_____

_____

Prompt: What have been your 3-5 most important achievements to date that may be of a different type and category than what you documented in Chapter 1? They may have been related to helping someone or overcoming a challenge…

_____

_____

_____

_____

_____

How do you see them as a whole; productive and worthy or lacking as higher achievements? _____

Reward yourself! Take a rocking chair moment and reflect on how these accomplishments have molded you and your life for the better. The benefits of achievement journaling and collaging these uplifting moments and challenges are long lasting.

This is another tool to clean our windshields of life and something that I journal consistently. You can use the journaling or collage as a springboard to new and more complex achievements. I have been utilizing several other formats that include collages, pictures, scrapbooks, DVD's and cloud-based options. They provide me a tremendous amount of self-fulfillment, self-confidence, and self-esteem. Become more self-aware of your achievements on a consistent basis to drive higher emotional wellbeing.

Project: Begin the collage with a background that exemplifies your overall interests, passions, and goals (I chose a ski trail map from one of the mountains that I frequent). Use a large piece of construction or backer board in a lighter color. Print out names, alma maters, achievements, places, and prior interests. Cut out pictures of achievements like graduations, weddings, family and friend's pictures, goals attained, pets, high honors, or other items that define your life and accomplishments. Below is one of my attempts a few years ago. I also have a picture collage and another one of concert and event tickets that I attended that span a lifetime.

It is important that we are committed to documenting and celebrating our achievements routinely to boost our emotional wellbeing. It's a strategy and defense counteracting the negative problems and challenges that confront us. I have worked on a daily achievement journal when the going gets tough by writing down simple and basic daily wins. This is another way I use positive reinforcement to help me, and I encourage you to think about incorporating it into a weekly or monthly routine. It is a beneficial way to document great efforts and your growth and development. The Workbook provides additional focus and space to reinforce consistency to begin or continue this process.

A footnote on the positioning of mentors… although not discussed in detail within the initial cornerstone footings as a pivotal competency, the benefit of connecting with and utilizing coaches, trainers, managers, teachers, and mentors should not be overlooked. Successful individuals consistently note that mentors play a key role in their growth and development. We will review this in more detail in Chapter 6. Mentors are a central component and play a key role in the strategy of the Diamond Cycle of Achievement as discussed in Chapter 1.

Prompt: Mind bend and write down other accomplishments in addition to the ones you noted prior. Include anything of value that may be more detailed and personal. Maybe it's a relationship, challenging situation, artwork completed, something physical, child related, volunteer initiative, financial independence, intellectually or socially based, or career related.

Personal achievements _____

_____
_____
_____
_____
_____
_____
_____
_____
_____
_____
_____
_____
_____
_____
_____
_____
_____

Oftentimes our honors, accolades, and achievements lead to our mission and future occupation and career. This may or may not be the case with you, but these achievements can help define us and some of the skills that we learn and retain. We might receive honors or distinction regarding certain subject matter in school, and then pursue a career path within that field of knowledge. We may have exceled on the sports fields, become a captain that may lead to a career as a coach or trainer, or similar related sports marketing career.

We may have achieved a solo or lead part in a play or music repertoire that led to developing this art form in the future. Maybe we volunteered for a service or became interested in something from Boy or Girl Scouts. We may have helped rescue someone. You may have volunteered on the Emergency Squad or at a local hospital or similar medical/emergency field opportunity. There are often many tie-ins to our future from some of these introductions at an early age. We will discuss this correlation further within the career development section.

Are there skills and honors that you may have learned and received through your accomplishments that are a potential part of your overall mission and vision? How may you incorporate these into your vision and future development?

_____

_____

_____

Achievements are the byproduct of our hard work and commitment. Taking the time to document and celebrate them provides a continuous positive feedback loop that helps improve our self-confidence and self-esteem. They are not necessarily an end, but can potentially reset more advanced objectives and goals that build upon themselves.

They can also allow us to review situations from a different perspective and vantage point, and afford us the ability to move in a different or parallel direction. Some of these skills, honors, and distinctions may even direct us toward a certain hobby, vocation, or career path. Utilizing available formats to memorialize these beneficial results to keep them in front of us visually can help with this positive reinforcement and feedback loop. The achievement collage is my favorite and makes for a great party theme, but achievement journaling has been a consistent routine of mine that I benefit from regularly and have for a very long time. I encourage you to do the same.

PART TWO

The Structure and Building Blocks
of Achievement and Prosperity

CHAPTER 6

The Structure and Building Blocks of Achievement and Prosperity with Foundational Competencies

"One beam, no matter how big, cannot support an entire house on its own." — Chinese proverb

The structure and building blocks vision grew out of an attempt to consolidate most of the key components, elements, and competencies to realize prosperity, success, and wellbeing. A great deal of time and energy was spent researching, reading, and analyzing what successful individuals and businesses determined to be their most critical elements of success and prosperity. By using a multi-level structure, I was able to group and, to some degree, rank these building blocks and competencies in a manner equivalent to how they may be grouped and ranked toward our overall growth. I utilized the shape and composition of a building or structure since it aligns with building and growing as individuals. The process of adding layers to the structure parallels layering individual competencies on top of our own foundational ones.

Planning and designing begins with blueprints, which the structure resembles. Our ability to understand, review, develop, and implement these competencies for our benefit is the basis of this guide. While I was developing, reworking and organizing the orders of the building blocks, it dawned on me that the cornerstone competencies that make up the strategy of the Diamond Cycle of Achievement and Prosperity should be set in a way to illustrate and define the process and strategy. They create the footings of the structure just as we need each of them to be able to build upon for support and structure in our lives. They similarly act like the mechanical systems that drive the comfortable climate and free-flowing systems of the structure that we are accustomed to. Without them being positioned in this defined order and having a hierarchy, the structure and its associated layers and components would deteriorate rapidly. This is a parallel analogy to our lives' stability and our potential for growth. With each cornerstone competency functioning properly, we can adapt this strategy and focus it on each of the remaining competencies.

Our structure needs to have solid footings for stability and be anchored. This will allow each of us to form a solid base, stay strong, and endure. Any deterioration of these footings and competencies can adversely affect the whole structure. The foundational competencies correlate and grow out of the cornerstone competencies. It is the layer necessary for stability of the core level that will provide additional support for the higher level and peak competencies. These higher level and peak competencies enhance stability and development of our character and growth while allowing us to be more flexible. Each of these components are linked to and correlate with others.

As the proverb above states, no one element or competency can support our ability to be structurally sound, stable, and be able to help us properly progress. The structure and our lives are the sum of the components. We are the sum of our unique and combined attributes, traits, and competencies. This blueprint grows out of an attempt to illustrate as a visualization tool the critical elements that each of us need to develop and implement to reach our potential. You as the designer and architect of your own future and wellbeing may focus on some, all, or a few; it's completely up to you.

There are other elements of success and prosperity where it could be argued that they warrant their own section or building block. If we analyze these deeper, we will find that they are similar or are aligned with at least one of the competencies and building blocks imbedded in the structure.

STRUCTURE & BUILDING BLOCKS
OF ACHIEVEMENT & PROSPERITY

© Copyright 2017 Richard S. Olin

Chapter 6: The Building Blocks of Achievement and Prosperity | 61

Foundational Competencies:

The foundational competencies grow out of and correlate to the cornerstone competencies reviewed. We will take a closer look at the first four competencies that have been touched upon already with a slightly different angle and perspective. They include planning and journaling that emerge from vision and goal planning. Incorporating a positive attitude, correlates to having positive and beneficial beliefs. Having productive habits was touched upon in the chapter on actions and is a critical element required for each of us to be successful. The benefit of having mentors and coaches to assist in developing and implementing competencies was also reviewed in the chapter on the diamond cycle of achievement and prosperity.

The last two competencies have not been expanded upon prior. Gaining knowledge and continually learning ties into every competency and are key elements of our growth and success. A significant portion of this chapter is on financial planning. This is central to having a balanced wellness environment and consists of subject matter that I will share in a detailed manner. It also includes its own blueprint, structure, and building blocks of financial wellbeing. This rounds out these six foundational competencies, which complement the cornerstone competencies. We should make it our mission to implement all of these into our strategy and growth moving forward to transform our futures if they are not a part of it already.

Planning & Journaling

It has been noted earlier that people don't plan to fail, most just fail to plan. I read an article that stated that approximately 20% of American adults spend more time planning for their summer vacation than they do on their financial plan or wellbeing. Since I have drilled down into the benefits of journaling, I will only provide limited correlations moving forward with each competency. There is a significant amount more to consider with planning besides journaling and the financial component that will be detailed later within this section.

It has been said that high achievers plan their work and work their plan. As my children transitioned into high school, college, and then into the work environment, I observed this firsthand. The young adults who are furthering themselves and are intent on becoming accomplished have a plan in place to succeed.

They are in high school or college connecting with their mentors, guidance counselor, or teachers that they have a connection with. They also are connecting with colleges and networking early on to develop a potential curriculum and career path. The importance of parents and mentors with this planning process continues to be a key component and will be reviewed in the personal branding and career development section. It is also a key driver of young adults' initial planning.

If you are a young adult, this is a critical time to visualize one to two years ahead and develop the mindset that you are out of high school or college and/or moving on to the next stage of your life and career. That is why finding a college curriculum with a Co-op program or intern program can be a huge benefit to those students eager to get a foothold onto their next stage and network to make these connections stick for their future career paths.

My daughter is in her sophomore year at college and is already looking toward a second co-op program and planning out her degree requirements for her post-graduate studies. There are a finite number of spots within each company and the planners and networkers often get first choice. This planning methodology instilled at an early age will continue to afford those the ability to visualize what can and may lie ahead in the future toward their success and prosperity. High achievers plan their work, use the assistance of mentors, and work their plan. I encourage you to do so as well.

The planning process can be used with any of the competencies in the structures. I have tried to complete a thorough review of gathering critical data and information, analyzing and developing a plan of action for you, and providing ways to implement these plans for each competency. The review, implementation, and monitoring are up to you. Be patient, there are always setbacks and challenges even for the best laid plans.

Here is an overview of the planning process:

1. Gather the necessary data to better understand the specific elements needed to be included.
2. Analyze and evaluate the data and its importance and characteristics of this information, data, and the processes that have been laid out.
3. Develop the plan by breaking it down into smaller key manageable sections and steps. Provide a reasonable timeline for each of these steps.
4. Implement the plan in a meaningful and precise manner.
5. Monitor the plans progress and reevaluate when necessary. Rebalance expectations, goals, and results.

The prior example describes how planning can help us develop skills and competencies and position us for our futures. What follows is just one example of how planning effects our environment in general.

I love maps and have been a part-time collector for many years. I think this passion arose from my 20 years as a real estate appraiser when I used maps to locate properties. When you look at a map, it seems as though streets, houses, and neighborhoods have been randomly placed on it, but that generally is not the case.

The planning process of many towns, cities, developments and their associated commercial centers was borne out of the Spanish planning process for formulating a cohesive development plan. This "master plan," as it has come to be termed for our local and state planners, in its early infancy consists of a town park and central gathering area surrounded by certain types of structures, homes, and properties that assimilate within the context of the master plan. Key transportation hubs and arteries, commercial, mixed use, industrial and higher density areas are then planned out and sectioned accordingly.

There are so many variations of these types of town, city, and state developments and transportation arteries. These master plans are a work in progress that will grow and adapt to changes in what the habitants feel is important in the form of redevelopment. The same can be said for our own planning when it comes to all facets of our lives and the competencies detailed. It is important to journal plan these details and changes.

I am reminded of a time when I played the board game called Life, with my children that took us through Life's journey on a map. It's a great visualization tool and game to map out and plan your life's path. Use the tools and resources available in this guide as a starting point to map out and plan your game of life. It is intended to be the springboard for your creative energy.

Think about the three or four major life events that you wish to accomplish and start planning. Draw a starting point, then the roadway to the next stop in 1-3 years that includes a vision. Then the roadway to the next stop in 1-3 years that includes life events related to health improvement/education/career; then roadmap and next stop 2-5 years later. Maybe include a financial pit stop of a home purchase, renovation, or career development (you get the picture). Try and take a detour and add something "outside the box" like learning a new vocation. There is a blank page toward the end of the Workbook that you can utilize for this task.

Here is an example of an interesting landscape design planning project I just completed. I sketched out our property with the house and property boundaries on the plan using my survey. I then planned out a new landscape design that included certain types of trees, bushes, flowers, garden area with new walkways, paths, varying topography, retaining walls, shed (man shed, not a she shed) play areas, and dog run. I spent some time visualizing this in my yard to see where I wanted some screening to be planted, special lighting installed and directed at the house and trees, color combinations and specimens that required more or less sunlight.

When the garden was complete, the arrangement and color combinations reminded me of the collages that I completed with bursts of color and varying plants. I completed a similar planning project for my new kitchen and master bathroom layout using my original drawings. They provided me a sense of accomplishment and were included in my achievement collages.

Prompt: What planning projects are you interested in creating? Maybe it's a new house, renovation, landscape or crafting project or a career planning project. How about a financial plan with a savings, investment, and retirement plan or a startup group that you have been wanting to join or grow or a side business that you want to start with a business plan.

_____

_____

_____

_____

Once written, take that first small step you need in the gathering, analysis, and planning phases to see it through to fruition.

Planning and journaling are important components of future success and help us visualize what can and may lie ahead in our futures. Without it, we are left behind by those that do, as high achievers are planners and doers. These techniques can be used for the various other competencies to help us become more successful. We can create a plan for any of our physical, emotional, intellectual, financial, occupational, or social growth transformation. The key is to think of your life in stages of 3-5 year periods of progress. Use the cycle strategy and develop a planning process to help visualize and lay it out like the game of life and then act upon it.

Positive Attitude

One of the most poignant quotes I have ever read came from Charles Swindoll on one's attitude. He noted that, "The longer I live, the more I realize the impact of attitude on life. Life is 10% what happens to us and 90% how we react to it…we are in charge of our attitudes" It is our attitude that guides us daily and has a profound effect on our outcome and destiny.

My family relocated to a small hamlet of Millington, NJ in 1998. While moving in, I noticed that the owner had left a page with Charles Swindoll's quote taped to the inside of the cabinet. I read it often and even taped it onto the cabinet when we moved into our new home and left it near my work desk. I gave it to many relatives, friends, and coworkers when they fell on hard times and needed some guidance and a constructive perspective.

Think about your own reactions to things that happen in your daily life. When things don't go your way, how do you react? When you have a disagreement or fight with someone, how does that generally play out? Calm cool and collected or anger, resentment, yelling or worse? I know for me, this is something that I continually need to work on; just ask my wife!

When these situations arise, it is always best to take a step back and ascertain what is the effective outcome that we desire for this situation. Easier said than done! Another tip is to take a few slow deep breaths while using a breathing technique to try and draw out the amount of time between when something "comes to a head and surfaces" and your reaction to it. Often, when I look back at how I or others reacted to things, I wished I or they had done what I am describing. How do you think you react to things?

Quickly, without much time between the incident and your response or a slower response with a more drawn out period between the two? _____

The next time something unexpected happens to you try and stretch out the timeframe between the trigger and your reaction to it by taking a step back and using breathing techniques and mindfulness to draw this reaction time out. Another tool you may want to incorporate into your toolbox is the response to an offhanded comment. Why would you say that? This will deflect the reaction back to where it originated and afford you the opportunity to stretch out this timeframe and provide additional time for a thoughtful response versus an unwanted confrontation.

Controlling your emotions is critical to your success and how others perceive you. Successful people note the importance of filtering their emotions because they realize that if they let their emotions control them, relationships could be affected adversely at work and at home. If you want to be successful and have higher Emotional Intelligence or EQ (we will touch on this in Chapter 9) then try and filter what comes out of your mouth. Provide some time between when there is a trigger and when you respond to it, and react with mindfulness and slow deep breathing. Be careful not to always say what's on your mind by filtering your responses. Try and take a step back and wait until you're calmer and have had a chance to analyze the situation objectively before you respond. Keep your emotions in check.

Our own attitude toward ourselves is also an important element in our demeanor and perception. This attitude factors into the importance of having a high self-concept or the combination of having higher self-esteem and self-confidence. How we view and evaluate ourselves plays an important role in our overall attitude. If our perception of self is continuously negative, then it will significantly affect our attitudes. We will provide a cursory review of our attitudes toward our physical identity of self as a subsection on self-esteem. Throughout the guide, we will provide some tools and techniques to improve this view of self and how we can improve our level of self-esteem and our overall attitude.

A friend of mine once told me that, a bad attitude is like a flat tire, you can't go anywhere until you change it. Attitudes are with us from the minute we wake up to the time we fall asleep. As I touched upon in Chapter 3 on beliefs, we seem to either have a positive or negative attitude towards our physical, intellectual, and financial beliefs, among others. It is common notion that a significant portion of these beliefs and/or attitudes are something that we are born with, as well as cultivated by our surrounding environment. I am focused on providing some resources and techniques related to how we should self-reflect regarding our attitudes so that we are conscious of them and then discuss simple ways to make them more positive. My simple tool each day is to read or note the quote presented at the beginning of this section. That is why I adhere to the mantra of "if you want something, put it out in front of you to focus on." It's a way to visualize your next move.

Prompt: What is your general attitude, positive or negative? _____

What is your attitude toward yourself physically, positive or negative? _____

What is your attitude toward money and your financial situation? Are these indicative of those that attract and help us maintain wealth or the opposite?

_____

What is your attitude toward your intellect and career options _____

_____

We will review additional tools, resources, and techniques to assist with improving our attitude in the next chapter. Something else I have noticed throughout my life is how infectious attitudes can become while in the presence of others. People seem to generally gravitate toward individuals that exhibit positive, energetic, and vivacious attitudes and demeanors.

I worked with a very successful manager named Palak who was not only energetic, but always had a very positive attitude. Working with her helped me stay in this frame of mind. Other times, I have worked with individuals who were very negative, lacked energy, and often spoke poorly about others. I monitored my attitude when I interacted with them because it could quickly change in a negative way.

Attitudes seem to feed on themselves and others if left unchecked. It is up to us to decide who we are associating with daily. I will touch on this in a later chapter when we dig into our inner core social circle and their significant effect on us. For the time being, think about the people you associate with on a regular basis be it family, friends, colleagues, coworkers, etc. What is their general demeanor, positive or negative? In what way does it or will it consistently affect you? It is very important that we monitor our own attitudes and those who surround us to determine how we can better understand, acknowledge, make the necessary adjustments of our attitudes and the time spent with those who may influence us.

Prompt: Who among the people you spend the most amount of time with has the most positive and energetic attitude and demeanor and WHY?

_____

_____

Who among the people you spend the most amount of time with has the most negative and pessimistic attitude and demeanor and WHY? _____

_____

_____

The individuals above are a part of your inner core circle reviewed in the next chapter. This exercise may afford you the opportunity to rethink who you may want to include or exclude in your inner circle based on their attitudes. Keep this in mind moving forward as you want to gravitate to those positive and energetic individuals and avoid the downers and blamers at all cost!

Having a positive attitude toward certain aspects of life and ourselves is an important subcomponent of having positive beliefs. We should be mindful of checking how we react to things when they occur. Often, I am guilty of overreacting or reacting poorly to situations and incidents when I don't take a step back and insert some space and time between when bad things happen and when I react to them. Taking a moment to assess our thoughts would afford me and others the ability to change our response.

Reacting more positively will inevitably help enhance our EQ with others. We also need to be mindful of our attitudes toward ourselves. The more positive and higher self-concept we have the better we can become. Take another look at the Target of Belief and Self-Concept and note the verbiage in each segment. Which reaction describes you the best? The added benefit of being open-minded and growth minded can help with our attitudes. We also need to get a handle on who we are spending quality time with and how their attitudes and beliefs may have a significant effect on our own as being infectious. I can't stress enough the importance of having positive beliefs and attitudes especially related to personal future transformation.

Productive Habits

"We are what we repeatedly do, excellence than is not an act, but a habit. We form habits and habits form our futures; we are then creatures of habit." — Aristotle

There are many facets to habits. So much has been written about and opined about them. It is not my intention to provide a broad-based analysis of the topic. I view this as more an opportunity to impart some of the basic considerations. They include self-reflecting upon your own habits, what are your most prevalent current habits, what are some of the habits exhibited by successful versus unsuccessful people, and simple ways to make a potential change regarding some of yours. I have touched upon a few of these related elements in the chapter on actions, since it correlates and grows from our actions and behaviors.

Habits are a continuation of behaviors and routines that we exhibit often enough to become lasting. There are many studies that show differing intervals as to when a repetitive behavior becomes a routine and then a habit. We can debate this all day long. The important thing to understand is that with repetition and some conditioning comes a routine and then followed by a formed habit.

However, the missing piece of the puzzle or strategy in changing bad habits into better ones that is often overlooked is the belief and attitude that a change needs to be made. This belief may come in the form of knowledge, confidence, enthusiasm, motivation, and persistence to make the change. The wildcard element is knowing the WHY or impact benefit in visualizing this change and what the result looks and feels like.

It's great to say, "I want to lose weight or start saving money for an emergency fund." But the reality is that we need to create the vision or plan, believe and have the mindset that we can accomplish these tasks, know the

WHY, visualize the impact benefit, and then take the actionable small steps necessary (maybe with the help of a mentor) to create the transition and new formed habit. This hopefully sounds familiar to the Diamond Cycle of Achievement and Prosperity. Please don't discount the importance of positive beliefs and mindset in this strategy and formula.

Habits generally follow a three-step process which include either the trigger, cue, or reminder, the routine, and the reward. The trigger, cue, or reminder sets our mind in motion to start the process. The routine is the behavior or action we are taking, and the reward is the benefit from the process. Take for instance my former habit of sitting in my Lazeboy every night after dinner, turning on the TV, eating snacks, and vegetating.

The trigger may be a sporting event that is coming on or just that dinner is over, and then the routine and reward follow. Once I determined that I could use this time more effectively and that this process and routine was unnecessary and visualized the impact benefit of changing this habit to playing and practicing guitar or reading an article, I was halfway home to making the change.

The next step is introducing an interruption and potentially linking or pairing up the new routine with another routine. In this case, instead of sitting in my Lazeboy, I went into my office and sat at my desk or the kitchen table. Interrupting the old habit may delink it and the routine process. In this different environment, I began to focus on other tasks not associated with watching TV or surfing the internet.

One of the results of making this change is that I became more tired focusing on reading or guitar and forgot about the snacks and went to bed sooner to wake up earlier. This allowed me more time for my morning pairing routines to improve my emotional wellness! That's a threefer!

I provided some examples of pairing and linking new emotional hygiene routines to other morning sanctuary ritual routines prior. My commute and lunchtime routines are paired up with other more productive habits. It's critical that we find the trigger or cue, interrupt the routine, have the belief and know the WHY, then potentially pair it up with another routine. I don't want to mislead here, sometimes depending upon the habit, this is easier said than done. It's one thing to stop sitting in a Lazeboy, it's a whole other level to stop a smoking or gambling habit. The reality is that this same strategy and continuum of the process can also be utilized.

A study of how and why the Alcohol Anonymous AA programs are so successful conveys the critical elements of "someone having the belief, confidence and often faith" that this change can be made while incorporating the assistance of a social network of mentors. We will explore the importance of this social network in detail to follow as key to our growth or lack thereof. It seems evident that smokers form the habit of hanging out with smokers, drinkers tend to hang out with drinkers, studious individuals hang out with smart people and spectator sports minded people have a hard time relating to those who aren't spectators! Be careful who you hang out with and chose your friends wisely.

Prompt: What are some of your worst, destructive, or poor habits currently in addition to the ones noted in the beliefs chapter?_____

_____

_____

_____

_____

_____

_____

_____

Don't forget about your screen time habits. We reviewed the importance of time management in the chapter on actions as critical to one's success. The focus was more on screen time as a crutch and an unproductive habit when it is not educationally or financially based. We also touched upon commitment devices and behavioral change triggers as beneficial tools and techniques. Within your phone settings there is a screen time tracker and limit settings. It can be set for your phone or your children's phone, so be aware of this great commitment device app for your kids to be able to control the amounts of screen and text time they are using.

You may want to set up their content and privacy restrictions as well. If you find that you are spending too much time on your phone and the apps, internet, communications and email, then it is a great opportunity to not only track your time spent, but also input limits on certain apps and sites that you visit too often.

Prompt: Take the time now to set up these app and communication limits if you are spending way too much time on your phone and not on other important wellness activities and think it's necessary. You may also want to set reminders on your calendar to review the screen time tracker to get a better understanding of your time spent on each of these apps and activities.

Prompt: What are some new more productive and beneficial habits that you want to incorporate into your daily or weekly routine? Review some of the vision goals and your rocking chair moment notes you made prior to facilitate some tie-in ideas. _____

_____

_____

_____

_____

_____

_____

Successful people, it has been noted, form the habits that unsuccessful people are not willing to form. It's easier to binge watch Netflix movies and YouTube or Tiktok videos than it is to read, study, and learn a new skill or subject matter at the end of your day or on weekends.

But these successful people continue to grow, learn, plan, save, invest and connect with mentors. Learning and reading are other reasons why they may become successful. I once wrote an equation for my son, Jon, when he was younger. It read, hard work + enthusiasm = the potential for success. Many of these elements noted are prerequisites for the potential to be successful, but they will not make you successful generally on their own. I find this to be an important distinction.

Statistics and studies show that certain habits of wealthy individuals include saving and investing, consistently learning and reading, connecting with mentors and working longer than expected. The structure provided has many of these quality habits embedded in the competencies for your review. The section on conditioning mind and body has several habits and routines for you to pair up. As an example, the upcoming financial planning section conveys many savings and spending habits to consider and change.

We will review our physical and emotional habits. It might be a good opportunity now to take a second look or self-reflect upon and appraise the habits you exhibit based on these other wellness competencies. Other habits that include being grateful, generous, confident, phone detox, spending more time outside, exercising, reading, and exploring can help increase your overall health and wellbeing.

Our actions, behaviors, and habits play a key role in our overall success. We form habits and habits form our futures. It is evident that successful people form the habits that unsuccessful people are not willing to form. Several elements have been reviewed to illustrate how we can transition from having unproductive habits to more productive habits. One of the most helpful techniques that I have utilized is pairing up or linking emotional hygiene routines and habits with other daily personal hygiene habits that I complete in the morning. This has led me to a more balanced wellness environment focusing my time and energy investing in myself on more productive routines and habits.

Mentors

"If you want to find out about the road ahead, then ask about it from those coming back." — Chinese proverb

One of the reasons I wanted to write this guide was that it would be a mentor resource for my children during their adult lives and potentially for you. Utilizing the benefit of mentors, coaches, buddies, trainers and others to assist in your pursuits is critically important to your growth. I have touched on their ability to play a pivotal and centralized role in the Diamond Cycle of Achievement. I have alluded to the fact that successful organizations and athletes have their own mentors, coaches, trainers, and Board of Directors or Advisors. These mentors and coaches can simplify and expedite processes related to the competencies and building blocks of achievement and prosperity.

They can be someone you already know within your family, school, organization, or core circle or outside. Our parents play a pivotal role as our mentors early on, which can be both good and bad. Teachers and other family members can also play a mentoring role. My sister-in-law, Joan, was a great role model and mentor for my wife during my wife's career and had great insight related to her career progression since Joan was working in a similar occupation. She was an advocate on my wife's behalf.

A mentor may or may not have a vested interest in your success. Successful people, when surveyed, consistently rank having a mentor as being one of the most critical elements that helped make them successful during their growth period. This is a powerful statement and one you should consider. This section will primarily focus on if you have mentors currently in your life; how you should consider incorporating them into certain aspects of your life; examples of some great partnerships and next steps on how to drive these important connections.

Prompt: Who in your life do you consider to be your biggest advocate, supporter, and mentor to date and WHY?_____

_____

_____

_____

_____

Mentors can assist with one's personal life or professional career and image, help manage time productively and help with building personal and professional confidence. They may assist with developing skills like being proactive instead of reactive, as well as help you focus on shorter range milestones in addition to larger goals. This relationship may be either informal or formal. The mentor can assist with branding, imaging, problem solving, role playing in a career setting, skill building, conflict resolution, communication skills, and developing better listening skills to name a few benefits.

    Many larger organizations offer mentorship programs to help foster career development and growth. They pair up junior managers with tenured senior or executive level management, often with an executive coach. This helps not only the mentee or junior manager learn new skills, but also allows the corporation an avenue for leadership development that can fill gaps in future job openings. It can also foster a clear communication of the corporate mission statement and culture that the enterprise wishes to disseminate and endure. If you work for a company, does the company offer a formal mentorship program? If not, is there an option to connect with a well-positioned manager or executive?

Prompt: If the above mentorship opportunity is available, begin the process of signing up for this initiative by contacting the appropriate department or lead liaison. If it is not an option, then think about someone who can assist with your most critical need to progress by reviewing some of the challenges you noted related to your habits and beliefs or potentially help with your career planning. There may be someone within your present circle of family and friends that may act as a mentor without being in the career path that you are pursuing. Write down a contact name and the next steps you will take to pursue an initial connect or meeting via call, email, LinkedIn, etc. Add a potential second contact in case this individual is not willing to assist.

_____

_____

When I was starting my career as a financial advisor at a reputable firm, I was paired up with a mentor that was going to assist me in launching my practice and teach me many of the processes and responsibilities of a successful financial advisor. However, due to many unforeseen circumstances and family responsibilities he had, and a lack of a true connection between us, this initiative and collaboration was never a real benefit to me.

My mentor was not really invested in me and because of this, I was not invested in dedicating additional time and energy to this relationship. It was not a good fit. We all need to be prepared for this as a potential outcome and adapt to it. We should never assume that it is the mentor's responsibility to drive the relationship. We should take the initiative and schedule meetings to continue to drive activities that the mentor is willing to assist with.

It is the mentees responsibility to be prepared to drive the interactions, bring up some of the things that they want to focus on, and what goals they want to accomplish regarding this relationship, not the mentors. You should be more invested in the relationship than they are as you are the one who primarily benefits from it. If you find that you are contributing enough to the initiative and the mentor is not contributing toward your growth and success, then you will need to adjust, adjust, adjust.

There are so many great examples of fruitful mentorship relationships throughout history. Those that come to mind include: Aristotle being mentored by Plato; Mark Zuckerberg of Facebook being mentored by Steve

Jobs; Warren Buffett being groomed by Benjamin Graham (the father of value investing) early in his career; John Glen being mentored by his high school civics teacher who pushed him to become a fighter pilot, and who later became an astronaut and a true American pioneer! Many successful people, including those noted, have learned to model themselves after others who have already achieved success.

Another important element to consider is that we need more than one or two mentors in our lives. As we grow older and our lives become more complex, there becomes an increased need to incorporate other mentors or advisors into our lives. Some of the mentors that you should incorporate into your center or sphere of influence (SOI) would include health care providers, accountants, counselors, attorneys, financial advisor, teachers, and managers related to your career vision and goals.

These SOI's can form the basis or core team also known as your personal Board of Directors or advisors to help cultivate your growth. This is a good way to create ties to mentors and learn from successful individuals. Corporations need competent board members and you need competent advocates on your team.

Here is a potential list of those individuals that you need on your side as advocates for your success. My hope is that this guide acts as a mentor resource for you. There are so many different aspects of life where we can use help and assistance from trainers, coaches, and mentors. It would become overwhelming to list all of those that have potential. This is considered a consolidated team of advisors and mentors that should be the starting point for your sphere of influence and Board of Advisors. I have tried to group them together more cohesively.

- Occupational Specialists — Career and branding specialist; Career counselor; corporate mentor; Co-op advisor; Business strategist; Recruiter.
- Physical Specialists — Doctors; Exercise trainer or coach; Nutritionist;

Health care associate; Team coach.

- Emotional Specialists — Doctors; Life coach; Clergyperson; Confidant; Partner; Social worker; Health care associate.

- Financial Specialists — Financial Advisor; Insurance Specialist; Attorney; Accountant; Realtor; Benefits Specialist; Banker; Mortgage loan officer.

- Intellectual Specialists — Teachers; tutors; managers, and all of the above.

- Social Specialist—Social worker; Psychologist; Matchmaker.

These individuals can provide you with knowledge, direction, encouragement, inspiration, and motivation toward your growth and prosperity. There are several online sites that offer mentorship and coaching options and groups where you can locate mentors who are willing to help.

Athletic coaches are mentors and guides for our young athletes regarding life lessons and overcoming adversity. The impact they have on the trajectory of a player's life can't be overstated. There are so many examples of this growth partnership both in and outside of sports.

I spent the greater part of my adult life coaching and training my children when it came to team and individual sports such as, baseball, softball, soccer, tennis, and skiing. It was an opportunity for me to become involved and make a difference in their lives and has become a focal point of my earlier adult life. My advice to you is to also look at this wildcard in reverse and volunteer to mentor in some way so you can make a difference in your life and others and create your legacy.

Prompt: Review the list above and write down some names and contact information for each of your mentors. Document them in order of importance with the most needed mentor as a starting point for the area in your life that requires the most attention and improvement (that may be lacking or more important at this time). Contact them via telephone, email, Linkedin, website, etc. Ask them for a short amount of time to connect to advise you on some next steps for success. Maybe that is a quick cup of coffee or a phone conversation.

Don't discount family members or close friends of your family, teachers, managers, coaches, and volunteer organizations as potential mentors as they have a vested interest in your success.

Career/Occupational mentors _____

_____

_____

Physical mentors _____

_____

Emotional mentors _____

_____

Financial mentors _____

_____

Intellectual mentors _____

_____

Social mentors _____

_____

It is important to consider building teams of mentors, advisors, coaches, and friends related to several or all of the above groupings. These are your Board of Advisors. This team structure will give you a broader overview of the challenges, opportunities, resources, tools, and next steps needed for success.

Start with your health teams comprised of your physical and emotional BOD's. Then comprise a financial team of BOD's and the others to follow. These teams will increase the probability that you will move toward a successful outcome. Find a friend who will act as an accountability confidant or partner who shares similar visions and positive motivational beliefs that you may have. Work with them to build similar teams of mentors and trainers for the same end goals. Think of them as your "health buddy" and "money buddy" who will motivate and challenge you just like the mentors. We will discuss this element in more detail when we review your inner core social circle in the chapter on core competencies.

The power and benefits of having mentors, coaches, and teachers in your corner for support, feedback, and planning are undeniable. History is inked with so many great examples of how successful organizations and individuals utilized the knowledge, resources, and guidance of these advocates. They are a support system that helps develop, sequence, and institute an action plan and progression for your transformational growth and development. Don't expect them to lead and do the work as it's up to you to drive this relationship and beneficial outcome. Build teams of advocates as your Board of Advisors and work with a friend as an accountability buddy.

Successful individuals note that having a mentor as a positive influence in their lives was one of the main reasons for their success. Make the connection today and follow through. Think about reversing this notion and becoming a volunteer and mentor. A great place to start are volunteer organizations like the Boys and Girls Clubs of America, Big Brothers Big Sisters, United Way, and other local non-profit organizations that help drive these beneficial relationships.

Learning and Knowledge

"An investment in knowledge pays the biggest dividends."
— Benjamin Franklin

Continual learning is a key element for success and prosperity. That is why Benjamin Franklin noted it as being critical. This guide is devoted to providing knowledge regarding multiple key competencies within each chapter. Based on this, I will impart some other important considerations around this subject matter and not duplicate information. Learning and knowledge are the base line components for the intellectual competency that eventually leads to, and connects with, the occupational competency and career growth and our associated earnings potential. These are just a few reasons why it should be a main focus.

One of the key elements to be reiterated is the importance for each of us to be growth minded instead of fixed minded. Our intellect is not fixed as it was once believed to be. If you have a growth mindset, you desire to experience, read, learn, understand, improve, grow, and prosper. We all differ when it comes to experiences, aptitudes, attitudes, and competencies. Being open-minded and adaptable will enhance your abilities. The important consideration is that having this open-minded growth mindset will allow you to learn, gain knowledge, have new experiences, and improve as an individual as you move forward on your journey.

Studies and surveys consistently document how successful people spend a significant amount of time reading every day. They do this to learn and increase their understanding of life, career, business, and subject matter that is important to them. This makes them more valuable to organizations, superiors, customers and/or clients. A high majority are reading content on current events, personal development, and career and financial related material that will enhance their knowledge and growth.

Nowadays, these growth minded individuals note that they are using resources like podcasts, audiobooks, and online educational and lecture material to supplement their reading. Online sites catering to these individuals include: EDX.org; Coursera; Khan Academy; LinkedIn, Skillshare, and Udacity to name a few. These other delivery options allow us the opportunity to drive this beneficial activity linking it as a twofer with other daily activities.

This was a technique that I touched upon in the action section on time management. It is also one that I have incorporated into my daily routines. Reading was never my forte, and I shied away from this early on in my career. However, as I grew to understand its importance, I took it upon myself to create an action plan of utilizing these podcasts and audiobooks as my preferred delivery method. I spend a great deal of time reading for my career and keeping up with the ever-changing laws, regulations, and procedures in addition to better understanding market valuations and economics.

Prompt: What learning method mentioned may be a good fit for you to incorporate into your daily routines as a twofer? How can you move this process forward with next steps to capitalize on the benefits? _____

_____

_____

Many of us, including myself, are visual learners. That is why I often present the material in picture or a structured format. It is also an opportunity to make the content more of a visualization tool and resource. Knowledge and learning can be captured anywhere and in many forms. From a simple walk down the block mindfully observing a hawk overhead in search of its prey or a trip to the local museum. Every library, museum, local community and groups have their own sponsored free events. Search them out, connect with them, add them to your calendar and benefit from the dissemination of knowledge to learn new things and grow.

The vast network of museums throughout our states offers us many possibilities to learn and grow. Many of these are free to enter if you review the details as they may only request a donation and entrance fees may not be mandatory (I learned that at the Museum of Natural History). Also, some companies offer free admittance as a member organization (as a former Bank of America/Merrill Lynch employee and customer, they offer a "museums on us" program).

These visits expand our mind and may lead to a new vision, hobby, volunteer initiative, and/or branding or career development consideration. One of my favorite things to do is to check out the planetarium and telescope observation nights that are routinely available. Zoos, aquariums, memorials, tours, and sculpture parks can also be great places for growth and learning opportunities.

Side note: if you are ever near central New Jersey and can plan a day trip, search out Grounds for Sculpture in Hamilton, NJ. This is one of my favorite day trips and not very well known outside of the area and state. These park grounds were grown and sculpted by renowned artist Seward Johnson and encompass hundreds of his bronze life size statues. Think of the huge statue known as "Unconditional Surrender" of the sailor kissing the woman at the end of World War II or the Marilyn Monroe statue. It's worth the visit and experience.

Many of us who have not attended school recently may not have picked up a book in a long time. The average American reads 4 or more books per year, but a high percentage of these are fiction related. Successful individuals are generally avid readers, whether it is a book or periodical. Building this routine will inevitably help you learn, retain knowledge, and potentially apply this knowledge to your life in one capacity or another. It may be a good opportunity to take a moment and determine and appraise what your reading habits are currently and how you may adjust them to a well-rounded beneficial approach.

Prompt: Search out 1 or 2 opportunities for you to gain some knowledge in an area outside of your career path. This may encompass a hobby, pastime, art related, self-help, etc. Write down the interest and how you are going to search out learning possibilities surrounding it. Don't forget to provide the WHY and a time frame. _____

_____

_____

_____

Take the first step now to research and put a hold on a book or audiobook or download a podcast. Add as a phone reminder if necessary.

It is apparent from my own personal experience that those with higher levels of education and advanced degrees are more likely to be occupationally successful with higher and quicker career development. This will also help them have a more balanced wellness environment to be reviewed moving forward. That is why in many cultures, not only in the US but throughout the world, children and adults are consistently growing by learning. We all have a finite amount of time so it is important to utilize it beneficially. There are currently so many distractions and I refer back to the paradigms noted prior. I have touched upon the negative time management effects of the constant proliferation of social media sites and its focus by our youth.

Knowledge regarding our personal security is more critical than ever. Since my vision in the guide is to present and impart important information that may help each of us be successful, I want to touch upon specific topics of security and protection. These are lessons and issues that you don't want to learn the hard way.

Cybercrimes account for billions in financial loses every year. While identity theft accounts for a significant portion and grabs all the headlines, other types of fraud cost consumers more. Since I have worked in a bank for many years, I have seen some egregious situations arise, often on a daily basis, that primarily affect seniors.

The first incident I witnessed happened back in 2012 when I was an advisor in a bank branch in northern New Jersey. It was a quiet Friday in June when in walks an elderly lady who approached the teller and mentioned that she wanted to send out a wire transfer. The teller who was trained and coached to ask questions regarding these transactions began her process, when the customer abruptly and rudely interrupted her and told her that she was in a rush and needed to get this wire done quickly. She was then escorted into an office and asked several of these questions again. She told the associate that she had won a large lottery prize and in order to collect it, she needed to wire out a significant amount of money to claim it.

Eventually, due to an escalated situation, the police were brought in to assist and explain to her that she was being scammed. As she hastily left the branch on the phone with the perpetrators, you could hear her saying to them that she was leaving and going to another branch to make the wire transfer. That was the first of many similar situations over the next many years that I was privy to.

Just this year, I was in another branch when another elderly lady walked into the bank requesting the same wire transfer. After some time discussing the situation with the branch manager, it was discovered that this customer wanted to wire out another $50,000 after she had already wired out $50,000 to the same individual just a week prior. She noted that this was going to a friend of her late husband's that he had gone to school with who was in Africa. The "friend" needed help with some business issues he had encountered. She told the manager that this person mentioned that her late husband had told him that he would always help him out in times of need if they ever arose. Even though the requested wire transfer was denied, it turned out that she eventually sent him the wire from another bank. Over the course of eight years, I personally witnessed at least one of these incidents every year.

There are so many internet and phone scams. If you have not done so already, I recommend that you have a conversation with your family members about the following:

1. Email or server compromised: Scammers target us by hacking and/or phishing through bogus emails or through online internet access to request wire transfers or online tech support.

2. Phone scam purporting to be the IRS: Callers purport that you owe the IRS back taxes and that there is an outstanding arrest warrant that needs to be paid for through a wire transfer in addition to the back taxes.

3. Home purchase and closing scam: A phishing attempt borne out of realtor information that requests a wire of funds for the escrowed closing costs for the closing associated with your home purchase.

4. Lottery scam: A request to wire transfer funds to allow for the lottery winnings to be released to you.

5. Apartment security deposit scam (often on Craigslist): Request for wire transfer of security deposit and first month's rent for an apartment listed where you have not connected with the right owner. This happens when scammers post real addresses of vacant properties they found online and renters release a deposit without inspecting the property or connecting in-person with the true owner.

6. Confidence fraud: A similar wire request based on a previous or current relationship where people have never met.

7. Non-delivery due to cancelled payment: Scammers request wire transfer to deliver free or won items where payment was denied previously for shipping and handling fees.

Several of my friends and relatives have been scammed by a few of the above!

Other security features to consider:

- Be careful what you put in a safety deposit box in the bank as they may not be insuring your items. Check the agreement for details and waivers.

- Never post future vacation dates online or on Facebook as it will alert potential thieves.

- Never post your correct birthday or log this date into non-critical websites as they can be hacked. People routinely ping me for my birthday on days that are not my birthday. Makes me happy multiple days of the year!

- Never use your birthdate in your email address! I have clients that have them in their addresses.

- Don't post your newborn's birthday online.

- Install a comprehensive firewall or Antivirus, anti-spyware software package on your computer. Your company may offer discounts.

- Check your credit score and sign-up for free credit monitoring of your report for errors regularly on Credit Karma or other free sites. This will also allow you to monitor who may be pulling your credit information without your consent or permission as potential fraud.

- Add your emergency contact information into your phone in case it gets lost so that you can be contacted.

- Add your medical ID information into your phone health app such as blood type, medical conditions, allergies, and medications. Be careful not to input critically private information like your date of birth. You can also add your emergency contact information.

- If interested, you can also add into the Health app, under medical ID any organ donor information you may wish to disclose.

- When using a ride sharing service or any car service, confirm prior to getting in the vehicle that the driver knew beforehand where your destination was and about the fare. There have been many instances, especially in college towns, where young women were preyed upon by individuals posing as these drivers. This can lead to serious consequences.

Prompt: Take some time to connect with family members, especially grandparents and parents, and have this overview discussion so that everyone is aware what not to do and what information not to provide to strangers.

These security scams and concerns connect with our financial priorities as they can affect the bottom line. Financial literacy is the bedrock of a successful financial plan and one's success and prosperity. Yet, most of us don't spend the time to read and learn how to be financially literate. What follows is one of the most important sections of this guide.

Studies document that wealthier Americans consistently rank reading, knowledge, and thus learning as the top two or three most important factors, after savings and often hard work, in their success. Having mentors, networking and setting goals also ranked high. Learning is a continual process as we learn new things every day. Today for instance, I learned that trees in the rain forest emit vapors that form clouds that rain down in certain areas; barre guitar chords are hard to play, and financial markets don't necessarily care that another 7 million people filed for new unemployment benefits in one week.

The best way to learn for me, and many of us, is by doing or working through something. If I write the information down, I tend to remember it more often than just reading it. So, my recommendation to you is to complete the prompts and repeatedly work through some of the elements within these sections that resonate with you that you may benefit from. Complete the vision and achievement collages, put it up on your wall; write down and document your goals, beliefs and habits, and work through some new strategies and techniques to transform your future and wellbeing and get to a better place.

I have to reread many sections of my own guide to remind myself to work on my EQ and what to say in certain situations and not reacting immediately among others. It has helped me, and my hope is that it will help you. If you are a visual learner, then this guide and its pullout pages in the Workbook should be helpful to you.

Learning and building up your intellect ties in with your branding and career development. This, in turn, correlates to our financial success regarding our salary, income, and cash flow reviewed in the next section. The three wellness competencies of intellectual, occupational, and financial wellbeing are interdependent and critically important to our overall success and prosperity. Gaining knowledge and learning is time well spent and it is making an investment in yourself as noted in the tenents.

Financial Planning

Successful financial planning and wellbeing include a comprehensive financial, investment, retirement, and estate plan. Having a written, well-documented and detailed financial plan and executing on this plan forms the basis of having sound finances. Financial planning and wellness encompass many competencies including: proper budgeting, saving, borrowing, investing, retirement planning, protection planning, and estate planning among others. I consistently note that financial success is not driven by the performance of the investments, but by the behaviors of investors.

Financial security affords us independence and prosperity. Often, attaining a solid financial footing may depend on having a solid financial plan. In the introduction of the guide I detailed several paradigm shifts taking place that we all should understand and account for. One of these is related to the shift in burden of planning and preparing for our retirement from institutions onto us.

In the past there was a three-legged retirement stool to provide for most corporate and government retirees. Currently, most of us are down to a two-legged one in addition to having to prepare and account for investing for our health care related costs. These are in addition to the usual pressures of keeping up with the neighbors and continually being egged on by our kids to buy them the newest iPhone, gadget, or gaming system. It is a battle and one that you need to fight daily and win by properly saving and investing.

Studies related to financial literacy in the US consistently convey that barely half of the adult population is considered financially literate and that we rank poorly compared to other first world countries. The lack of financial literacy can carry high costs in fees, debt and interest payments, fraud as noted, and mistakes.

One of the main missions of this guide is to instill the importance of proper financial planning early on in one's life. There is a lack of financial education at an early age in the US. Too few states and schools require financial education in their curriculum. Over 50% of high schools don't require students to complete a personal finance course. It is not a surprise that many individuals don't understand how to budget or save and are falling so far into debt that they are mortgaging their futures and independence. Our media and society glorify spending and instant gratification over long term fiscal responsibility. This has far reaching effects for us individually and collectively as a nation.

Since I was a child, I was a saver. When I earned an allowance cutting the lawn and completing chores, I always saved some of the money and had a passbook account at the local bank. At that time when you made a deposit, you gave the passbook to the teller and they added the deposit to your passbook as your receipt. At that time in the 1980's savings accounts were paying around 10% and I was even getting a 12% yield. Oh, how times have changed. The point I am trying to make is that by being a saver (and my wife being a saver as well) and having a written plan that we have stuck to, it has helped us build savings, investment, and retirement funds that have afforded us this elusive financial security and independence.

There have been several references prior to studies on the benefits of writing down one's written goals. Instead of citing others that may be relevant, I want to reiterate that this task has always worked for me personally. It is something that I have been completing for decades and can honestly say that many of these goals have been completed successfully. This task also affords me the opportunity to revisit and review them periodically to keep them top of mind. The strategy of having a written financial plan and saving for a rainy day or an emergency fund is paramount to one's financial success and survival. I encourage you to transform your financial future by setting this process in motion.

A recent survey of Americans noted that 63% don't have $500 saved to pay for an emergency. These individuals are a significant portion of our society and have given up their potential financial freedom. Many Americans prioritize spending over saving and are more focused on the short term instead of the beneficial longer-term planning.

Sound financial planning calls for a first step in saving an emergency fund equal to a minimum of 3 to 6 months of your monthly expenses. My recommendation to my clients is that they have a minimum of 6 to 9 months liquid assets in a checking and high yield money market savings account to cover their expenses. For the average person that does not have a large amount of overhead expenses that may be $2,000 to $5,000 per month. Do you have an understanding of what your monthly expenses are on average over the past 6 months? What are they? $ _____

How much is your 6-month emergency fund? _____

Budgeting and Saving:

Budgeting is a great first step in taking control of your finances. A proactive approach, along with a disciplined savings plan, can help you pursue your financial priorities and goals. If you monitor your expenses closely through receipts and credit and debit card statements, you have an opportunity to make the necessary adjustments to your spending. By doing so, you will have additional capital monthly for your savings plan and build up the necessary emergency fund for unexpected expenses with the proper disciplined approach.

Below, and in the Workbook, is a Budget and Cash Flow Analysis for your use. Additional copies will be needed as your life situation, expenses, and income change. I have tried to make the spreadsheet as inclusive as possible so that you don't miss any miscellaneous expenses.

Supporting documents you will need are: payroll credits or paystubs, checking account statements, credit card statements, checkbook, bills, receipts, etc. Spend the time now to invest in yourself and understand your budget. Some line items may not apply to your situation now. Please make sure that you are being inclusive and thorough in your review and are not leaving anything out.

Budget & Cash Flow Analysis	Monthly $
Housing	
Rent or Mortgage & Taxes	
Homeowners Assoc fee	
Utilities (gas, electric, water/sewer)	
Cable & Internet	
Phone	
Insurance: Homeowners or renters	
Repairs / Maintenance contracts	
Lawn, cleaning, other services	
Other - streaming services	
Auto - Transportation	
Auto Loan or Lease Payment	
Second Car payment	
Auto Insurance	
Gas	
Maintenance / oil changes	
Parking, Uber or Public Transportation	
Other	
Medical	
Medical/Dental/Eye Insurance Premiums	
Deductibles	
Presription Drugs/Pharmacy	
Life Insurance Premiums (LTC/Disability)	
Other	
Personal	
Groceries Supermarket	
Dining out/Takeout	
Entertainment	
Gym or Club memberships	
Personal Care/Hair, nails, etc.	
Clothing	
Vacations & Travel	
Gifts & Occasions	
Hobbies & recreation - other	
Child care	
Child support	
Alimony	
Loan payments - student/personal	
Charitable contributions	
Other - credit card	
Other	
Other	
Total Monthly Spending	$
Monthly After-Tax Income	$
Surplus or Shortfall	$

Monthly Income	Monthly $
Salary 1	
Salary 2	
Freelance income	
Investment income	
Dividends	
Social Security 1	
Social Security 2	
Pension 1	
Pension 2	
Annuity 1	
Annuity 2	
Alimony	
Child support	
Rental income	
Rental income	
Other	
Monthly Income	$

Transform Your Future & Wellbeing

What is your monthly cash flow, positive or negative? $ _____

If negative, then you should take immediate action to reduce your expenses. We will review several options later in the section to assist with reducing expenses. If positive, then this is your available amount to place into savings to first build up your emergency funds and then your investment accounts. If you have difficulty with willpower and this exercise, then your bank or company may offer an automatic savings plan that allows payroll to automatically transfer a set amount from your paycheck or checking account to a savings account. This is a great alternative way to force yourself to start saving.

Here are four things you should ask yourself prior to buying something:

1. Is it a need or a want? We need to distinguish between the two!
2. Do I really need it to better myself?
3. Can I afford it, will I be putting myself in debt, and what are the consequences of my actions?
4. What is the true cost of this product including tax and any financing involved?

PAY YOURSELF FIRST! This is similar to investing in yourself. Having a substantial emergency fund by budgeting and saving and not overspending are the first cornerstones and competencies for a sound financial plan. Setting goals and creating written budgets give you a monthly and yearly blueprint that you can revisit and revise accordingly.

Prompt: Pinpoint one or more expenses that you are incurring that can be reduced or eliminated altogether in your budget. Maybe you can bring lunch to work 3-5 days per week and not go out to breakfast or lunch on weekends; stop going to Starbucks daily; reduce your phone or triple play expense by switching or changing plans and/or stop gambling. Write these down and add the actionable next steps you will take and a timeline to complete. Track your progress until you achieve the desired result. Add phone reminders as a trigger.

Savings plan 1 _____

Savings plan 2 _____

"You need to tell your money where to go instead of wondering where your money went." — Dave Ramsey

In 2020 my coworker and I would connect on planning and how she was investing in herself as I completed instructional meetings and reviews for the bank branch employees as an advisor. She noted that she was accomplishing learning about financial planning and investing by listening to podcasts given by Dave Ramsey, who offers a great analysis of and insight into personal finance. The strategy of using educational podcasts is one that I noted earlier as a value add and potential twofer while commuting to work. This quote resonated with her and me and should resonate with you.

Let's review some meaningful ways to reduce your monthly expenses:

1. I finally returned an unused cable box that I was paying $8 per month for unnecessarily or $96 plus fees and taxes per year!
2. Cut the cord or reduce your cable bill by getting a basic package. Call the cable provider every year and renegotiate any yearly cost increases that occur.
3. My family uses a lower cost smaller phone carrier that saves us hundreds of dollars per year. You can lower your phone and cable fees by reducing content or band width options. Get rid of the unused home phone.
4. Reduce your takeout coffee bill with an in-home Keurig. A friend told me that instead of ordering a menu triple from Starbucks, you could order a baseline coffee, add the flavor pumps, and save a lot more per cup.
5. Brown bag lunches for work instead of ordering out.
6. Eliminate your banking and ATM fees by not using outside banks ATMs and keep sufficient balances in your checking and savings accounts.
7. Eliminate late fees on all accounts and bills by paying on time with a

plan and having overdraft protection on your checking account.

8. Takeout from restaurants or reduce the amount of times you dine in.
9. Become an informed supermarket shopper with coupons and price checking for sale items.
10. Join Costco or BJ's and buy in bulk. This has been one of the best budgeting techniques I have ever utilized over time. Many members go for the $1.50 hot dog and soda lunch and free samples! Homage to my dad.
11. Cut your lawn and do the landscaping and upkeep. I did this for the past 30 years and saved a ton. Great exercise as a twofer!
12. If you carry high credit card balances (which you should never do as it is a financial plan killer) call the company and negotiate down the interest rate. Only do a balance transfer without a fee, which there almost always is.
13. Clean your own house if you use a cleaning person. Great exercise as a twofer!
14. Stop buying expensive bottled water and get a filtered pitcher.
15. Skip the car wash and do it yourself. Have car repairs and maintenance done at a discount service shop instead of the dealership. You would be surprised what the difference is and the additional add-ons that they get you for.
16. Not using that membership or subscription, get rid of it. Cancel Satellite radio.
17. Buy clothing from discount stores like TJ Max or Bob's Stores instead of the mall and full price stores. This is my wife's favorite!
18. If you are paying PMI insurance and you have 20% equity in your home by now, take the steps necessary to cancel it.
19. If you're a drinker, have a few (not too many) before you go out to

dinner or start going to BYOB's to reduce your checks.

20. Stop buying iPhones every few years. You and your kids don't need them just because everyone else has the newest and best!

21. Start to take on some simple home repairs yourself if you're handy. I was never handy, but when I became a homeowner, I renovated 3 houses, finished a large basement, and added on a bedroom to another.

22. Do your own manicures and potentially pedicures.

23. Skip the dry cleaners if you can and iron the clothes yourself.

24. Stop gambling period; on lottery tickets except for an occasional one, sporting events or anything else besides a box for the super bowl or a bracket in March madness!

I could go on and on… like refinancing any high rate car, home, and student loan debt that I will touch on later. The point I am trying to convey is that there are ways for you to save money if you are willing to make the effort. It is the media and advertisers' job to keep you watching their hyped "breaking news" and commercials to retain control of your eyeballs and make you believe that you need these products. We are a consumer driven society and we buy way more than most of us truly need.

If you find yourself upgrading your phone every year or two because the phone company has enticed you with their high fee plan in place, you should reconsider your options. If you are leasing cars every 2-3 years and/or buying the newest gadget or outfit, rethink and evaluate you're spending and savings habits as you are weakening your savings, investment, and retirement plans and longer term security and independence every time you take their bait.

Prompt: Take another look at your budget and spending over the past few months and the list of potential savings options I have provided above. Write down two or more other savings plan options not noted in the prior prompt that you can implement over the next week to help you save a substantial amount of money toward your savings and investment plan.

Savings plan #3 _____

Savings plan #4 _____

Savings plan #5 _____

If you have significant credit card debt and need to kick start a savings plan into high gear, then you will need multiple savings strategies. Don't succumb to peer or societal pressure as they won't be there to help when a job loss, recession, or retirement happens! I would recommend writing down everything you spend money on for 1-2 months in your journal. Then group these into your budget line items. This will give you an accurate overview of where you have gaps and shortfalls in your budget.

How often on average do you eat out per week (includes all meals)? _____

What is the total cost per month on average $ _____

Take a moment and think about ways to adjust your schedule and reduce these weekly by eliminating some, if necessary. Think about getting takeout for one weekend dinner while setting up theme movie/music/game/romantic/outdoor or creative nights eating and drinking at home. If this isn't your greatest weakness, then review the list and plan and execute your strategy to transform it.

Once you have successfully tackled your budgeting and cash flow management and set up a savings account linked to your bank checking account, then it is time to take the next steps for your banking needs.

Please note that there is no benefit to having multiple checking accounts, especially in multiple banks and this will end up costing you money in fees. The only time this comes into play is exceeding the FDIC limits over $250,000 per account or for a unique situation if this applies to you. Set up direct deposit of your paycheck into your checking account to hopefully waive any bank fees and research other bank offerings if you are paying fees without having sufficient balances in each account.

Local banks and Credit Unions tend to have less fees and costs and higher yields than the larger national and regional banks. Multiple savings accounts are also unnecessary in most cases as well and should be consolidated whenever they can to be eligible for a higher yielding account and no fees. Bank employees often encourage customers to open multiple accounts since they get credit based on these new accounts, so don't get enticed into doing this with no benefit unless you need to keep them separate based on different account titling's for unique situations.

Set up overdraft protection by linking your checking, savings, and credit card accounts to avoid additional and higher fees. Use account alerts with online banking to notify you when you're checking, or savings account, balances drop below the levels you set. This will automatically transfer money from savings to checking accounts prior to your account balance going negative and incurring fees with a purchase or overdrawn check.

Several bounced checks will incur very high fees. If you use ATMs often, which you should not, make sure that you are using your own bank's ATMs, otherwise you are incurring additional fees by both banks involved in this transaction, which is a big waste of money. I know I repeated this, but it is very important to consider and account for.

Prompt: Review your bank statements over the past 3-6 months for your bank fees paid. Include ATM fees, statement fees, account level fees, overdraft fees, etc. Create a plan and visit the bank(s) to make the necessary changes to accounts and processes to eliminate them completely. These can add up monthly and be detrimental to your budget and savings plan.

Total average bank fees paid monthly $ _____

Studies show that the average person incurs $290 or nearly $300 annually in bank fees.

Once this emergency fund is established and you have accounts linked and the minimum balance to avoid fees, the next step would be to set up more advantageous savings and investment options that offer higher yields on your assets. There are a few high yielding online money market accounts available.

One option is a Marcus account offered by Goldman Sachs and another is Ally Bank high yield account. Research current offerings and best options regarding the amount of money you have to apply to a high yield money market account. These assets are liquid and should have no penalty for early withdrawal and should be FDIC insured. Note to leave a sufficient buffer in the checking and linked standard savings accounts monthly, and account for your credit card spending. Then, keep the remainder in this high yielding account. Often, you can link it to your primary banking institution's accounts for seamless asset transfer through an Electronic Funds Transfer (EFT).

Note that you should never leave substantial amounts in your checking account of more than what's necessary and reasonable. Your debit card and checks are tied to this account and you don't want fraudsters to have an access point to this account, even though banks should credit you back your lost assets with any theft.

It is much more difficult for con artists to access a savings or money market account where you should leave the bulk of the assets. I have witnessed times where someone has very little funds available to pay for their monthly expenses and their checking account gets hacked. Then, the bank freezes or closes it. It can then take a while for the bank to investigate and pay the customer back when they don't have that financial leeway to wait.

There are other higher yielding bank accounts offering fixed rate products like CD's that will not be covered here. Currently, we are in a very low interest rate environment and the benefit of locking or tying up these assets for long periods of time may not be worth the lack of access and not investing the money for the longer term. At some national banks, the yields can be lower than the higher yielding money market accounts noted and offered that are liquid, so be aware.

Credit and Borrowing:

Building credit and its benefits and consequences are far reaching throughout your adult life. The minute you start applying for credit through a credit card, car or student loan program, or mortgage you are building a credit score that is tracked by credit agencies. Your ability to pay bills and loans off on time and handle credit effectively will help dictate these scores.

In turn, your credit score will determine who will be willing to provide you a loan and at what rate and terms. This can save or cost you a lot of money over your lifetime and is a critical element in your financial planning and accountability. It is also why you should monitor your credit report and scores regularly, and use tracking apps and companies that offer these services.

My goal throughout my life was to never pay a bill late and never carry credit balances that were unnecessary. It was also to never pay fees for banking products or credit card balances and have the bank regularly pay me to use their credit card products (how sweet is that; more to come later). My wife and I have stuck to this mantra for decades and it has helped us toward our financial independence. You don't want to put yourself at the mercy of a loan company on their terms, you want to purchase something and pay for it on your terms. If you buy a $100 item, then it should cost you $100 all in. But if you buy a $100 item on your credit card and make minimum payments and not pay it off prior to your next billing cycle, it will cost you a much larger amount based on high card interest rates.

That is why it is critical to get your budgeting right from the beginning, because credit debt can and may snowball out of control. So many people end up in bankruptcy court because they don't have the budgeting in place, they can't control the credit borrowing element and the loose lending practices that allow us to fall into this trap.

Note: The number two cause of divorce in the US is due to financial difficulties between partners.

If you are just starting out and have a budget and you are fiscally responsible, you will want to open a secured credit card to begin to build your credit rating. Secured credit cards generally start at age 17 and only allow you to spend up to your cash limit that has been deposited into the account. The key here is to build good credit and continue to strengthen your credit score, which you can access for free online, using one of several free sites. Never pay for this service as your bank may offer it for free or research other free options at Creditscore.com.

As noted, this one aspect of your financial life dictates a tremendous amount of access and costs associated with any borrowing or financing that you will do over the course of your lifetime. A high credit score will afford you the opportunity to borrow money at much lower rates. The lower your score, the higher your costs and potential lack of access to borrowing and capital. It is imperative that you are careful with borrowing and using credit cards for only purchases that you can pay off monthly. If you can't afford to pay off the debt monthly and not incur interest payments and fees, then you should not make the purchase. My advice is to wait 3-5 days to purchase it. If after that timeframe you really feel as though you need it to better yourself and the purchase will not be a financial hindrance, then go buy it.

Prompt: What is the current balance on all your credit cards, if any? $ _____

How much interest have you paid over the past year in balance fees? $ _____

How much outstanding credit balances do you have between your credit cards, car, and student loans? _____. I have included a liabilities section in the total net worth analysis below for you to evaluate your total debt load including mortgages.

Think about the budgeting and spending plan you noted that you should institute today to account for any shortfall and recurring balances on the cards. Then, provide a timeline for paying these off completely.

Based on our yearly spending, my wife and I receive hundreds of dollars, and sometimes more, at the end of each year in point's rewards on our credit cards based on relationship credits. This can pay for a family vacation every year! **I like when the bank pays me instead of me paying the bank!**

Do you know what your credit score is currently? Find out what it is. _____

If you find that your score is not within a reasonable range of 670-840, depending on which reporting agency you used, then you should immediately reevaluate your budgeting, spending, and savings plans. Then, you should make the necessary adjustments and execute on the revised plan. Longer term, not doing anything to repair and increase your score will hinder your overall financial plan, success, and prosperity. Once you have the basics down, open an unsecured point's rewards card at your discretion to build credit, increase your score, and start earning points rewards.

Prompt: Add a phone or calendar reminder to check your credit score and sign-up for free credit monitoring regularly of your report for errors on Credit Karma or other free sites. This will also allow you to monitor who may be pulling your credit without your permission as potential fraud.

Other factors that will help or hinder your credit score include:

- Paying all bills and loans on time, every time with a plan and schedule.

- Having a few credit cards open and paying them off in full and on time.

- Always keep the credit lines open that you have had for the longest as closing them out will hinder your score.

- Checking your credit report yearly or more often to make sure that it is accurate with no errors and quickly correct errors if uncovered.

Student loans, grants, scholarships, and merit aid options will be detailed in the section on career development. SOFI.com will be referenced as an option to refinance loans to lower overall rates and fees.

Practical tip: If you do not have a Home Equity line of Credit or HELOC open on your home, then you should open one (as long as you don't have significant spending issues). This line of credit can act as an emergency fund to tap into the equity in your home, if there is equity. This is a good strategy in case you or your partner lose your job or have some budgeting or emergency issues where timely access to funds becomes important. If you are not employed, the banks will not approve you for this loan, so now may be a good time to research and pursue. You may also be able to consolidate higher rate loans into a lower rate HELOC to reduce your costs but be very careful with these credit lines. I will touch more on mortgages and home loans in the section on home financing.

Investment Detail, Beneficiary Designation, & Net Worth Statement

Prompt: Take some time to fill in your liquid net worth statement. This will include your liquid assets such as, banking, investments, and retirement assets and will not include any real estate holdings or other non-liquid assets. This is a good opportunity to review the average rate of return for each of the accounts which may be found on your monthly and/or yearend statements. You can also use the spreadsheet to determine any maturity dates, as well as who you have designated as the beneficiaries for each account titling, which will assist with your estate planning to be discussed later. The below total net worth statement will illustrate your total debt versus your total liquid assets. This analysis will provide a review (potentially on a yearly basis) for your overall net worth.

Net Worth Analysis: Investment Detail - Liquid Assets

Institution - Bank - Brokerage Co & Account #	Account Owner - Ind. or JT	Asset Value	APY/Avg rate %	Maturity Date & Beneficiaries; Notes
Bank cash assets: checking/savings/CD's				
Investment Brokerage - Non Retirement				
Retirement: 401/403/IRA's/Pension/HSA/ESOP				
529 - Annuities - Funds - Stock/Options - Bonds - Life Ins.				
Total liquid investment assets		$		

Total Net Worth Analysis

Assets & Liabilities	Owners (Individual - Joint)	Market Value	Cost Basis	Other - income cash flow
Total Investment Assets (from prior page)		$		
Real Estate Holdings				
Primary Residence				
Secondary Residence				
Rental Property				
Business Property				
Other:				
Other Assets				
Vehicle				
Vehicle				
Jewelry - Art - Collectibles				
Other - Business Inventory				
Other - Business - LP's				
Total Assets Calculation		$		

Debts - Liabilities with Start Date	Owners	Outstanding Debt Owed	Interest Rate % & Term	Refinance notes
Primary Mortgage				
Home Equity Line				
Primary Mortgage - second property				
Home Equity LOC				
Auto Loan				
Auto Loan				
Student Loan				
Other loan - credit card				
Other loan - credit card				
Total Liabilities Calculation		$		
Total Net Worth Calculation (Assets - liabilities)		$		

Investment planning

The most simplified and practical book on investing that I have come across that will apply to all of us and our situations is The Intelligent Asset Allocator by William Bernstein. He provides a great strategy and summary for how each of us should invest and the WHY behind the theory. He advocates, as does John Bogle, who we will discuss later, a low-cost strategy of investing in Index funds or Exchange Traded Funds or ETF's.

If you are going to invest yourself, and even if you use a professional financial advisor, this is a must-read book. Another must read book with a similar theme of low-cost indexing being the wisest strategy is *A Random Walk Down Wall Street* by Burton Malkiel.

What I am hoping to impart and communicate to you in this section are the key competencies that you should account for due to their importance of helping you become financially secure without the burden of taking on too much risk while noting other potential investment mistakes. These would include proper diversification and asset allocation of your portfolio, the benefits of dollar cost averaging, rebalancing, low cost investing, tax efficient strategies, retirement income planning, and a buckets of money strategy.

There is a tremendous amount of information related to this subject matter. The Structure and Building Blocks of Financial Wellbeing that has been included in this section, and many of the associated building block elements, are outside the scope of this guide. My vision is to provide enough information to assist with your basic financial priorities and provide introductory and ancillary information on the most important aspects of a successful investment strategy.

If you want to take investing to another level and are now in a higher net worth category where you have the time, knowledge and motivation to better understand markets, indexes, investor psychology, and individual security valuation, then a great read is *The Intelligent Investor* by Benjamin Graham. Benjamin Graham, better known as the father of value investing, was also (as noted) the mentor of Warren Buffett. He provides detailed analysis on company valuation methodologies, proper diversification, and risk versus returns. There is not a one size fits all investment strategy due to our individual time frame, risk tolerance, and liquidity needs among other considerations, but there are several prevailing strategies that everyone needs to understand and implement.

The buckets of money strategy illustrated below provides a visual understanding of a financial plan. It is a blueprint that segments assets and protection plans into buckets as a simplified approach. It also guides you to consider percentages of your assets to be split into different buckets based on certain criteria, and other buckets to focus on your protection planning strategies.

You can conceptually think about where your assets and planning should be pinpointed. It coincides with the previous strategies of creating an emergency fund as part of the first bucket; taking on some moderate risk for your medium term funds, and taking on greater risk for your longer term retirement assets in the other bucket.

Each of the buckets' yield or potential return is correlated with its risk return profile of its associated investments and strategies. The bottom line is that it allows you to not put all of your eggs in one bucket, but spread out the risk within three top buckets based on your timeline for needing the money, your risk tolerance, and age profile among other considerations. The bottom two buckets guide you to focus and prepare your protection planning strategies for life, health care, property and casualty, disability, and long-term care insurance options. They also provide a focal point on potential guaranteed income streams at retirement within the last bucket.

This is a strategy that I used to train my financial advisory teams to utilize with their clients. I have adapted and updated the approach that I have utilized over the years with my clients. I have found this to be helpful as many of us are visual learners, and the conversation and strategy should be easy to understand as a simplified approach.

Buckets of Money Strategy

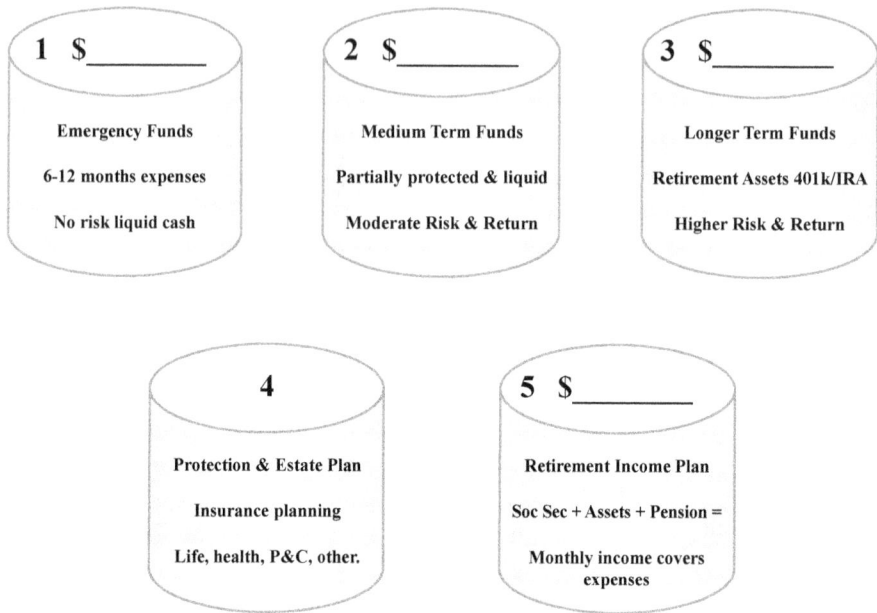

A more detailed review identifies the upper left number 1 bucket as containing a six to twelve-month liquid emergency fund that we discussed. These assets should be allocated within your checking, linked savings account, and then a higher yielding money market account discussed. These are no risk FDIC insured liquid funds and may incorporate other larger amounts of assets than the 6-12 months emergency funds that you may soon need to access.

For instance, you may have additional liquidity needs within the next 1-2 years due to upcoming college, wedding, new home, or other major expenses. The strategy here is to have a liquid emergency fund and other shorter-term assets that are not at risk, and to keep pace with inflation and not lose purchasing power over this period of time with these funds.

The second or number 2 bucket is medium risk and has a mid-term time frame of approximately 2 to 5 years. This bucket may contain assets that can take on some risk, be potentially protected, and should provide a higher rate of return than the first bucket. Some potential strategies and products that may be used include longer term or market linked CD's, lower risk bonds and bond funds, preferred stock, fixed and indexed annuities and market-based indexing strategies with a lower risk profile based on your individual needs. This bucket will be the one that varies the most for each of us depending on our age, risk tolerance, and profile. It may be more conservative for those that can't stomach the risk or more aggressive for those that can and are looking for higher growth potential. The strategy here is to outpace inflation (having a real return of 1-3% above the inflation rate) and not take on too much risk in doing so with a medium term time horizon.

The third bucket is your longer term (over 5 years) retirement funds that may take on a higher risk profile if you have the risk appetite for it. It will include your company's retirement accounts, individual IRAs, and other tax deferred vehicles to allow your assets to grow pre-tax at a faster rate. We will review some options in more detail within the retirement section. It may also incorporate mutual funds, ETFs, stocks, variable annuities, higher risk bonds, and other higher risk strategies that are outside the scope of this guide. The overall strategy here is to take on more risk that you can accept due to your longer time horizon that may level out or reduce the volatility in the return over time. It is also to outpace inflation with higher returns while minimizing one's overall risk.

As we fill up these three buckets through a comprehensive budgeting, savings, and investment strategy, we will need to periodically rebalance them. The cash bucket should be maintained for your 6-12 month needs in addition to any other upcoming larger cash needs.

As excess funds become available, they should be distributed into the other two buckets to capture higher rates of return using a dollar cost averaging strategy to be discussed. Some of these assets can also be repositioned into lower risk profile assets like structured products, tax liens, bonds, and higher rate CDs. If you have a higher risk profile and a longer time horizon then you may want to fund the last bucket with a higher percentage.

As noted, the lower two bucket strategies are for protection planning and retirement income strategies that are addressed later in this section.

Prompt: Write down all your assets on your net worth statement. Compare the asset mix of the accounts with the top three buckets in the figure. Do you have the right mix according to your time horizon, age, needs, goals, and risk tolerance? Are you overly aggressive with no emergency or liquid funds? Or maybe you have everything in a checking and savings account earning far less than 1% and not keeping pace with inflation. Separate the assets according to your comfort zone in the buckets. Make the necessary changes to each account if you find investments are not aligned with above and your "comfort zone."

Total Liquid Net worth? $ _____ excludes real estate and businesses

Emergency liquid money market funds bucket #1 $ _____

Medium term moderate risk funds bucket #2 $ _____

Longer term retirement funds (higher risk) bucket #3 $ _____

There is an old saying in investing that "diversification and asset allocation are your only free lunch." Don't put all your eggs in one basket. By having a diversified and proper asset allocated strategy, you can avoid some big mistakes and reduce your overall risk profile. By spreading around your investments in cash, stocks, and bonds and their subcategories, it will help you reduce the effects of various market swings and corrections. These are two foundational principles on sound market investing that should always be adhered to WITH NO EXCEPTIONS.

By purchasing broad market indexes with low cost ETFs, you are easily able to broadly diversify, and asset allocate, all of your market-based funds.

This is also the low-cost indexing strategy of John Bogle. These are passive funds where individual securities are not picked by portfolio managers as active managers and funds do. They purchase all the securities in the market or a sub-set or asset allocated portion of the overall market. Vanguard's Total Stock Market Fund is an example of this type of investment where, with one vehicle or fund, you can own the entire stock market.

Another example is the S&P 500 Index ETF. This eliminates the risk of having a lack of diversification, asset allocation, and avoids you managing your own mutual fund with too many positions. The appropriate asset allocation is an evolving target that is based on your needs, plans, age, risk tolerance, and time horizon. It will need updating as your situation changes.

Over time, your portfolio's asset allocation will "drift" as market fluctuations effect the asset allocations of the investments. Rebalancing is the process of bringing your investments back to their target allocation that was set up initially to counteract this drift.

At times, bonds outperform stocks and vice versa depending upon market changes and volatility. Rebalancing is periodically selling some of the outperforming investments and buying some of the underperforming ones. So, when do we rebalance? A common rule of thumb is to consider rebalancing either once or twice a year, or quarterly, which I recommend for clients. Some accounts, as well as these indexes, should have automatic rebalancing features, but do your due diligence and make sure that you are periodically rebalancing these accounts. Please refer to the yearly calendar in the workbook for direction in adding this rebalancing plan into your yearly routine.

Prompt: Take some time now to review all your asset mixes in the three buckets. This will afford you the opportunity to determine if you are over or under allocated within certain asset classes and your overall diversification.

Asset allocation breakdown of liquid assets and investments:

Cash, MM, CDs and fixed annuities $_____ _____ % total

Total Bond Funds: $_____ _____ % total

Total Stock Funds: $_____ _____ % total - includes individual stocks

Prompt: Do you feel this mix is appropriate? _____

Review Asset allocation of each:

Large cap stock $_____ _____ %

Mid cap stock $_____ _____ %

Small cap stock $_____ _____ %

International stock $_____ _____ %

Emerging Market stock $_____ _____ %

Real Estate Investment Trusts (REITs) $_____ _____ %

Commodities $_____ _____ %

US Treasury bonds $_____ _____ %

Municipals bonds $_____ _____ %

Corporate grade bonds $_____ _____ %

Other: High yield, Junk, Emerging market bond aggregate

$_____ _____ %

Individual Stock $_____ _____ %

Prompt: Is the asset allocation mix you input above appropriate? _____

What changes may be/are needed to this asset allocation and why? _____

_____

_____

_____

List stocks owned_____

_____

_____

_____

List individual stocks (if the number exceeds 15, then you are managing your own mutual fund and should rethink the excess positions above 12-15 as being too many). If you are a seasoned investor and primarily an individual stock owner, a portfolio of 10-12 positions each with an 8-10% allocation is recommended, unless you also own in addition, index funds like the S&P 500 or a total market index; Dow Jones Index; Nasdaq Index or International index. These can be of a much higher percentage due to their diversification. Note that no individual positions should be more than 5-10% of your overall investment or liquid funds. Are any industries positions too overweight where the portfolio is not diversified enough?

Another strategy used by successful investors is dollar-cost averaging. This is investing a fixed amount of assets at regular intervals. By doing so, you will buy more shares when the prices are low and fewer shares when prices are higher. This is a continuous disciplined approach to investing new capital into your portfolios. This goes hand-in-hand with the notion of not timing the market as a losing strategy. A proper investment strategy is not about timing the market, but time spent in the market that counts.

Much has been written about the benefits, or lack thereof, between active versus passive investment management strategies. I would include anyone day trading in the active management category. Many online articles tout how this person made a fortune trading stock and online high frequency trading platforms will promote this strategy for their own benefit.

The reality is this—For all my friends and acquaintances and I who have worked on Wall Street and for the large Brokers, **trading has been and continues to be a losing strategy.** For every person who suggests that they have outperformed the S&P 500 Index, there are at least 9 or more who did not. I also question the validity of the returns for that one individual. Investing is not gambling, and day trading becomes a form of gambling. The real proof lies in the Standard & Poor's published yearly SPIVA report (S&P Indices Versus Active).

Every year returns are published by the S&P providing the ratio of active managers that beat the S&P 1500/500 and other associated indexes. Large Cap active management funds have been beaten at a 64%-70% rate over the past 10 years by the index. Some Mid Cap and Small Cap ratios show better active management returns.

However, those who may outperform the index one year are most likely, or generally, not beating the index the next. One of the many reasons that active managers have a disadvantage is the fee that they charge (on average around 1% +/- .25%) versus the very low fee structure of passive management.

Do yourself a favor, buy a super bowl box or a bracket or two for March Madness or a scratch off ticket if you need to, but don't gamble in the market with your investments and retirement. This is at best a losing proposition and at worst can be devastating. Use low cost passive indexing as a primary strategy. If professionals with large knowledgeable teams generally can't consistently beat their associated index, then you should not believe that you can either. This advice is coming from a professional.

The fees noted above that are a part of the investment industry are at times very elusive to determine by the average investor. These fees can be charged on a quarterly basis if your portfolio is being managed, they can be imposed when you purchase the investment upfront and/or may be charged periodically by funds and may be a combination of these fees.

Brokers will charge you for the management of the account (if they are managing it, anywhere from .4% for an online robo advisor to 1.5% or higher for a full-service advisor per year, charged on a quarterly basis). In addition to this, you are charged a fee for the actual mutual fund or ETF investment known as an internal net expense ratio or 12b-1 fee.

Some brokers may offer you "clean or institutional shares" where these fees are much lower in comparison to other fees. These 12b-1 fees range from .25% to 1.5% or higher based on if it's a bond or stock fund and US or international fund, the latter of which are generally higher. These fees come out of your investments pre-returns and are provided in their prospectus's for your review and analysis. The total fee you are paying most of the time is a combination of these fees, if it is managed by the broker.

Mutual Funds, which also have the 12b-1 fees, have sales commissions in addition, which can be either up front when purchased or back end when they are sold. There are "no load" funds, which are the ones you should be utilizing. Exchange Traded Funds (ETFs) if purchased by you in a trading account, also have internal expense ratios or 12-b 1's similar to the mutual funds. Look for lower cost 12b-1 fees of .1% to .4% to reduce your overall fees by utilizing the approach of Bogle and Bernstein. You can review these fees for each associated mutual fund or ETF at Morningstar.com or the required prospectus and/or plan notices.

Individual stocks do not have any fees or 12b-1's other than a potential cost to buy and/or to sell them as a flat fee charged by the brokers. Fixed and fixed indexed annuities don't have front end fees generally, but there are early liquidation charges that can be levied on withdrawals. Variable annuities are high in fees and can range from 1.5% to over 4%. Advisors are paid higher commissions for selling these, so buyer beware.

Prompt: Look at the statements and (Morningstar.com) for the fees you are paying for your investment accounts. If you have a managed account, then add the quarterly/yearly management fee with the internal expenses to find your total cost. Determine if they are warranted or not and if they/you are using lower cost index funds. Review ways to reduce them.

What average fee are you paying for your investments? _____ %

Some securities pay a quarterly dividend. The yield is the relationship between the amount it pays the stockholder for the year and the stock price. It fluctuates but most high-quality companies, which have been listed for a long time, pay a dividend of between 1% and 5% per year.

There are many tech and newer issue companies that don't pay a dividend. There are many companies that pay higher dividends, which are the ones you should be careful of investing in as these companies can cut their dividend, which would adversely affect the stock price. There is an old adage to never chase yield, meaning be cautious of these high yielding companies or bonds as they may be riskier.

Most mutual funds also pay dividends and interest on quarterly intervals similar to some stocks, ETFs, and bonds also found on Morningstar. Most bonds and bond funds pay yields (unless they are zero coupon) at different intervals. They are known as fixed income instruments because they pay a fixed amount as income. Bonds also have a period of time known as their term for how long they are in circulation or in the market. Additional detail on these investments and their fees are outside the scope of this guide.

What average dividend yield are you receiving from your funds & stocks?_____%

Some other important investment considerations, if you are investing in individual stocks, include the following:

- **The man who begins to speculate in stocks with the intention of making a fortune usually goes broke, whereas the man who trades with a view of getting good interest on his money sometimes gets rich.** Charles Dow
  Be mindful of this one as all studies convey that a high percentage of day traders will lose money over a longer period of time.

- Diversification is not owning 10 stocks (they may all be in similar asset allocation and/or industry).

- Tips are for waiters so don't buy based on them! Been there and wished I hadn't.

- When you are first investing outside of your retirement plan and have less than $20,000 (in addition to your emergency fund assets); buy low cost index funds or ETFs that diversify out your portfolio. Some examples were provided above.

- Never buy more than a 5%-10% position in any one stock position. This is in line with diversifying and having proper asset allocation. Learn from my mistakes!

- Never buy on margin unless you are a professional.

- Invest in companies that you understand and potentially are a customer of.

- Buy only the highest quality and dominant companies in their sector.

- Don't sell your winners and keep your losers in the hopes of getting back to even.

- Don't keep dollar cost averaging lower as a stock trends lower or tanks. Cut your losses. Learn from my mistakes!

- Find the highest quality dividend paying stocks to add to your potential investments.

- The long-term return of equities or stock puts all other financial asset returns to rest. This comes with a price that is volatility.

- Don't buy stocks under $15. Learn from my mistakes!

- Cut your losses at 8% and sell the position.

- Never buy all at once, scale into a position and scale out of a position.

- Don't own more than 12-15 individual stock positions as it's too many to research and keep track of.

- Make sure that you don't have any individual stock or bond certificates in paper or non-book entry form as they can get lost. They should always be registered in an account with a holding company or Broker Dealer account.

Some final thoughts on the stock market and trading in general:

Frequent trading will lose you money as a poor strategy. It will also increase anxiety, stress, and generally reduce your overall emotional and mental wellbeing.

The talking heads in the media create headlines and stories for the action in the market.

The longer-term trends in the markets are up due to our retirement contributions.

The fourth quarter and November through April are historically good months and time periods in the stock market.

Follow the above strategies on the bucket approach, emergency cash position, low cost indexing, diversification, dollar cost averaging, and rebalancing.

Prompt: Review the list above and make note of any strategies that you are not following and/or breaking. Seriously consider making the necessary changes for successful investing. _____

_____
_____
_____

A note on ESG investing: There has been a recent surge in interest in directing and applying investments to socially responsible "Green" investing in Environmentally, Socially responsible and proper corporate Governance of companies (ESG). There are numerous platforms, ETFs, and mutual funds to assist with these options, one of which includes the Newday app. Other online investing sites like Wealthfront, Betterment, Wealthsimple, Robinhood and Acorn offer savings plans, low cost investing options, and valuable content. This is in addition to potentially utilizing licensed professionals.

Retirement Planning

In the introduction and earlier in the section, I noted one of the main paradigms that we all should be aware of and account for as retirement income transitions from a three-legged stool to a two-legged one. In the past, many retirees were able to rely on a company or government pension, social security payments, and savings to account for their retirement income.

However, recently many of these pensions have been either frozen or no longer offered. This trend has transitioned the burden of investing for retirement from the institutions to the employees. Retirement income now more than ever will come from a combination of social security and our savings and investments in Defined Contribution DC plans like IRAs, 401Ks, 403B plans, and the like. That puts more of the onus of saving and investing for this goal squarely on us. This is another important factor as to why we all need to learn and understand how to be more effective investors to account for our retirement income planning.

Retirement planning is a part of the financial planning process. It is generally the longer-term portion of your portfolio and it is extremely important to contribute from the time you start working. Your ability to save and invest from your earnings and utilize corporate matching funds within these plans is very important. Investing these assets appropriately will also be critical in determining the outcome of your success. I have clients that have saved, invested, and accumulated substantial amounts within these company retirement plans by way of dollar cost averaging, rebalancing, and proper asset allocation over long periods of time. The benefit of having a longer timeframe within your retirement accounts affords you the potential ability to be more aggressive with your investment options even with the higher risks. Where many of your non-retirement accounts have assets earmarked for shorter-term needs, like a home purchase or renovation and/or college funding, retirement funds generally are longer-term.

Some, or all, of the prior considerations noted within the investment planning section are also relevant here, including the importance of diversification, proper asset allocation, rebalancing, reducing costs, and dollar cost averaging. The key elements to consider as an employee are to have a good understanding of the company plan and its associated investment options, potential matching funds it offers and their terms, other types of accounts that may be offered like stock options, stock purchase, and restricted stock option plans and savings plans.

The focus of this guide will only be on defined contribution plans like 401k, 403B, and IRAs since these encompass the larger portion of plans that most of us have or are offered to us. They all offer the ability to invest earnings pre-tax, grow tax-deferred, and then are taxed when assets are withdrawn. This tax deferred growth is a substantial benefit that is offered within these plans that we all should be taking advantage of.

Prompt: Review your retirement plan investments, your contribution rate, company match, if any, and the fees associated with each investment. Is it diversified, low cost and aligned with your time horizon, risk tolerance, and objectives? You can and should make a note of your online ID and passwords in the Workbook at the end of the guide.

Contribution percentage _____ %

Company matching funds _____ %

Average fees for investments _____ %

Changes that you may want to make _____

_____

_____

My recommendation is to speak with a plan sponsor financial advisor for a complimentary review and receive a financial check-up. You should continue this review activity at least yearly and add a reminder to your calendar and/or phone.

Always make sure that you are contributing what is needed to receive the company match. Otherwise, you are leaving free money on the table. Also, note that these matching funds often have a period of time that you need to stay with the company in order for them to vest and be retained by you.

Review any company vesting schedules for each plan. Also, think about increasing your contribution rate if you have sufficient cash flow, an emergency fund, and other assets as a back-up plan outside of this corporate DC plan based on the buckets noted.

Look to contribute approximately 8% to 15% of your pretax income if you have the necessary liquid funds in place already. I would also recommend using low cost index funds for the investment options, if they are available options. Usually, corporate plans have lower 12b-1 and management fees associated with them in comparison to other broker dealer investment accounts. Companies are consistently reviewing and implementing ways to reduce these fees for employees as a benefit.

If you don't work for a company that offers these types of plans or any retirement plan, then it is incumbent upon you to set up your own IRA or (if you qualify after review with your tax advisor) a SEP IRA. Each has its own contribution limits and offers a much wider range of investment options including individual securities.

The first step is to open the appropriate account and encourage yourself to start saving on a quarterly basis for these contributions. It is a good idea to add this to your calendar and phone reminders. I would also recommend investing in similar low cost funds and ETFs that track indexes and stay away, at least initially, from individual stocks (until you have the time to devote to researching and following them and doing your due diligence).

This is the type of account where you should set and review it, and only occasionally revise investment options when necessary. Trading within these accounts is a losing proposition, take it from someone who once fell victim to this inferior strategy. Focus on the strategy of making quarterly contributions to account for 8%-15% of your pre-tax income, diversifying, and properly asset allocating investments that you are comfortable with, using low cost indexing options, automatically rebalancing and reviewing the plan at least semi-annually or yearly.

There are online sites that offer a free analysis in the form of a retirement plan. These programs will show you if you are on target or off target to reaching your retirement goals. They will offer what's known as a Monte Carlo simulation of your individual situation and illustrate via graphs if you are on target.

Most, if not all, of the company plans offer this analysis on their own or on their plan administrator's websites. Although Roth IRAs are a great compliment to other retirement assets, they are beyond the scope of this basic financial planning review. Please consult your tax advisor and financial professional for more information on their benefits and requirements.

One thing to consider is to be very careful about taking loans out from your 401k or retirement plan. Often, employees fall trap to the easy access of money if it is an option, thinking that they will pay it back quickly. Some issues that arise are that one loses the growth of the loan assets during the timeframe that it is being paid back and their associated compounding effects. If an employee is displaced for any reason, the terms of the loan may change and/or it may become more difficult to continue to pay off the loan due to other cash flow needs.

Prompt: Set aside time to visit one of these sites and review your retirement plan to see if you are on target or how far off target you are. This can act as a wakeup call to reconsider your contributions and appropriate changes that may be needed in addition to your overall cash flow management. Spend the time now to Invest in Yourself!

Tax Liens and Tax Deeds

One of the least risky investments with a higher return profile are tax lien and tax deed sales. Every state and county sells either one or the other or both when a property owner does not pay his/her property taxes and certain utility bills. They are sold to investors to pay the related fees owed to the municipalities or cities.

Tax liens and tax deeds have different procedures, processes, risks, and potential returns. A high-level overview of both is that as an investor, you are paying these costs (taxes and fees) on behalf of the owner for delinquent non-payment. If and when the owner pays off the lien or sells the property, you are first in position to get paid similar to the government getting paid.

Therefore, regarding tax liens, you almost always (unless the property becomes worthless due to environmental or other issues like fire, flood, etc.) will be paid back your investment premium and interest or take ownership of the property. In some cases with tax deed sales, if the owner does not pay within a certain period of time, you may be able to take over the property as the owner.

There are many instances where a tax lien certificate and/or tax deed investor has taken over a property for far less than the actual value of the property or its current market value. There are groups of investors that purchase large blocks of these investments. Tax liens sell tax certificates and are sold by bidding down the rate of return in an auction process. Some of these begin at 18% in certain states. Tax deeds are sold to the highest bidder.

As an appraiser, I know of investors that have received high rates of return on these assets with a much lower-risk profile than investing in stocks, bonds, or mutual funds.

Note that many of these investments are illiquid for an extended period of time until you get your premium and interest payment back. They may also require additional capital investments regarding tax deed sales as well, so do your due diligence. My recommendation is to always personally inspect the property and the surrounding neighborhood prior to buying any of these. It is a good idea to speak to the owner and/or the neighbors to get a better understanding of the value of this investment.

A footnote on other investments like real estate and market based derivatives. Most of these are outside the scope of this guide. There are companies that sell non-listed Real Estate Investment Trusts (REITs) that offer brokers high commissions. An investor can accomplish owning publically traded REITs with similar dividend structures that are liquid and preferable. I would be careful prior to purchasing any non-listed REITs with better alternatives available that offer liquidity.

I have several friends and clients that invest in flipping single and multi-family properties and knockdowns who have made a successful career out of these strategies. I have also had clients and colleagues who have ventured into this arena and gotten burned and even went bankrupt. I had former clients who opened self-directed IRAs and used their IRA assets to invest this way; one of whom was successful and another who lost a lot on the venture.

Timing and risk are important considerations and doing your due diligence and understanding all of the critical elements of these strategies are paramount. My personal analysis of low cost indexed investments in the stock market over the past 20 and 30 years noted that these investments have outperformed investments in singe family real estate. Once we account for the value of our time spent, vacancy rates, and operating costs, as well as taxation concerns, and review true capitalization rates, the evidence to me seems overwhelming. That said, many of these individuals noted above may disagree.

Insurance Planning

Life insurance protection is the backbone and foundation of a good financial plan and potentially critical to your family's future wellbeing. It provides peace of mind knowing that if there was a premature loss that the financial wellbeing of the family, or anyone who is dependent upon your life, will not potentially further suffer financially.

It is hard enough to go through a difficult situation, it is that much harder to do so in a financial hardship. One must consider several factors when determining the amount, type, and term for these insurance contracts. When we think about the amount of the death benefit, we should consider two things. The ability to pay off a mortgage on the house with potential car loans and college funding also hanging in balance. This is in addition to needing to potentially replace the income of the one who passed away. This income replacement is critical to the overall planning for the term and the total death benefit amount.

There are two ways you can retain a life insurance contract. The first is through an employer group life insurance plan, if this benefit is offered, and second through a private life insurance contract. The cheaper and easier way to obtain life insurance is through your employer group plan if it is an option. There are no applications, waiting periods (generally) or approvals needed, only to go online and make your election on what is offered.

Since it is your cheapest option, I recommend electing a higher amount of benefit. Please note that this policy is only good while you work for the company and may or may not be convertible to another policy if you are displaced and no longer working there. Also note that you can only be approved for life insurance when you are healthy and insurable, not if certain conditions arise. Because of this, it is good to have a private transportable policy at all times and complete this process now when you are hopefully healthy. Life insurance proceeds go to the beneficiary's income tax free at passing. They may be subject to other estate and beneficiary taxes.

There are two types of life insurance: term policies and permanent policies known as cash value policies. Term policies are equivalent to renting as you own the policy for a certain number of years and after it expires (if there is no conversion option) you no longer have this life insurance death benefit. The term or period of coverage is very important. This is a much cheaper option than permanent life insurance where you pay premiums and have either a guaranteed death benefit or a non-guaranteed death benefit. Permanent policies are much more complicated contracts with their own associated investment options within the contract. Permanent policies also come with long surrender periods (some of which can go for 15 years) where if you liquidate prior, there are fees associated with this withdrawal. Permanent policies, depending on the investment options and their fee structure, will eventually build up a cash value portion within the policy.

However, these cash positions can only be borrowed against while you are living and may need to be paid back and can cause other issues with the policy down the road in terms of proper funding for the associated death benefit. There are so many considerations when it comes to these options that are outside the scope of this guide.

My advice is to keep your cost low by increasing or maxing out your company plan option. Look to get a term policy in force for a minimum period of time where your children are under your care and dependent upon your income. The death benefits should in aggregate be able to potentially pay off the home mortgage, car loans, and provide enough in return to replace your income over a certain period of time.

I would recommend discussing these options with a financial professional to help create a detailed plan. There are some situations where a permanent policy can be a good supplement for these other basic protection strategies. However, it should not be the primary focus for younger families starting out as term and group life policies are the more affordable options. Permanent policies will always have higher costs associated, as well as the complicated investment crediting features and surrender periods.

As a footnote, if you are looking to purchase a permanent policy, I would recommend an indexing investment strategy similar to the ones I previously described rather than a variable investment strategy. This is due to the indexing strategy being a lower cost option and the potential downside risk associated with variable policies to name just a few of the many concerns and differences.

Prompt: Document your life insurance and other insurance coverages in the analysis below with your liquid assets. Compare this total to your outstanding loan balances. Add in the income that will need to be replaced over a 20-year period depending on your age and family needs. There is no magic formula, but if for instance you make $100,000 and have a $1,000,000 death benefit only to replace income (not including loan balances); if we were able to get a 5% return or $50,000 per year (there is no guarantee of this, just an estimate) and added to that yearly a portion of the principal, then we may be close to the replacement value over a 12-15 year period of the original $100,000 income.

Once you review your total "in force" death benefit, then take appropriate actions in applying for an additional contract, if underinsured. Both spouses and partners should consider their own needs and responsibilities and dependents separately when necessary. Especially when both are working and contributing to a family budget and cash flow plan.

Life Insurance Analysis

Owner/Insured & Type (Term or Permanent)	Death Benefit	Cash Value	Annual Premium - Term	Beneficiary
Total Death Benefit & Cash Value Calculation	$	$		
Total Liquid Investment & Retirement Assets	$			
Total liquid Assets	$			
Total Debt: Loans + Mortgage + College	$			
Total Income Replacement	$			
Asset Shortfall or Surplus	$			
Long Term Care & Disability Analysis				
Owner/Insured & Type	Yearly maximum benefit	Monthly maximum benefit	Annual Premium	Notes - Benefit & Elimination periods

Transform Your Future & Wellbeing

Your health insurance plan will depend on if you have access through a company or the Government Exchange after you move off of a parent's policy by age 26. Vision and dental plans will also be part of corporate or private plan options.

Disability insurance coverage may be an option in corporate plans. Long-term care insurance options should be a consideration if it is a concern, and there is evidence of a prior condition in your family medical history.

When searching for insurance, companies like USAA or Manufacturers Insurance are quality options that have helped friends and family. You may have an insurance broker that assists with lining up pricing for multiple insurance lines of coverage.

Senior Financial Considerations

Seniors should sign up for Medicare 6 months prior to your 65th birthday or at most within three months of turning 65, if you are no longer employed. Otherwise, after 90 days from your birthday, you are penalized progressively per month when you don't sign up unless you are still employed and have insurance through your employer!

When you sign up for Medicare, you are making a very important insurance decision and one that may be permanent. We have a choice between Medicare with a Medicare Supplement Plan or Medicare Advantage, the privately offered managed-care alternative. By choosing Advantage, it may become effectively irreversible later in retirement. The reason being, is that the best time to buy a Medicare Supplemental Plan or Medigap supplemental plan is during the six-month period after signing up for Part B and any future medical or pre-existing conditions may negate a later purchase of this plan.

During this six-month enrollment period, Medigap plans cannot reject applicants or charge higher premiums for preexisting conditions. After this period, you can be rejected or charged more (unless you reside in a state that has guaranteed issue rights). It is very important to have supplemental coverage due to the high out of pocket costs. Advantage plans may also restrict one's choices and ability to choose a physician or medical facility that is out of their network.

Although Advantage plans have attractive lower premiums and add on prescription drug coverage and other perks, it is wise to research options as Advantage plan's denial of care and claims could, and have become, potential issues and concerns for many. A better alternative option for most of us would be traditional Medicare and Medigap with a standalone Part D drug plan. These plans are offered through AARP or AAA and other organizations. They may provide discounts for your health insurance. Due your due diligence on www.Medicare.gov

Make sure that you take your Required Minimum Distributions (RMD) the year you turn 72. Otherwise, you may lose 50% of the RMD to an IRS penalty if you don't take it. Review with your tax advisor!

Don't leave your social security card in your wallet or purse in case it gets stolen. Only take it with you the day you need it for proof.

Seniors and retirees whose income is under $69,000 a year (2019) should explore IRS Free File for free online tax preparation. Go to IRS.gov/FreeFile to see all free filing options. Free file providers also offer state tax return preparation, some for free, and some for a fee. Seniors who are not comfortable preparing their own tax return have other free options. The IRS helps support the Volunteer Income Tax Assistance Program and AARP supports the Tax Counseling for the Elderly Program. Volunteers will prepare your tax return for you for free. Use the VITA locator tool to find a VITA/TCE location near you. My daughter has volunteered to assist with this tax preparation initiative as a generous networking and growth opportunity to be reviewed later.

New Jersey seniors may qualify for a Senior Tax Freeze based on annual income limits. This will prevent yearly increases that you would pay on property taxes once they are frozen. Applications can be requested from your township or city clerk's office. Other states may offer similar programs.

Estate Planning

No matter who you are and where you are in this life, everyone over the age of 18 or 21 (age of majority) needs these three documents:

- A valid will
- A valid durable power of attorney
- An Advanced Health Care Directive or Living Will

Studies show that 30% of American's don't have a valid will, which can cause some significant challenges and problems for your family in the event of premature death.

A will states who will inherit your assets and who may become the guardian of your minor children upon your death. Where your assets end up may be determined by the will or by the titling on the accounts of these assets. It can preempt disputes among your heirs. A will can also stipulate who will become the legal guardian(s) of your minor children if you and your spouse/partner both pass at the same time or in close proximity to one another.

This is a very important determination for parents of children whose relatives may, and probably, have differing opinions from one another on how they should be raised. In the case of my wife and I, when my children were minors, we named one family member in our wills the financial administrator for our children and another relative the caretaker guardian. This is provided for example purposes and not advice.

The way assets are disbursed when you pass away is first dependent on the titling of each asset and its account, potentially not the will. The will disburses assets only when there is not a surviving individual on the titling of the asset (deed, title, account). If an account is titled jointly, then depending on that titling, the survivor will get some or all of the account balance and will not pass through the Probate County Court system by way of your will.

Depending on how deeds, titles, and accounts are titled, they will ultimately be distributed by this legal disbursement. Not having a will or being intestate, as it's known, can be very costly and time consuming. I have spent a good deal of time consulting with and assisting people to account for their estate planning needs.

Earlier in the section and in the Workbook in the back of the guide, I have provided a net worth analysis that includes how each account is titled and who the beneficiaries are for each. This includes if it is held individually or jointly as to who will be the beneficiary on each account. This will provide you a better understanding of who will inherit these assets upon your death. Selecting beneficiaries for your accounts is an important step in the estate planning process.

Major life events including marriage, divorce, birth, or loss of a loved one can create a need to change these beneficiary designations. It is highly recommended that you take the time, at least yearly, to review these beneficiary designations on each account and make appropriate adjustments as needed.

When I worked for an estate planning company, I often came into contact with people who had stressful and unfortunate estate situations within their family. I could write another book on just these stories and their outcomes. Just one example of how this distribution can go terribly wrong by not reviewing beneficiary designations is: let's say you intend to leave your assets 50%/50% to your two children and you own a house with one child as Joint Tenancy with the Right of Survivorship and you have a bank account jointly held with that same child. The other two accounts you have at the bank or institution have no specific beneficiary titling on them. The potential distribution will not be 50% and 50% as the property will be owned

100% by your surviving child who is jointly on the deed, as well as the joint bank account. The remaining two accounts not held jointly, as well as other assets and personal property, may then be distributed through your will and the Surrogate Probate Court according to you wishes. Generally, the one child has no obligation to split all the assets 50% and 50%, even though your intention was that way.

My informal study of clients noted that many don't know where their will is and have not told their executor where it is located. You should keep a copy in the file within an estate planning folder noted in the Workbook and not only in a safety deposit box, where it may not be accessible. I have also included a detailed section in the Workbook on many other considerations to think about and needed related to your estate plan, important documents, burial and funeral service information for your family, and executors to utilize to simplify the process.

Durable Power of Attorney

The will only takes effect upon your death and does nothing while you're living. The POA, as it's known above, is a legal document that you use to name a guardian while you are living to take care of your financial affairs in the event that you become incapacitated and can't exercise them yourself. Even if you are legally married, most states and institutions will need proof of the POA prior to you handling certain affairs. That is why it is critical that you have this valid document in place prior to any issues. This provides the conservator the ability to: pay your rent or mortgage and bills, access your bank, investment and/or retirement accounts, if necessary, as well as other critical timely functions that you would normally handle if you include these options within this document.

It is durable in the sense that it is revocable, and you can change it at any time while you have your faculties in case you need to and only comes into play if and when you become incapacitated. Most banks, brokerage firms, and insurance companies have their own Power of Attorney documents that will also need to be filed in conjunction with your Durable Power of Attorney (DPOA). However, the beginning point of the process is to have your own valid DPOA to start.

Advanced Health Care Directive or Living Will

This important legal document is intended for your medical wishes to be adhered to in the event that your health care professionals need to make critical medical decisions on your behalf. It is also known as a DNR, or do not resuscitate document. Oftentimes, it can be provided and signed in the hospital, but don't assume that is the case and make sure to account for this now while you can.

Other estate planning documents may also be needed like certain trusts and codicils, etc. These are outside of the scope of this guide.

Prompt: Today, do the following and put into force the above three documents if you have not done so already. If you have them, then it's a good time to review them for accuracy and any necessary changes. If you need to produce them or make changes, you can do this in one of several ways:

1. Find an Estate Planning Attorney in your area and consult them on fees and next steps to complete.

2. Go you your library or online and locate the book, Quicken Willmaker. This has templates for all three documents where you can input the proper information and then print them out for free.

3. Go online to sites like Legalzoom and research associated fees and next steps.

Please note that some of these documents, in addition to being signed, need to be witnessed and notarized to be valid. Your city, township, or county clerk's office is a good starting point for this step.

Prompt: Take some time now to input and review all your assets by account level and determine who the beneficiaries are for each. See the net worth spreadsheet as a guide. Make the appropriate changes through the bank, brokerage, or institution holding these assets. Don't forget to review deeds, titles, and retirement account beneficiaries.

Home Ownership

Owning a piece of the "American Dream" is another key element of successful financial wellness. Although, it is not so much a part of traditional financial planning since advisors are not generally focused on this part of one's financial life other than a cursory discussion on goals. The ability to purchase a property and pay off a mortgage through amortization is similar to having a forced savings plan in place. Each month that we make that payment we are paying off the interest and some of the principle of the loan, which is the savings portion.

As property values generally increase over time, our equity position in the property or the difference between what the property is worth or its market value and how much we owe on the mortgage gets larger. The ability to leverage this investment also plays a key role as an investment vehicle. When you add this equity to your Total Net Worth Statement, it enhances your bottom line.

My vision here is to impart to you some of the important considerations you should think about when you are ready to purchase a property as a primary residence to live in. However, there are many costs and factors related to this purchase that should be considered prior to taking the leap. One of the most important criteria is the timeframe associated with staying in the property. Many studies show that the breakeven of costs associated with a home purchase is near 3.5 years. This means that it will take around this amount of time to recoup all the costs associated with the purchase related to fees, applications, approval, inspections, appraisals, insurance, repairs, escrow costs, and other closing and loan related costs. These can add up quickly.

So, if you are wanting to buy a property but don't intend to stay there at least this long or longer, than I would highly recommend you rethink your intention. You also want to make sure that you have a sufficient emergency fund in place, in addition to the down payment needed and closing costs as a backstop for some unforeseen events like significant repairs or job downsizing.

You have probably heard this "location, location, location" as the critical factor in where to buy a house or property. This can take on different meanings to different people. Some view this statement as meaning, don't buy a house on a busy street or next to something that hinders its appeal and value. Others may view this as a strategy to buy the property on a dead-end street or a town that is desirable. Others may see it as a reason to only buy a home in a town with a Blue Ribbon School district and top rated high school. There is not a one size fits all meaning. They all matter.

You should avoid purchasing the biggest house on the block and neighborhood as it could be considered an over improvement for this market area. You may want to also avoid older homes that need a lot of work if you're not handy, not willing to learn, and don't have family and/or friends that are willing to pitch in to renovate it. Generally, the best option is the worst house in the best neighborhood with a good school district, as this does matter.

Another recommendation you should consider is to rent for a period of time, potentially a year prior to purchasing a property. After doing so, you may decide that some things are more important than others like changes in the property location or looking at different towns. It will allow you to get to know the area prior to making this big decision especially if you are new to this market area. You may want to seek out the help of not one, but a few realtors to get a better feel for who is truly assisting you in the search, adding value to the process, knows the local market well and provides you with the best choices and advice.

This similar approach should be used when looking for financing options. Work with several loan officers to see what their rate and terms will be for a similar 30 year or 15-year fixed rate mortgage and what the closing costs are associated with each. By finding out the closing costs and the rate, you will have a better understanding of the "all in" cost of the loan.

In the current year (2020) very low interest rate environment, you should only consider taking out a fixed rate mortgage. If and when rates move higher, an adjustable rate mortgage could be a lot more expensive longer term. There are some hybrid options that may apply to your situation, but generally a fixed rate is the better option as the only change in monthly cost will be increases in taxes and insurance.

Other great strategies include; making one extra mortgage payment early on in the life of the loan as you may save approximately 4 to 8 years on a 30-year mortgage depending on the interest rate. Another strategy to reduce your total interest paid over the life of the mortgage is, instead of taking out a 15-year mortgage and being locked into higher payments, take out the 30-year mortgage and pay the equivalent of the 15-year payment monthly.

My mortgage amortization schedule and others show that this will reduce the timeframe of the 30-year loan down to approximately 15 years and 9 months. If you can afford to convert to a 15-year mortgage, it may make sense to do so to reduce your overall interest paid based on a lower rate. One of my clients recently noted that the smartest financial decision he has made was paying off his mortgages early by making additional monthly contributions above his standard payment. He now owns three properties free and clear with no mortgage.

You should have a general sense of where mortgage rates are and their link to the 10 Year Treasury Index. If and when rates are much lower than your existing mortgage rate, and you plan on staying in the house for several more years, it may be worth refinancing to a lower rate. Review options with several mortgage loan officers and companies.

If you have equity in the home and are fiscally responsible not to put yourself in more debt, then it is always a good idea to have a Home Equity or HELOC line of credit open in case of emergencies. As noted prior, the reason being, if the primary earner loses his/her job, it may become impossible to open up this line of credit from lenders. There is no cost to opening it until you borrow money and it should be completed when you are gainfully employed, otherwise, it may be too late. It is a way to access assets if cash flow becomes an issue.

Lastly, if you have owned your home for some time and took out Private Mortgage Insurance because you made a down payment of less than 20% for the purchase, it may be an opportunity to remove this cost. The burden to remove the PMI cost is on you in proving that your equity position in the property is above this 20% threshold. It is a good idea to save the original appraisal and contact local realtors and/or appraisers to determine the current market value of the property in comparison to your loan balances.

Connect with the PMI lender to better understand their requirements and process to remove or cancel the insurance. FHA mortgages may require you to refinance in order to drop the PMI insurance. You may also want to periodically review tax appeal options with these same professionals if and when your property taxes are out of line with similar properties in your town or city to reduce your tax burden.

Prior to purchasing a property, always get a home inspection, even if it is not required in your state. Make sure you tour the property with the inspector without the homeowner being home and getting in the way. You will learn a great deal about home maintenance and nuisances with the right inspector. The report the inspector generates may allow you to negotiate any repairs that surface during the inspection that can easily negate the cost of this inspection.

Once in a while, serious structural issues may be uncovered where you would want to walk away from the purchase. My last inspection (although required) uncovered a serious Radon gas issue common in this area where the homeowner had to spend several thousands of dollars for a Radon reduction system to be installed prior to closing. I also negotiated several roof, skylight, and electrical repairs after the contract was signed with adjustments made at the closing. Make sure that there is an inspection clause in the contract to allow for this potential renegotiation.

As discussed in the knowledge section, never wire closing costs to the attorney as there are phishing scams out there preying on people who are closing on properties. See #11 below for removing PMI insurance in the future.

Important Things to Do After Your House Closing

My wife and I put ourselves into debt until the year 2028. After 60 minutes, numerous signatures and initials, we had a pile of papers, a set of keys, a bottle of wine, and an electric garage door opener to our new home. What next? I want to share with you some thoughts I had throughout my first few days of home ownership.

1. Call a locksmith and change all the outside door locks. You don't know if somebody's buddy still has a key and might decide to let themselves in and crash on the couch. Also, leave a hidden key somewhere outside the house.
2. Change the garage door opener codes.
3. Check, clean and/or replace the furnace and/or air conditioning filters and mark your calendar for the next replacement date.
4. Check the batteries in your smoke and Carbon Monoxide detectors and the pressure in the fire extinguisher periodically.
5. Create a file for all closing documents: copy and keep handy the survey for future property boundary disputes with your neighbors! Create a separate file for all appliance paperwork (received at the closing) and one for all the warranties on everything. Mark your calendar for inspections prior

to their expiration (especially the termite contract). Create another file for all house receipts for future stepped up cost basis on the property. Copy the appraisal for a possible future tax appeal. Copy the HUD 1 statement and keep it with your tax records for current year tax deductions. When you receive your deed in a few weeks, put it in a secure place.

6. Recommend chronicling your possessions after you have moved in. Video everything in the home as well as the home itself. This will serve as an invaluable tool in the event that something unfortunate happens. Your memory will never be able to take the place of the video and you will encounter less resistance from your insurance company if you have to prove something was present. Also, make a detailed written list of all the costlier items. Keep a copy of both in at least one location outside of the home, such as a safety deposit box.

7. Recommend changing washing machine rubber hoses to braided metal hoses and attach metal safety cables to garage door springs.

8. Go over second floor and upper floor emergency evacuation routes and main water and gas shutoff valve locations with family members.

9. Find a neighbor and give them your phone number for any emergencies prior to you moving in and also retain their name and number.

10. Mark your calendar for garbage and recycling pick up days.

11. Keep the name and number of the appraiser handy. If you are paying Private Mortgage Insurance PMI, check yearly if the equity in your home exceeds 20%. When it does, get an appraisal at a reduced cost to prove your 20% equity, and remove the PMI insurance costs.

12. Finally, you might want to pick up some toilet paper, towels, sponges, soap, air fresheners, garbage bags, extension cords, flashlight, bucket, broom, basic tools, extra light bulbs and toilet plunger and a battery backup for the sump pump, as they may be needed prior to moving in. Good luck!

College Planning - please see Career Development section.

Corporate Financial Benefits

For employees of larger corporations, there are often an abundance of benefits that one should consider. In addition to the retirement plans and company matching previously discussed, some companies offer Health Savings Accounts HSA's and some offer Flexible Spending Accounts FSA's. They have different requirements, but offer savings accounts to employees to pay for out of pocket healthcare expenses. HSA's have the additional benefit of allowing individuals to invest their assets dedicated to health care related costs. When utilizing the benefit of an FSA one needs to accurately account for and determine yearly spending within this account as assets may not be able to be rolled over into the following year. HSA's do not have these same requirements and assets can be used throughout one's lifetime although generally contributions will stop at age 65 unless employment continues. They also have an additional benefit of being triple tax advantaged. It is important that beneficiary designations should continue to be updated on these accounts to avoid the probate process.

Employees should consider and analyze all plans if spouses and partners have their own plans and coordinate these benefits advantageously. Sometimes, there is duplication of plan coverages that can and should be avoided. Employees can find themselves over insured if this yearly analysis during open enrollment is not performed.

Employees should also take advantage of their yearly medical checkup as it should be covered at 100% as preventive, in addition to being good common practice to catch medical issues early one. Other considerations include making sure providers utilized are in network prior to the visit to avoid unnecessary and costly fees.

When receiving prescriptions, it may be wise to request generic brand medications to reduce overall costs. Companies may offer prepaid legal services, childcare and commuting benefits, cybersecurity plans, identity theft, and other benefits that you should consider carefully. Tuition reimbursement plans are a great way to develop your career by completing degrees and certifications and will be reviewed in a later section.

Some of the larger corporations even offer financial wellness incentives, credits, and activities that are available for your benefit. Many of these offer wellness incentive credits that will pay you for healthy activities and lifestyles.

An example of this is that my employer offers up to $600 per year in wellness credits for certain completed health related activities yearly. I did a survey of associates that I work with and concluded that less than 10% were utilizing these benefits! These activities fall into my twofer category as great for savings plans and improving one's healthy lifestyle.

Prompt: Review your company's benefit options. Make sure that you are receiving the company match on your retirement account if offered. Make a list of other benefits that are offered to you that you can utilize now or in the immediate future. Discuss options with your benefits manager or online contacts. If you work for a smaller company, or are self-employed and don't have these options, then take note of how you can better utilize your health care benefits, add additional benefits, and/or improve your retirement planning.

_____

_____

_____

_____

_____

_____

_____

STRUCTURE & BUILDING BLOCKS OF FINANCIAL WELLBEING

PROSPERITY
FINANCIAL WELLBEING
SECURITY & INDEPENDENCE

PEAK COMPETENCIES - DISTRIBUTION
- Alternative Investments
- Tax Efficient Strategies
- Philanthropic & Grateful
- Complex Estate Planning
- Hedging & Risk Management

CORE COMPETENCIES - ACCUMULATION & CONSOLIDATION
- Real Estate Ownership & Income
- Investment Planning
- Retirement Income Planning
- Debt Elimination
- College 529 & State Prepaid Planning

CORE COMPETENCIES - ACCUMULATION
- Low Cost Indexing
- Asset Allocation & Diversification
- Career Development
- Dollar Cost Averaging & Rebalancing
- Retirement Planning

FOUNDATIONAL COMPETENCIES - PROTECTION
- Budgeting
- Good Savings & Spending Habits
- Emergency Fund
- Insurance Planning
- Basic Estate Planning

CORNERSTONE FOOTINGS & CYCLE OF WELLNESS
- Vision & Goals AND
- Beliefs FEED
- Actions CREATE
- Financial Wellness

© Copyright 2019 Richard S. Olin

Financial Wellness Checkup

Day 1 – Complete your budget and cash flow analysis.

Day 2 – Complete your Investment Detail and Net Worth Statement.

Day 3 – Complete your changes in your spending and savings plans by taking the first step toward a sufficient emergency fund.

Day 4 – Review higher rate money market options for your excess cash.

Day 5 – Checkup on your outstanding credit balances and your credit score. Create a new savings plan if there are balances and look to renegotiate down your high credit card rates with the bank. Review better cash reward programs online.

Day 6 – Review options to refinance higher rate student loan, car, or mortgage balances to a lower rate or potentially a shorter term to pay off loans quicker.

Day 7 - Review the buckets of money and the three options to determine if your strategy is on target.

Day 8 – Review or set up your company retirement plan, your IRA or SEP IRA accounts, and options. Make sure that you are receiving the company match and determine if you can contribute more moving forward. Set up a contribution schedule for your IRA contribution quarterly or yearly.

Day 9 – Perform portfolio reviews for all accounts for diversification, asset allocations, rebalancing, dollar cost averaging, and fees. May take longer…

Day 10 – Begin to consolidate or close out any unneeded bank accounts and old retirement accounts into your existing accounts or IRA through a direct rollover.

Day 11 – Begin reading the book, The Intelligent Asset Allocator. Create a college savings plan or open a 529 college account if you have children and have not started these.

Day 12 – Checkup and analyze your life insurance protection and death benefits and terms. Use the life insurance analysis provided and, if you are underinsured or do not have an individual non-company policy or need to reapply for a higher benefit, begin this process today. Add in any company paid life insurance benefits to your total policy benefits.

Day 13 - Review your company benefits for additional cost saving options like commuter, legal, child care, wellness credits; review your disability and long- term care options either within the plan or outside of it.

Day 14 – Review or complete all of your necessary estate planning documents.

Day 15 – Review all account beneficiary designations for possible updating on your bank accounts, investment and retirement accounts, life insurance policies, deeds and annuities, etc.

Just as we should visit our doctor for an annual checkup, similarly, you should complete this 15-day financial checkup. This will put you on track for financial wellness and determine where you may have gaps in your financial plan that need to be addressed today.

Financial planning is a foundational competency that is critical to our success. Yet so many of us spend very little time reading, learning, and planning to understand these important strategies. This section is much larger than any other section due to my expertise in this area as a financial advisor and Registered Supervisory Principal. My goal is to share some of the most basic considerations and elements of your financial plan so that you have the basis for a sound and thorough plan of action.

We all need to pay ourselves first by saving and not mortgaging ourselves and our futures through credit card debt and excessive fees. By doing this we are investing in ourselves for our futures. If you want to be successful, then you MUST master this competency and the prompts and spreadsheets that I have included. Successful people are generally savers and investors who are knowledgeable about investments and finances.

There is a direct correlation between one's occupation and one's potential earnings power. A large portion of our financial picture grows out of our ability to earn an income based on our career and invest the savings. Start your savings, investment, and retirement planning early on in your career. Being financially secure is critical to our overall wellbeing. So often stress and anxiety are caused from a lack of planning, budgeting, saving, and investing.

Once you create the habits necessary, which were documented in prior sections, regarding your spending and savings habits, you are most of the way there. The rest of the investment and retirement planning can be put on autopilot with a buckets of money strategy using high yielding savings accounts, company retirement plans, low cost indexing, and diversification strategies. My wife, who is an employee benefits professional, often uses this quote that may be attributable to Gandhi—The world is not your mother! I think it is appropriate here as this is a key competency and one that is our responsibility to facilitate our financial wellbeing. The key is to not make it overwhelming but to put a thorough plan into place and then review and revise.

"Wealth is the ability to fully experience life."
—Henry David Thoreau

CHAPTER 7

Balanced Harmonic WE Wellness Environment

"Prosperity is achieved through balanced harmonic wellness." — Richard S.Olin

I began this project in an attempt to uncover and learn more about what it takes to attain success and prosperity, and what that truly means. Was it about getting rich or wealthy? Probably not since I know many people who are wealthy by most metrics that have missing elements of success in their lives. Is it being lean and fit and heathy? Or is it about being the career scientist that lives to find the next cure for a disease?

My research brought me to Aristotle's teachings touched upon earlier in the guide about prosperity and wellbeing, or living the good life as he noted it to be. His revolutionary interpretation was that prosperity and wellbeing came from a balance between one's physical, emotional, intellectual, and political (later interpreted to be social wellbeing) self.

He noted that it was a combination of these factors and competencies that makes each of us thrive and prosper within our society. A more recent interpretation of his theory has also included financial and occupational or career wellbeing as part of these original elements to round out. Some would separate spiritual, environmental or other elements, but these are included in one form or another in these core six elements noted above. Attaining this balance between these six different competencies is what most consider to be a prosperous and successful result, and what I have tried to achieve.

There are an abundance of community-based wellness activities and groups available to facilitate this end result. A cursory review of the local paper or activities calendars and/or blogs often provide details on these events. I would encourage you to seek out some of these opportunities for walks, free classes, lectures, and other valuable options. The library and non-profit organizations are also good sources and/or reference points.

One of the main tenents of this journal is to share with you these thoughts, resources, and tools and to inspire and challenge you to find your Harmonic WE. You can, and should, be able to accomplish this by finding a happy successful median between these six competencies. Retirees and seniors could replace the occupational or career wellness with other opportunities like volunteering or mentoring. These six often tend to interplay with each other as we progress through our days and lives. There is a parallel between intellectual, occupational, and financial wellness.

There may be times in your life that you discount one or more of the components to focus on the others, but one should strive toward a balance of all six. What follows is my adaptation of my Structure and Building Blocks of Achievement and Prosperity as a blueprint for a balanced wellness environment. It includes all of the competencies and illustrates them in a cohesive fashion.

STRUCTURE & BUILDING BLOCKS OF BALANCED WELLNESS

PROSPERITY
BALANCED WELLNESS
HARMONIC WE - WELLNESS ENVIRONMENT

PEAK COMPETENCIES
| Genuine Integrity | Confident | High Self Concept | Adaptable | Motivated & Persistent |

HIGH LEVEL COMPETENCIES
| Social Circle & Mentors | Generosity & Gratitude | EQ Emotional Intelligence | Overcome Adversity | Enthusiastic & Happy |

CORE COMPETENCIES
| Financial Wellness | Physical Wellness | Emotional Wellness | Intellectual Wellness | Social Wellness | Career Wellness |

FOUNDATIONAL COMPETENCIES
| Planning & Journaling | Positive Attitude | Productive Habits | Conditioning & Mindfulness | Knowledge & Learning |

CORNERSTONE FOOTINGS & CYCLE OF WELLNESS
| Vision & Goals | Beliefs | Actions | Wellbeing |
| AND | FEED | CREATE | |

© Copyright 2017 Richard S. Olin

Prompt: Review the Structure and Building Blocks of Balanced Wellness. Rank each of the six wellness competencies from 1 being the most time spent (outside of work and/or school) to 6 for the least amount of time spent. Take some time to think about how you can spend more time on some of the others and less time on #1. Review the sections related to these less focused competencies to learn more and cultivate some ideas and strategies around how you can facilitate growth.

1 most time spent _____

2 good amount of time spent _____

3 some time spent _____

4 some time spent _____

5 little time spent _____

6 very little or no time spent _____

Next, take small actionable steps toward creating new tasks and routines related to those at the bottom and little, if any, time devoted to them.

The time management aspect of this task and prompt is important to consider on a daily and weekly basis. That is why I have tried to provide some ideas and considerations on incorporating these into a 30-minute routine, phone reminders, calendar prompts, and other next step elements to get these moving in the right direction.

I have provided a yearly calendar in the Workbook as another guide for you to keep a higher degree of focus on all six competencies and some of the tasks associated with each of these six. I think it's important to keep these in focus on a routine basis, as well as a longer-term basis especially the ones at the bottom that may require more of your attention.

Prosperity, success, and self-actualization come from a combination and balance of competing wellness competencies based on the teachings of the masters and history's great thinkers. In using this as a template for my own personal success and prosperity, I have committed to incorporating all six into my daily and longer-term routines. I have created short tasks and routines and paired them with other routines and habits. My intention is not to overwhelm you by suggesting that you should routinely incorporate every one of these on a daily or weekly basis. It is to provide some context on how they may be more balanced and which ones, if any, should garner more of your attention. Think about how you want to adapt your wellness competencies so that you may aspire to reach your highest potential toward self-actualization.

I encourage you to find your Harmonic WE…

CHAPTER 8

Core Competencies

The core competencies are the spine that steadies us and our wellbeing. They incorporate several key competencies that correlate and grow out of the foundational and cornerstone competencies to enhance them.

I begin with conditioning mind and body, which could be a part of either the core or foundational level. This is due to its key role in our health and wellness. Described in detail is the importance of creating your brand to develop your career as being critical to your earnings and savings plans. Reviewing and understanding the makeup of our inner core social circle will help us obtain better potential advocates and advisors.

I am hopeful that this may challenge you and cause you to choose your friends and advocates more wisely and effect your social wellbeing in a positive way. Later sections will be devoted to two key competencies also touched upon briefly within the other two levels in nurturing gratitude into our lives and having the ability to overcome life's many adversities that often interrupt and sabotage our focus. Without the tools, resources, and strategies for these core competencies, we are left along the roadside without the vision to have a map, spare tire, an advocate, or the mindset and strength to endure the unique situations at hand and that await us further up the road.

Conditioning Mind & Body

Are you committed to changing the aspects of your life that truly need to be changed? If you are, then this section will assist in building routines and strategies to help you. I noted earlier in the guide that some of us (including myself) are good planners, but many of us (including myself at times) are not such good doers. It's the commitment with adding a repetitive process to our routines described within the actions and habits sections that afford us this necessary consistency and conditioning.

Conditioning entails taking a systematic routine approach to these aspects of your life. Think about how athletes, military personnel, and artists condition themselves to perform different motions, plays, and strategies. They do so by repetitively practicing drills and skills daily until they no longer have to think about it or concentrate on them as a routine habit.

Military drills and conditioning programs are the primary strategies that affords military organizations and their ranks to perform at peak levels in highly stressful and unique circumstances. This is the same approach we need to take when it comes to conditioning our minds and our bodies. It does not always need to be the same drill, but constantly running through drills and skills so that at some point, it is purely muscle memory. I recall when I first started playing guitar last year and was discussing how difficult it was to remember all the different cords and strumming patterns—My friends commented that with practice and repetition will come the muscle memory and it was so.

When I played tennis in high school, we would all stand at the baseline and practice our serves daily. Coach made us take 20-30 serves every practice focusing on both our first and second serves. He drilled into us how important it was to place your foot pointed and legs apart in a certain direction and at a certain angle depending upon which serve you were initiating. He imparted the importance of repetitive focus on the toss at a certain height that worked for each of us and the spring needed for velocity. Next followed a discussion on focus, aim, consistency, and the psychological commitment to the competition, all critical to the result similar to a successful champion.

Tennis is a great game and participation sport. The individual and team sports that I participated in helped teach and define me as a young adult. I never worked very hard at conditioning until I got older and understood more clearly its importance. It was the early introduction, coaching, and mentoring that I look back on as a significant part of the foundation and core of who I eventually became.

We go through school and life learning so much. It is the critical element of how we are able to approach and apply it into our daily lives that separates each of us. The repetitive nature of practicing and conditioning ourselves is critical to our physical and emotional wellbeing. Just as we swing a bat or club, throw the ball repeatedly, react to a specific situation, so do we need to repeatedly condition ourselves using emotional hygiene and physically demanding techniques to refocus our vision and overall health. Repetitive routines and conditioning create the muscle memory and habits needed for better results and wellbeing. A disciplined approach plays a big factor in our success. Find a repeatable process as the strategy, be disciplined in your approach and use conditioning techniques for your physical as well as your emotional wellbeing.

Conditioning Mind

"The greatest weapon against stress is our ability to choose one thought over another." — William James

Take another look at the target of belief and self-concept and which segment number you chose. We discussed the importance of moving from the outer segments toward the inner ones with the help and support of advocates and available resources. This is in addition to our own self-discipline and using willpower to fight off the negative fixed mindset and focus our attention on a more positive growth mindset.

You owe it to yourself to invest in yourself and reach a better place both mentally and physically. We spend time every day on our physical hygiene including washing and brushing and flossing. We need to make time for our emotional hygiene and our focus on using some mental cleaning and flossing techniques to remove the undesirable. What follows are strategies and resources that may assist with these next steps.

Remember the depiction of the car windshield and cleaning off our emotional mindset with emotional hygiene techniques? Our daily lives throw so many things at us and our windshields. We need to have determined wiper blades to condition our minds and the cleaning solutions to cleanse our self-talk and mindset. It's a battle for self-compassion.

My goal recently has been with each negative event or situation thrown at me, I meet it head on with one or two positive thoughts. It's a mind game and a numbers game. Every time someone cuts me off on my commute, I think that the guy's wife is probably giving birth to their first child in the back seat, and I hope he makes it to the hospital in time! Each time an appliance breaks (as they often do), I think about how thankful I am to have 10-15 others that work (at least for now). Every time I have an issue at work often in succession, I am thankful that I have a job and a place to hang my coat every day. Meet your negatives head-on with exponential positives. It's important to note that we need to love ourselves first, before we can effectively allow others to love us. Self-compassion with positive self-talk is critical to our emotional success and to our overall balanced wellbeing.

As I speak to friends, clients and family, I realize that very little time and energy, if any, are being devoted to discussing and improving our emotional wellness. There is a compelling argument that each of us needs to spend more time on this competency and have a better understanding of tools and resources available to us. The tools and resources I am providing may be basic, but they work for me and I am hopeful that they can be a good starting point for many of you.

Some of the emotional hygiene tools that were touched upon include journaling some positive affirmations and self-talk or reciting them off a list. It may be by adding gratitude into your life daily by thanking someone you care about that has been helpful and supportive. By recognizing their hard work and support, you should feel positive vibes. Send a text, email, gift, or call someone to share your gratitude.

When I led the firm's regional volunteer initiative and we completed the volunteer work to support the local non-profit and community, I always felt a true sense of pride. It's tough to describe the feeling I get when I volunteer, but it's worth the effort and experience, so commit to giving it a go.

One of the elements that I struggle with the most is the benefit and strategy of forgiveness. Full disclosure (my wife will attest) that I tend to hold a grudge and it lingers. I have tried to take a new tact in that I don't look back through the rearview mirror as often. The more I look back, the more things deteriorate. I now try to drop the baggage and leave it and don't look back.

Optimists look forward, pessimists look back. I once read when something unexpected happens that's negative you should say to yourself "plot twist" or "shit happens" and move on. Try not to dwell on the negative and focus on the future; it will help. Anger, resentment, and playing the blame game are not going to help you. It is a loser's attitude and you will lose altitude on your growth. It's a choice we make each and every day; growth minded or fixed minded, positive or negative, forward focused or backward looking.

Prompt: Think of a situation where you felt angry, resentful, or blamed someone else and could have been more forgiving. Could you have handled it in a different way with a preferable outcome? Describe how you may take a different approach to forgive and move forward.

_____
_____
_____

SMILE often! Act "as if" you're happy! Walk with a big stride and keep your chin up. William James challenges us with these tactics. It's been noted to "fake it, till you make it" so why not fake it and maybe you will make yourself happier by just doing it!

Prompt: Try it now, smile for the next few minutes, walk with a big stride, arms flowing by your side, chin up, and see if you have a different frame of mind. When you meet people, smile as much as you can as it leaves a great impression. You should elicit a better reaction more often than from what you would normally receive. Condition yourself to smile and make these small adjustments daily.

Over the past three to four years, as I focused more on this project, I have continued to be more mindful of the things, situations, and vibes around me. It has helped me focus in on the positive and reframe the negative. I have started to position this focus with my inner core social circle. If I encounter a negative situation that I can remove myself from, I do. I am working on reducing the negative confrontations more often, even though it is difficult to gracefully remove myself.

We will review the importance of this to utilize with others to gain a higher Emotional Intelligence EQ as a benefit. We should also consider this as a technique to gain a more positive mindset when it comes to dealing with others and their own unique issues and shortcomings. Mindfulness can enhance our ability to allow us to comprehend our emotions in real time and slow down our reaction times. It can help us recognize emotions of others and be empathetic to their feelings while strengthen our ability to control our own.

Evidence is mounting on how mindfulness, meditation, prayer, and other forms of interpersonal reflection like Ikigai, Hygge, Wabi sabi can help create a healthier wellness environment and overall greater wellbeing. They are the tools and resources to get you back on track and act as a shield against negative thoughts and triggers. These practices allow us to get a hold of our thoughts and control how our mind wanders. By controlling our wandering mind, we give ourselves time to react when a situation arises. If we can lengthen this timeframe and stretch it out, we may cause beneficial reactions and decisions.

I have practiced mindfulness to clear my mind; it's very calming, reassuring, and helps me better cope with situations and challenges. Try it sometime, you may end up utilizing it. It's all about controlling your thoughts, emotions, and reactions.

If you pair these as twofers you may be able to quickly and skillfully add them to your repertoire and routines. Journaling your daily achievements, gratitude, faith, prayer, thanks, generosity, forgiveness, or spending some time (the last 10 minutes of your day) on contemplating these can help. Some of us are more spiritual and/or religious than others and may feel that this alone should be its own wellness competency.

Although somewhat less spiritual, I can appreciate and have worked on realizing these benefits more recently. It seems best positioned as a subset and another great technique of emotional wellbeing that you may want to pursue. As I get older, I better understand the benefits it provides, such as comfort and reassurance.

The goal is to aim for the bullseye of the target, expand upon and use these emotional hygiene techniques paired with other routines. Our growth depends, in part, on moving from the outer edges of the target toward the bullseye as we sharpen our focus on our emotional wellbeing. Beliefs, attitudes, and the conditioning of our thoughts correlate with other higher-level and peak competencies of higher EQ and self-concept. Challenge yourself to sharpen these skills, and focus your energy on a wide variety of mindfulness and hygiene routines.

10 Day Emotional Wellness Checkup

Day 1 – Complete the positive affirmation and self-talk pullout in the Workbook and hang it in a place where you will view it often, like a sanctuary wall or desk. Recite the list and mindfully inhale the meanings and benefit.

Day 2 – Print out Charles Swindoll's quote on Attitude and hang it up on the inside of your cabinet.

Day 3 – Call, facetime, text, or send someone who is close to you and an advocate a message or gift that you are thankful that they are in your life (and that you love and worship their partnership). Smile while talking to them!

Day 4 – Complete your achievement collage and hang it up somewhere where you can enjoy it every day!

Day 5 – Complete the gratitude jar project and at dinner, go around the table and ask everyone to say what they are grateful for.

Day 6 – Forgive someone that has wronged you and make amends if that's possible. If not, drop the baggage, leave it by forgiving, and don't ever look back!

Day 7- Start taking a walk or meditating with deep breathing daily. Be mindful of the benefits of nature's beauty or what pure silence has to offer you.

Day 8 – Volunteer to help a non-profit organization.

Day 9 – Listen to podcasts of comedians or the comedy channels on cable or satellite radio. Smiling for periods of time is infectious!

Day 10 – Find and embrace meditation, faith, prayer, and positive belief into your life through religion and/or mindfulness. Use music as a conduit.

Prompt: Take time to review the emotional hygiene techniques and tools noted. Write down which ones are current daily routines or habits and those you will pair with as a twofer moving toward for meaningful change.

Mindfulness during a walk or meal _____

Forgiveness and drop the baggage _____

Thanking or paying it forward _____

Giving of yourself to someone or something _____

Meditation and deep breathing _____

Journaling positive affirmations _____

Positive self-talk at lunch or commute _____

Faith and prayer recital _____

Gratitude jar on table _____

Ikigai review _____

Reiki routine _____

Hygge time _____

Smile and act as if… _____

Achievement celebration _____

Wabi Sabi _____

Comedy classics review _____

Conditioning Body

We need to condition our body to be healthy. I previously alluded to the importance of athletic conditioning and repetition, which hopefully provided a good visual perspective. I began the guide with a review of how being a participant instead of a spectator is critically important. There was a significant correlation made between successful athletes and franchises and having a playbook, strategies, and drills, and how this influences our commitment, conditioning, and ultimately our wellbeing.

My goal regarding this section is not to provide diagrams, exercises, routines, and other tasks and functions of exercise regiments. There is an abundance of books, magazines, websites, blogs, and videos available.

Because of this, I will spend much less time digging into the details of these elements of this competency. I will direct the focus toward these following components: healthier lifestyle of physical conditioning and nutritionally related healthier options and benefits, simple daily tips and routines, pairing them as twofers and lastly, providing a 10-day checkup routine.

When it comes to exercising, taking an initial small step is a good start. In order to create a healthier lifestyle, it should be a repetitive part of your daily routine. Once it is part of your routine, you hopefully won't need to think about it or dread doing it anymore.

A potential start may be deep breathing and stretching and/or yoga. It can clear your mind and is a huge stress reliever after work or to start fresh at the beginning of the day. Yoga improves flexibility and creates better blood circulation and feels good. Superior blood circulation helps restore muscle, which is important for long-term mobility and joint health.

Each morning, I do 10 minutes of stretching and core exercises to get my mind and body ready for the day. It helps loosen my back, neck, hips, and legs. Since I sit at a desk all day, the stretching allows me to counteract some of the muscle tension. I have had chronic back problems in the past after back surgery. So, I find that this stretching has made my muscles less prone to stiffness and soreness, potential lower back weakening, and pain over the years.

Studies consistently convey that stretching, yoga, and exercise improves posture, builds muscle, which protects us from arthritis and back pain, prevents cartilage and joint breakdown, provides better bone health, improves blood flow, and reduces our blood pressure. Other routines like Tai-chi or walking are also good options.

The next step is regular aerobic exercise that helps keep your lungs, heart, immune system, and body healthy. According to the Mayo Clinic, aerobic exercise allows you to live longer, maintain mobility as you age, strengthen your heart, keep arteries clear, manage and reduce chronic conditions (blood pressure and blood sugar). It also helps you be less susceptible to viral illnesses.

Any type of exercise will be helpful in the long run, but I also want to stress the importance of building these routines by planning. I have found that forcing myself to go work out once in a while is a lot harder than knowing what days of the week I have dedicated as workout days. By getting into a routine I have conditioned myself for it to become a habit. As Aristotle noted, we are creatures of habit, we form habits and habits form our futures.

A weekly routine that I have is walking about 2 miles on the treadmill prior to dinner usually 3-4 days per week. I also supplement 2 days or so of strength training weekly into these routines, which may include yard work, gardening, and home repairs that I may do as a weekend worrier. My family members have committed to a routine workout plan each week incorporating cardio, strength, and stretching exercises into different days of the week. This diverse strategy is one that I am advocating. It's not just about doing one thing, but alternating or supplementing cardio with some strength training and stretching daily.

Prompt: How many times per week do you participate in physical exercise for a period of 20-30 minutes a day and which ones do you do (cardio, walking, strength training, sports, yard work, home improvement, hiking, biking)? _____

_____

If you are not participating in routine exercise a minimum of 3 days per week, what 1-2 activities would you choose to start from the list above? Write down which ones would be a good fit and why? _____

_____

_____

Add calendar notes or phone reminders on the specific days you are going to complete these activities. I encourage you to challenge yourself to try just

20-30 minutes a day.

Team sports and athletics are great opportunities for growth in so many ways. They are an opportunity to make friends, volunteer, and build your brand and network. Athletics cultivate participants and introduce children to life's realities of winning and losing with some hard lessons. This, in turn, helps them cope and understand the need to work with others as a group and how to deal with disappointment and adversity.

As a young adult, team sports filled a void and were a positive and motivational influence in my life. One thing that stands out as building character was that if we lost a soccer match, we were running hills, even in the pouring rain upon our return from an away game; thank you coach.

The importance of healthy nutrition also plays a key role in our overall physical health. This relates to both healthy eating and proper hydration. Since there is so much available information on this topic, especially regarding nutritional information, a general simplified approach will follow.

An Australian study followed the eating habits of 12,000 people and found that those who added 8 portions of fruit and vegetables a day experienced an increase in overall mood, health, and life satisfaction.

Here is my simple list of better and healthier choices (with the help of my health conscious wife). I stress the word simple as I don't want it engrossing my life so I have time for all of the other elements and competencies.

- Several portions of fruits (especially berries) and vegetables daily.
- Using apple cider vinegar in my salads.
- Avoiding fried foods and replacing with healthier grilled meals.
- Have a healthy smoothie, especially after a great workout.
- Using a lot of garlic in my cooking.
- Replacing potato chips with unsalted nuts.
- Enjoying a salad to start dinner.

- Swapping out the red meat for white meat.
- Laying off the cheeses and opting for plain yogurt with fruit.
- Exchanging soda for flavored water.
- Avoiding fatty fast foods and focusing on the healthier fresh options.
- Reducing amounts of bread and donuts!
- Having an orange instead of cookies at night.
- Eating a larger lunch and a smaller earlier dinner.
- Reasonable amounts of red wine.
- Having a cup of tea with honey after dinner when I'm hungry again.
- My favorite; adding cinnamon to sweeten it up and replace sugar!

These changes can make a big difference in our overall physical health. It's all about being disciplined and conditioning oneself toward better choices.

Here is my partial list of superfoods that you should consider adding to your shopping list, meals and diet as I have. Some are repeated for emphasis.

- Organic apple cider vinegar with the "mother" in it; great for a diet and cleansing.
- Garlic; for high blood pressure, heart, and high cholesterol.
- All types of berries, which are great for brain function.
- Oranges and bananas; potassium reduces risks of stroke, high blood pressure.
- Honey for a sweet choice.
- Salmon, love it! High in omega 3 fatty acids for your heart.
- Dark chocolate; antioxidant for cholesterol and heart; not as good a taste as milk or white chocolate though…
- Spinach; magnesium promotes energy and balances blood sugar levels.
- Popcorn; whole grain fiber high in antioxidants.
- Broccoli; high in calcium for soft bones.
- Turmeric; my clients swear by it; may help prevent heart disease, cancer, and they say dementia.
- Alfalfa; packed with tons of vitamins and helps with many health issues.

- Fish; all kinds for B12
- Coffee and tea time.
- Tomatoes and strawberries; melatonin helps with sleeping and feeling calm!
- Brussel sprouts; Omega 3 Fatty acids for your heart.

Now hear me out; I added brussel sprouts for a reason, because I used to hate them and would never eat them. However, now if overcooked and soft with the right amount of garlic, virgin olive oil and salt, they're pretty good. So with time, our tastes change and so too can our options for meals. Give these a try. I am not a nutritionist or doctor, but most tout these as being great for your overall health and wellbeing. This list can go on and on and is different for everyone. The key is to have your list of superfoods and incorporate them into your shopping list and daily diet regularly.

Prompt: Which of the above, or your own superfoods, do you eat on a weekly basis? Do you have at least 10-15 on the list? If not, which ones should you immediately incorporate daily? _____

_____

_____

_____

_____

_____

A good general rule of thumb for portion sizing is a palm-size of protein, a fist-size of vegetables, a cupped hand worth of carbs, and a thumb size of fat. There are a plethora of references to use online if you are unsure about portions or ideas for healthy meals. Free online resources for healthy recipes can be found at The Food Network or Good Housekeeping websites among others. For portion control, there are online options that detail recommended amounts and a government website on portion control and weight loss that are other good resources.

There are vast nutritional benefits to cooking. According to registered and licensed dieticians, eating out regularly can be detrimental to our diet because of the portion sizes, which are often two to three times the recommended daily allowance. It is much easier to overeat, since we generally do not know the correct portion size for the meal we ordered. Restaurants also need to make food taste good and are not often concerned about the calorie count. By eating at home you can control portion sizes and what is being added into the preparation to ensure the use of healthier ingredients.

It can be challenging and difficult for people with little cooking experience to make the shift easily. A potential way to start easing into this routine is to utilize a service like HelloFresh or Blue Apron because their meals often include a good mix of vegetables, protein, and starches. My daughter started using HelloFresh as a sophomore in college as she transitioned off the school meal plan to cooking on her own. This allowed her to get a better understanding of how to cook, ideas of what to make, and what a balanced meal includes. A year later, she cooks on her own by incorporating those lessons and skills she honed. This ensures that she is consuming proper portions for each food group.

Another option is to get a basic cookbook and explore. Utilize the back pages of this guide as the initial starting point for a food journal to document your fruit, vegetable, starches and overall food intake. It will also allow you to track calories and nutritional information for each day based on amounts consumed. It may assist in holding yourself accountable, documenting what you eat each day, and detail other nutritional information. Find your comfort zone with meal preparation and incorporate the best and healthiest options available to promote your overall nutritional health.

Another important consideration regarding one's physical health relates to proper daily hydration. Drinking water and skipping the processed fruit juices and soda will help considerably. The National Academies of Sciences, Engineering, and Medicine recommends 15.5 cups of water per day for men and 11.5 cups per day for women. This amounts to about 6-8 large glasses of water daily. These amounts are also dependent on one's size, needs, exercise regimen, and the environment in which one resides. Water is our best option as being healthier than sugary drinks with no nutritional benefits that add calories to our daily intake. Try and measure out your intake of water, soda, and juices for a few days to get a better understanding of the amounts you're ingesting and track it to see if you are consuming the recommended amounts.

Prompt: How many glasses of water on average do you drink per day? _____

What changes can you implement today to increase your water intake and reduce amounts of non-healthy liquids? _____

_____

Sleep is another important element related to our overall health and wellbeing. Most studies show that 6 to 8 hours of sleep is recommended. It is a time where the brain commits things to memory and improves your mood by keeping a normal schedule. Studies also convey that the proper way to lay down is to lie on your side, bend your knees, and put a pillow between them. This may take the strain off of your lower back, which for me is a true benefit.

Breathing techniques have been discussed throughout the guide as a benefit to certain situations and practices. It can be incorporated anyway and anytime with little disruption or notice by others. Adding in mindfulness techniques can result in a twofer and an increased calm demeanor. Lie on the floor and perform deep slow breathing. Focus on your chest movement and the oxygen moving through your veins all the way to the tips of your appendages.

I mentioned the healthy wellness credits and benefits that may be offered by larger employers. Many of these programs pay you for healthy lifestyle activities. So take advantage of what's offered as a healthy time management skill and benefit.

Prompt: Do you work for a company that offers these wellness partners, credits, and incentives? If so, put a plan in place, add reminders to your calendar, and take action to complete many that apply to your situation. List out notes here on the offerings. _____

_____

_____

If you don't work for a company that offers these partnerships, there are other options to create a plan that will guide you toward better overall health and wellbeing. Here is my attempt to provide you with a checkup list similar to the emotional wellness list. Work on tying in both as your overall health checkup!

10 Day Physical Wellness Checkup Routine

Day 1 – Set up your yearly wellness exam with your physician, as well as your six month dental checkup and cleaning.

Day 2 – Start a daily or 5 day per week walking routine (maybe with a dog) for at least a 20 minute half mile distance, potentially during lunch.

Day 3 – Get to the market and begin buying and consuming 8 portions of fruits and vegetables daily.

Day 4 – Make sure your daily sleep regiment is a solid 7-8 hours.

Day 5 – Start drinking 6-8 glasses of water daily of 8 ounces each.

Day 6 – Implement a 10 minute stretching and yoga, Pilates, Thai chi or other light workout routine daily. Add deep breathing exercises and/or meditation routines while sitting or lying on the floor.

Day 7 – Review the list of healthy superfoods provided; pick out some and add them to your shopping regiment.

Day 8 – Begin to reduce your fast food meals weekly by 50% or more; or reduce your fried food intake by 50% weekly.

Day 9 – Implement a 30 minute cardio workout at least 3 days per week.

Day 10 – Buy some organic apple cider vinegar and use it in your salads or daily meals.

Bonus – As noted, if you work for a large company that offers wellness credits, review the options and plans by adding them to your calendar reminders and take full advantage of the benefits!

Weekend Detox – Another great healthy option is to consider a one day or weekend to reset and detox from several unproductive and distressing elements of our lives. These may include our addiction to our phones and technology, it may include not being in tune and focused on our inner voice, it may include detoxing from sitting in a chair all week and not moving around much.

Whatever the case may be for your situation, it may be a great opportunity to detox from these sedentary, unproductive, and potentially destructive behaviors. Use the checklists for both competencies to create your plan and find some sanctuary environments both indoors and outdoors to get well. A friendly reminder to also put the phone away for your tech detox.

One of the most critical components of balanced health and wellness is related to healthy living and our emotional and physical wellbeing. These are two of the six elements of a balanced harmonic approach. The importance of conditioning using disciplined repetition to create routines and habits can't be overstated and is a strategy used by champion elite athletes and artists and successful individuals. The amount of detail required to fully review these would be overwhelming. My attempt is to provide a basic understanding of the important elements and common sense strategies for your next steps to success. Our culture has been and is more focused on the physical nature than the emotional aspect. The more critical element and focus for me is on the emotional hygiene techniques that are not readily available or often discussed. Discipline of creating conditioning routines and pairing habits is key. Have a plan and work the plan and be a participant, not a spectator.

Career Development & Personal Branding

Career and personal development are important steps towards success and prosperity and emerge from knowledge and learning. They are part of the occupational wellness competency and succinctly coincide with our financial wellbeing. They directly correlate to our potential salary and earnings power and derived from that, savings and investment opportunities. This section will start by focusing on branding and then tackle the broader process of your career vision and development.

A few key components that will be reviewed include: ways to approach your branding and development with examples, considerations for college career pathing, co-op opportunities, building your resume, networking, and best practices for interviewing. We will touch on a few important and previously noted correlating elements that you should consider, including the benefits that mentors and company benefit plans offer, such as guidance and tuition reimbursement.

Branding and career development is all about planning. We will review how high achievers and motivated youth who have the mentors and coaches in place with a strong support group get a head start on their branding and developing their careers. Others who are more reactive and fixed minded with limited or no support can be, and are often, left behind.

As the competition for high paying jobs increases with the paradigms discussed in the introduction, this process begins earlier and earlier. Young adults are not waiting until they get to college to determine a major and future career. Many, or most, of these high achievers are researching ways to get ahead through volunteering, networking, co-op programs, and building their brand, mission, and resume early on.

You may not know exactly what you want to do for your career later on as a young adult. However, our ability to utilize the tools, techniques, and resources now to learn about and experience different occupational skills can be a great primer in determining if a certain career may be the right fit for you or not.

Early on in life, it becomes more important to focus on learning, education, building your personal brand, and higher education as a roadmap toward your career aspirations and prospects. When we are younger, we have the time and ability to effectively connect with mentors, coaches, and guidance counselors to determine our career vision and aspirations. Branding starts out early and may be influenced by a parent's career or someone close to you.

I remember going to career day at my children's school to discuss my appraisal career and day-to-day skills and responsibilities. There was a time when my wife and I took our kids to work so they could get a firsthand experience for what we do on a daily basis. Many high schools require their students to participant in several extracurricular activities during the school year. This can include sports, the arts, music, theatre, clubs, volunteerism, part-time jobs, and other related activities to assist with introductions to building our brands.

These can be one of many avenues to build your brand, mission and your resume. Some of us may take the sports path like I did, others maybe the arts, but the growth minded individual will take multiple paths. Exposure to different activities opens unlimited potential and growth. This is the opposite of young adults spending their gifted time on social media and non-educational screen time that vies for their attention and limited resources. Many parents do not allow their kids to spend more than a limited time daily on their phones because they know the consequences. If social media occupies most of your time, you generally lose; if this does not interfere with studying and other focused growth activities, then you may win without this additional crutch.

Prompt: Take a moment and determine how many weekly activities you are engaged in other than your studies or work related activities and write them down. For high school and college students (and even adults), there should be multiple hobbies, part-time work and/or participation in sports/art/clubs/volunteer activities. _____

_____

_____

If there aren't a few, then think about challenging yourself to get started on building your brand. Here are just a few of many options:

- Volunteering is an important step in brand building and learning skills and connecting and networking. Find a local non-profit organization like United Way or Boys & Girls Clubs of America and get involved. If you want to learn a lot about building and construction, Habitat for Humanity is a great organization to get involved with.

- Join the local EMT Emergency Medical Technician Squad or volunteer at a local hospital if you are interested in a medical related field.

- Join the ROTC program if you are interested in joining the military or Junior Police Academy for law enforcement training.

- Join a local Young Eagles Program through EAA for a free flight and introduction to flying if interested in becoming a pilot or working in the aviation industry. The Aircraft Owners and Pilots Association (AOPA) also offers opportunities and programs promoting aviation related learning.

- Search out a Volunteer Income Tax Assistance (VITA) certification and help prepare taxes for the less fortunate to get a start on an accounting career.

- Clubs in school can open up growth opportunities in just about every area.

- Local museums and county or local libraries are a great source for other programs, clubs, and volunteer options.

- Sports are another avenue for athletes, trainers, coaching, and medical therapy related development options.

- Engineering has robotics clubs, events, and a multitude of competitions.

- Social media, communications, and marketing can be experienced by helping out local businesses, associations, or clubs with their branding efforts.

If you are involved as a participant then you're off to a great start. If not, then I challenge you to rethink your focus and time management and adapt by joining in and learning. Through volunteering and working in a field of interest early on you can make a difference in someone else's life. By doing so, you can also determine if you are truly interested in continuing that path.

These are just a few ways to set yourself up for college, as well as creating your personal brand. Oftentimes as young adults, we make quick decisions on what path we may want to take based upon a parent, friend, or career counselor's recommendation, which may be helpful but not the desired end. It is up to us to invest in ourselves and spend the time to research and determine these options for ourselves.

The process of building your brand starts out early and builds as you get older. As we grow, hopefully through college (but not always), we may determine that we want to make a change. Our ability to pivot and spend the time to focus on a career option and/or making a change is critical to one's success. A CareerBuilder survey found that only 32% of college graduates ever end up working in the field they majored in. Life is about learning, growing and transforming.

Prompt: Review potential career visions for yourself. Documenting some of your personal interests, priorities, skills, competencies, accomplishments, branding characteristics below that you currently employ, can provide great insight. Think about what excites you!

Specific interests _____

Primary skills _____

Subject matter & classes you enjoy _____

Knowledge & skills _____

Branding characteristics _____

Values & motivations _____

Accomplishments/honors _____

Organizations/clubs _____

Volunteer work _____

Career vision: My ideal position 3-5 years from now will include, and WHY...

_____

_____

_____

_____

These will be helpful to review later when we focus on your professional mission statement and at some point when you are developing your positioning statement for a resume.

As we become adults, we need to build our mission statement and narrow down our focus to a potential career opportunity and a path toward that end. College may not be the only path as some of us may join the military, go to technical schools (technicians, plumbers, electricians, HVAC are good opportunities, and somewhat recession proof), work in a family business or need to work full-time as a first step.

However, for most of us, based on the new paradigms noted with AI, Robotics initiatives and increased competition for jobs, we need to secure a college degree as only an entrance ticket to the main event. Without it, most will be left behind and struggle to attain significant career growth.

Higher levels of education and their associated degree are what employers and managers are initially evaluating. This is in addition to outside interests and how individuals are separated through their bio, resume, honors, and achievements. The plethora of career options and their associated incomes, future growth prospects, and opportunities are outside the scope of this guide.

College planning and funding options are interconnected as they effect one another. The financial burden of "all in" college expenses of tuition, room and board, and student fees and books is often large and overwhelming. Although colleges and universities post full-tuition and their all-in fees, these vary dramatically from student-to-student depending on multiple factors.

My goal is to share some college choice considerations and reference some good resources and tools for you to utilize for the process. Utilizing a guide and then a corresponding file system will help organize these key tasks. Journaling will help frame the information and allow you to conclude which college options would be the best pertaining to each of your considerations. You can list out the important dates within the journal to keep each deadline top-of-mind and document your thoughts and basis in making this important developmental decision.

The first consideration is what your major and focus will be. Begin to journal your interests and passions and highlight your options related to a few career fields and use the prior prompts. Some of the volunteer initiatives, interests, work and clubs that you belong to will play a factor. Your major and career development may also depend on guidance that comes from input from a parent that may have a financially vested interest, guidance counselors, friends, mentors, and associates.

Self-reflect on some skills that you may have, your strengths in terms of subject matter expertise, and the skills and interests that you want to develop. Connecting with some mentors who work within these occupations is highly recommended to get an inside analysis of the day-to-day focus, salary ranges, future growth options, and the basic pros and cons.

If you don't know anyone within these specific fields, think about how you can connect via LinkedIn or through school opportunities and your teachers and coaches. Once you have narrowed down this search, you can journal the pros and cons. Another planning process to review and analyze these options is to organize 4x6 index cards and similarly write down both pros and cons for each career option. A good starting point is Careerandcolleges.com that provides tools and resources related to both careers and college planning.

Once you have narrowed down a major, it is time to review school options. There are several considerations on which school you should choose including generally the most important factors of cost, programs related to your major, campus location and life and atmosphere, size, proximity to home (which can affect cost if in-state) and reputation and co-op programs among others.

Let's begin with the most critical factor, which is the financial implications of these costs which should be a key consideration in this decision making process. Too often, this is overlooked for the other benefits and ends up costing dearly in student loan debt for a long period of time. This is a financial decision first and foremost based on the high cost of "all in" attendance.

Let's break down some strategies that can be used to minimize the total costs. First and foremost, I discussed a student contract in the section on action to provide a commitment device for your consideration as both a student and a parent. This will hopefully prevent a 2 or 4 year experience turning into a long-term one at a higher cost. The main question to ask is: Who is paying for college?

If the answer is you the student, then you should be very careful about incurring a large amount of student debt to be financed and paid after graduation. Students who will finance their education without the assistance from parents, or parents who do not want to burden themselves with debt, should consider the benefit of the student attending a county or local college for the first two years and then transferring to a four year school to finish their degree.

By doing so, you can take advantage of one of the biggest tuition bargains in the nation. This can save you a significant amount of money initially and then even more based on associated loan financing costs. Please consider this option or at a minimum, an in-state public college with a 4-year degree. This way, you will not pay and/or finance the big loan debt of a private college or university or out-of-state school. In-state and prepaid college plans are a great option for cost conscious individuals and should be researched in advance.

The Naviance and Niche online platforms for searches related to college options and details are good starting platforms. Beware of the listings that show the best colleges to attend as they are often driven by college administrators who have alternative goals and partnerships to account for.

You will want to journal a thorough list of approximately 10 schools to start with that would include the in-state options and colleges that align well with your major and interests and other schools that are based on all factors that would be a good fit. This list should also include schools that you should be able to get accepted based on qualifications, and maybe a stretch school or two with about half in the middle bracket of qualifications that you possess.

Note that generally, the more you reach for a stretch school, the higher the "all in" cost will be. Schools have a way of providing large financial aid packages to students that they desire and that will enhance their metrics and not offer much to students that will bring the metrics down or who may potentially drop out.

The next step is to apply and make sure you are mindful of the deadlines! There are several good books on the application process that are also reviewed in detail in many schools. The interview process will be discussed as part of the broader job search process later in this section.

The financial award offers provided by the schools will coincide with the information you provide on the Free Application for Federal Student Aid (FAFSA) and your Expected Family Contribution (EFC) amount. These offers will document any merit aid, scholarship funds, and other credits each of these schools may provide and include to reduce the overall cost to you.

It may turn out that an offer from a more expensive out-of-state school is less than an in-state school depending on many factors and criteria for each school, including your standing among eligible incoming freshman. The discussion of all types of loan options, scholarships, and merit aid are beyond the scope of this guide.

However, a few things to consider are that you should spend the time in your journal listing out the most viable scholarship options to apply for, what your final awards are for each admitting school with merit aid, all in costs to you from least costly to higher cost schools, and requesting a review of the award to potentially increase it if this is one of your top choices.

Scholarship information can be researched on Scholarships.com and Fastweb.com websites that have the tools you need to complete this process. You should review and document each award from each college in your journal to see which makes the most sense based on all factors such as, cost, location, co-op programs, career focus, work study programs, certifications and job prospects after graduation to name a few.

You can also use the pro and con technique with the index cards. Once your attending decision is made there is an option to request a review of your award and financial aid for a higher award. These are all opportunities to bring down your total cost and fees. It never hurts to ask and request a review. Friends of mine have done this successfully in the past.

Other resources that can assist with these processes include: Finaid.org for cost estimators, calendar checklists and loan info; Fafsa.ed.gov for all financial aid info; Fastweb.com for everything college related; campustours.com for virtual tours and Thecollegeboard.com for SAT preparation. Sofi.

com provides refinancing options on accumulated student debt to potentially reduce the total interest costs. Good luck and plan your work and work your plan by journaling!

Once in college, branding starts to become more important for setting up your career path and future development options. Clubs are an easier way to start branding your interests, make friends, build a social circle, and connect with colleagues as a threefer! Holding a position within these clubs can also set you apart and add detail to your resume. Leadership positions convey one's interest in a discipline and can be vital when applying for your first internship, co-op, or job opening with a lack of work experience in your endeavored field.

Philanthropic work and volunteering in school can also be rewarding and provide details for your resume and a topic of conversation for future job interviews. My daughter became VITA certified in high school and volunteered to help prepare tax returns for several non-profit organizations as noted. It is another example of her ongoing commitment to build her brand and be generous by helping others while developing her career.

Now that you have defined your career vision, college options and initial branding, you should create your professional mission statement that will incorporate some of these elements. Your mission statement is one that will encompass what you want your professional brand to represent in a formal written format and may appear on your resume and LinkedIn profile. Companies have their corporate mission statement, and it is beneficial for us to have one as well. It is often a question that is asked during an interview process.

We all need to brand our life and live our brand. Your mission statement is a concise three to four sentence summary that communicates your brand. It describes who you are, your motivations, what difference you are looking to make, and the value and benefits you will share. You completed your personal mission statement in the introduction.

My professional mission is to be a mentor, advisor, and advocate for individuals to invest in themselves toward meaningful change. I have coached, trained, and managed both individual and supervisory relationships for the purposes of assisting others to reach their vision and full potential. This is accomplished through educating, inspiring, challenging, and empowering others with strategies and techniques to promote and realize these changes.

Prompt: Provide a professional mission statement that is approximately 3 to 4 sentences that explains and describes your vision and focus in a concise manner. _____

_____

_____

_____

_____

_____

_____

Your main achievements in life can lead toward a mission statement. Your vision and passions noted in the beginning of your journal should provide you with some guidance and potential talking points. What follows is an outline of some career development resources, resume building and interviewing tips, and networking ideas and strategies.

Network, Network, Network. From the minute you start your branding you should begin your networking strategies. With the introduction of Artificial Intelligence (AI), outsourcing of jobs outside the US, the use of employees on H1 and L1 visas, the new robotic workers soon to join us, the white-collar job market is becoming more competitive than it has ever been.

Thus, the need for networking has become increasingly important to securing a good position. This new paradigm shift is an important consideration for you to take note of and account for moving forward. US

News reported that more than 70% of positions are filled through networking. These may include job fairs, online resources, recruiters, local networking groups, family, friends, neighbors, alumni, professional groups, prior co-workers, your Board of Advisors or business connections, mentors, teachers, club and group members, and your sphere of influence among others.

If and when you need to map out your entire network, use the space in the back of the Workbook to break down these connections. I did this as a new advisor and journaled every individual that I had a connection with and segmented them accordingly. One of the firms I worked for made it an initial requirement for the position. It encompasses segmenting each of these groups and prioritizing those first connections as tier 1 or your inner core circle, or those who are very close to you, and tiers 2 and 3 for those that are somewhat, or not as closely, connected to you as your middle and outer circles.

Fortunately, technology has allowed the process of building and retaining your network online to be easier than in the past. LinkedIn is the go-to powerhouse for networking and other career related tools and resources. It allows users to communicate through connections via social media, IM, and email in a professional manner. The key benefit that LinkedIn provides is the ease of growing your network and connections. Using this platform and immediately adding connections from an early age allows you to grow your network for the future when you are interested in talking to someone about a career change, inquiring about a position at their company, or even just to catch-up with someone you met at a conference.

Other benefits include: The ability to ask others for recommendations, finding job leads, connecting with recruiters and hiring managers, and joining professional groups. Networking is also about connecting with mentors as they can help guide you and grow your network. Career mentors can be found through many avenues including LinkedIn, prior teachers, counselors, and coaches from your sphere of influence, locally within groups or organizations, close associates, or a formal program within your company.

There was a time that I addressed and presented to business majors at a local university on behalf of the company I worked at for their career day. I not only spoke to the body of students and engaged with them afterwards to discuss our opportunities in more detail, but then assisted and mentored an individual who requested some help. These are opportunities to network and request help from mentors.

Prompt: In the section on mentors, you provided the name of a potential mentor who can assist with your career development. Who is that person and what progress have you made since then to connect with them and grow this potentially great opportunity? If this person isn't the right fit or the relationship hasn't been helpful, who else can you connect with? Reevaluate and facilitate these first steps if necessary. _____

_____

_____

Other networking opportunities can come from organizations like Business Networking International (BNI), Rotary, Kiwanis, Women in Business Groups, local business associations, The Chamber of Commerce or corporate in house programs. Every contact you meet is a potential networking opportunity for your future.

Co-op programs, either through school or on your own, are an important career development opportunity, a firsthand career exploration initiative, and a networking opportunity. Careful consideration should be made to adding this initiative to your career development plans. This can be accomplished during the summer college sessions if they are not available while in school. Potential resources to gain insight into these include: company websites, LinkedIn, and your school's internship or job portal (for schools with co-op programs). Your ability to work in your field of interest and gain first-hand knowledge is helpful in determining if this is truly a good career match.

Your resume is your professional bio. Think of it as the recruiters, managers, or employer's first impression of you. It will act as an overview of your professional objectives and mission statement, prior positions, key skills, attributes, and competencies. It will include a summary of your educational background and achievements with degrees and certificates. This may include other technical training and/or professional development courses or instruction you may have completed. It will have a brief review of your professional associations and memberships, clubs, and other community and volunteer-based initiatives that you may be a part of and any offices you held within these organizations. Lastly, it would include any other relevant licenses, certifications, creative endeavors, skills, honors, and personal achievements that you have accomplished. Bottom line, it's your calling card and a one to two page sales brochure of you as the product.

The specifics on each individual section, the cover letter, and your references are beyond the scope of this guide. I have provided a template resume preparation form in the Workbook that you can copy and use as your initial guide, in addition to the Workbook journal. The prior mission statement, achievement and honors discussions, developmental skills, and memberships should help frame your talking points for sections of your resume, as well as the interview. There are an abundance of guides, tools, and samples online that provide the detail needed on content, style, form, and layout. Microsoft Word has preset templates that are available, and Google provides image examples for the style, formatting, and spacing.

To summarize the resume process, make sure you complete several drafts to ensure the resume is clean, easy to read, inclusive of all key and relevant dates, skills, and achievements, and has NO spelling mistakes. Recruiters read through hundreds of resumes, making it stand out may make them more inclined to contact you. It is a first impression, so make it a good one!

Lastly, I can't overemphasize enough the benefits of volunteering and adding that effort as a key line item and standout talking point on your resume. Generous people often get a second look. Your resume is the guide for the follow- up interview. When I hired advisors and private bankers for my team, I used their resumes as the general template for the interview, while adding notes as we progressed. More to come on this.

When I was downsized from my position as a market manager several years ago, besides updating my resume, my LinkedIn profile, and creating my networking strategy and sphere of influence list, I journaled a framework listing of my targeted job market.

Defining the available industries and associated companies that aligned with my list was a critical next step in my search process. It was one that I designed immediately and worked off to connect with recruiters. The beginning of the search process determines which companies and organizations need you and your services for their target market and where you would be a good fit. Make sure that this list is large enough to work off of but not too overwhelming that you can't manage it effectively.

You may narrow or broaden this list by the size of the companies, their locations for your potential commute, and other less critical factors. This targeted list will keep you focused and should be a work-in-progress to add and remove companies as they become more or less desirable. It is what you should use to connect with hiring managers and recruiters on LinkedIn and directly through Indeed, Careerbuilder, Monster and other online recruiting sites. Finally, execute on your marketing plan targeting the top opportunities on your list as it is revised, connecting with key players in your network and pursuing an initial interview.

The interview process is usually the final step in the search process, prior to an offer extended. Often, there will be multiple layers of interviews, depending on the position and its level of expertise. The following has been provided as a general guide for most interviews. It may not be inclusive for certain types of technical or other positions with unique needs. Note that the interview is a time for you to sell yourself. Be prepared to answer and ask questions. Always leave a good impression and ask what the next steps are even if you're not that interested in this position. You never know if another position is available that better suits you and your skills, or if this person could be a good point of contact in the organization and/or help to broaden your network.

Preparation for the interview is very important and often overlooked. Research the company, its industry, their mission statement, key executives, products and services provided, customers, history, etc. The company website is the best place to start, Yahoo finance for public companies and social media sites can also be utilized to learn these details.

It is also helpful to research the interviewer and know what his/her position is, how many people he/she manages, and other elements like, where they have previously worked noted on their LinkedIn profile. Take notes and then consolidate onto index cards if needed. Reviewing the details on the job description in the ad or website is critical and you should bring this with you to the interview as a reference point.

You will want to tailor your talking points based upon these associated skills, accomplishments, questions, and anything of relevance to these bulleted details. Frame up your discussion and questions directly from these descriptive responsibilities. In addition to the job description and company notes, bring 3-4 copies of your resume (one for you to use), your reference list, and a good list of at least five questions you will potentially ask. Know your resume, your mission or positioning statement, your questions to ask, and your general response to often asked questions inside and out.

Some of the more obvious things to note are to bring a notepad or padfolio, resumes and pen, any requested documents or drafts, and always overdress rather than underdress. Looking your best will make you feel more confident, so I encourage you to dress for success. Make sure your dress is appropriate to the corporate culture of this organization. Be well groomed and arrive 15 to 30 minutes early to use the facilities, take a look around, and have extra time for a wrong turn or traffic. Deep breathing prior to the interview can help with nerves and standing and stretching in the hall to get yourself pumped and ready to impress.

When first meeting the interviewer, look him/her in the eye, smile, and give a firm handshake as you introduce yourself. This shows the interviewer you are self-confident. You should continue to make eye contact with the interviewer during your conversation as it displays confidence in what you are conveying. Don't stare the interviewer down; mix it up by alternating with note taking and making eye contact.

If you are in an office, take note of pictures displayed, diplomas, or other items to make note of or find common ground during the interview. This helps to build some rapport and break the ice and tension when necessary. Pay attention and listen more than talk. Find a good balance and don't interrupt the interviewer. Be interested in the discussion by being positive and enthusiastic. Do not discuss or ask salary questions until an offer is extended. You should know the salary range for the position and where you stand prior based upon your tenure and experience.

I have a strategy that you should enter the interview with. It's known as the 5's. You should have 5 elements you know about the company and/or career path to refer to or impart, have 5 points of the job description to relate your skills to, have 5 good reasons why they should hire you, have 5 good questions at the ready; be ready for the 5 questions that are generally asked, and 5 things to close and leave them with. Exploring most of the potential questions that are asked is also beyond the scope of this guide, but we will touch upon a few noteworthy questions.

1. Tell me about yourself. You have your positioning and mission statement.
2. Why you are interested in working for our company? Why would you be a good fit and what contributions can you make? Respond with some company highlights and that you pay attention to detail and are a team player…
3. Tell me about your prior position and what skills and work experiences relate to this position? Think bullets on the job requisition.

4. Why did you leave your prior employer? Or … Where would you like to be in 3-5 years in terms of career goals? Don't say you want their job!
5. Describe your greatest weakness you have or a difficult time when you were criticized for your work, or a change was made that you weren't successful with. Turn a negative situation into a positive end result.

Here are the 5 things you want to leave them with:
1. Explain to them that you are a hard worker, have attention to detail, and will be a great addition to the team and organization.
2. Communicate that you are adaptable to change and wish to grow with an organization like theirs.
3. Ask if there is anyone else that you would need to meet with prior to a decision, the next steps, and when should you expect to hear back.
4. Ask for the job by stating that you would welcome the opportunity to work for a great organization and would add value to the division or company.
5. Thank them for their time and the opportunity to interview for the position. Retrieve all the business cards of those individuals that you met with for the follow-up thank you email.

The following Situation, Obstacle, Action, Result (SOAR) answer model for interviews will assist with your preparation for the interview process. It will also help frame up your answers associated with questions asked about challenging environments and your experiences often related to behavioral situations. It can be utilized in formulating a cohesive response to many questions related to an accomplishment story or a challenging situation you were involved in.

It begins with your brief explanation of the Situation and its details prior to your actions. It will also encompass your description of the challenge or Obstacle needed to be overcome. Next, you describe the effective Actions you took to resolve the situation and issue or challenge. Lastly, the Result will include resolution, honors, achievements, and/or any quantifiable results or deadlines met.

It is a good idea to visualize the interview process, questions, and your responses. Practice with someone in a mock interview. Research common behavioral based interview questions and prepare appropriate SOAR answers (weaknesses, strengths, leadership style, examples, etc.). There are websites that can provide sample questions to become more confident and prepared. Don't forget to send the follow-up thank you email.

Interviewing can be a daunting process for most of us. The best advice I can give is to prepare enough to where you feel confident in speaking about your resume, the company and role, ask certain questions, and understand why you would be a good fit for the role based on applying your skill set. A mentor can also be a great resource for preparation in terms of insight specific to this industry and the role.

Other opportunities to grow your brand and enhance your career development to consider include skill building classes provided by LinkedIn, Udemy, Toastmasters International, EDX.org, Coursera.org and Kaplan Institute. Local county libraries and community colleges also have great resources as they bring in lecturers and company representatives that may provide additional assistance similar to what I noted prior.

There are women's groups and other non-profit organizations that provide assistance with job searches, mock interviews, and counseling. Personal branding and career development are an evolving process. We all need to keep current by learning new skills to elevate our future options for employment and upward mobility. Continuing to network both formally and informally will enhance our sphere of influence and potentially create the connections needed for the next career transition. Studies show that the average Millennium will transfer jobs on average every 3.5 years. That portends to an important ability to redefine one's career objectives, search options and marketing plans, and job changing skills and opportunities.

If you work for a larger company, review your company's benefit program that may provide tuition reimbursement for continuing education and classes related to your position and field. This can help you pay to finish your undergraduate, graduate degree, or certificate program. It is often overlooked and under-utilized. There may be financial support for licenses, memberships for affiliate organizations, and additional career development planning and resource capabilities that you should research.

I have utilized these benefits to obtain my securities and insurance licenses and other membership benefits. The company may offer a mentorship program as well. Many organizations offer volunteer initiatives. Volunteering provides networking opportunities that has helped me and others with our career progression and it may help you as well.

Developing and implementing a brand and professional mission and connecting it into a career vision is critical to your success. You should strive to continuously focus on your branding and investing in yourself, especially when you're younger and have sufficient time to do so. This should lead to a broad successful career that will hopefully reward you with a great salary and benefits to promote your financial plan and priorities. We are CEO's of our own company's, Me Incorporated and head marketer of our personal brand called, YOU!

Have a mission statement that you can articulate and live by. The information provided is only a cursory review of the important elements, resources, tools, and next steps needed. I recommend that you seek out additional books and learning options for many of the components in this section. They will help fill in some of the details regarding your branding and career development, resume building, and provide more guidance on the interviewing process.

Every time you start a new class or go to a meeting or a seminar, introduce yourself to those you sit next to and who are at your table. Remember to get their card or contact information. This will help continuously build your network. As you move on in your career, there may be a need to transition to a different role or career altogether.

The ability to grasp these elements and competencies and be able to move the process forward becomes exponentially more important. As does connecting with a mentor for guidance. This component is one of the six core wellness competencies noted within the chapter on balanced wellness. It is one of the most important due to its correlation with the intellectual and financial wellness competencies as they go hand-in-hand.

Utilizing the strategy of the cycle of achievement and prosperity will help in your planning process. It's your ability to produce a written career vision with an associated timeline and have the positive attitude that will drive the behaviors for the interview process and feed an action plan for your marketing plan and associated networking. A knowledgeable mentor can be the pivotal person who streamlines these processes.

Achieving career success does not only entail hard work but also requires acquiring soft and hard skills. It also entails being passionate and loving what you do. Having this mindset will help you get out of bed every day and be excited about your work. If you are not passionate, it will lead to a less than ideal outcome. Continue to find your passion and build your brand and career upon it.

Social Circle Environment

"We are the average of the 5 people we spend the most time with." — Jim Rohn

It is very important that we choose our friends and close confidants wisely. Those that are close to us and surround us have a significant impact on our overall attitudes, beliefs, goals, habits, and more. We may not necessarily think that this is the case, but studies consistently document that it is. Who is in your inner core social circle? These are people that you confide in, are close friends with, but may not necessarily spend the most time with. What habits, attitudes, and goals do they have and aspire to? Are they positive or negative, proactive or reactive? Do you have any toxic people in this inner core group? These are some of the questions that you should be asking yourself as you reflect on the makeup of your inner core social circle.

We each have a few social circles that we are a part of—one being an inner core, a middle core, and an outer core. Many of us will take a look at our Facebook or Instagram feed and see that we have all of these friends. But in reality, we all know that most of these people fall into our outer core as just followers or people we rarely associate with or don't even know. The true focus of this section is your inner core social circle and to some degree your middle social circle.

Let's take a moment and frame our inner core social circle. Think about the 3-6 people that you relate to the most, spend time with socially, and align yourself with in your "off time." This may or may not include coworkers depending upon their social connection to you.

What type of personal goals, traits, and characteristics do they exhibit as a group? Have you ever given this much thought? I don't think it's a stretch to think that we generally like to spend time with and relate better to those that have similar traits and beliefs as we do. We like to hang out with those who are similar to us.

If we are studious and hardworking, we tend to frown upon and distance ourselves from those that aren't. If we are gamblers, we will spend more time with those that also like to gamble and distance ourselves from those that give us a hard time about this habit. Smokers tend to hang with smokers. When I was in high school and in college, it was apparent which groups were the partiers and which groups were focused on their classes and getting ahead with their education and career development. There were all sorts of other defined groups.

Prompt: Write down these 3-6 people that comprise your inner core social circle and then their most prevalent personal qualities, traits, beliefs and/or characteristics. Write down why you are friends with this person and what they may or may not do for your growth. Are they an advocate or not?

1_____

_____

_____

2_____

_____

_____

3_____

_____

_____

4_____

_____

_____

5_____

_____

6 _____

_____

_____

If you need more room, use the Workbook pages at the back of the guide.

Review what you wrote down for each of these individuals and note any similarities that define most or a majority of them. What are the 3 qualities, traits, similarities and/or characteristics that are most prevalent in all of them and you?

_____

_____

_____

What qualities and traits do you typically look for in determining your close friends?

_____

_____

It has been noted that your core social circle affects your thinking, goals, self-esteem, and decision making among a host of other qualities. That is why surveys of successful and wealthier people convey that they associate with other successful people.

    We should be strategizing on how to associate with people who are more successful than we are. In essence trading up instead of settling. If you want to make a positive change in your life, then you need to evaluate each of your relationships and determine if this person is a beneficial promoter (that can help you grow) or a negative detractor (that will hold you back).

    I think deep down we truly know who these people are and where they land. However, if you want to make it more visible, then try this test: Think about what you wrote down in the long-term goals section of your guide for where you truly want to be in 3-5 years. While spending time with each of these people alone (not in a group setting) mention these goals to them (they should be reasonable SWAT goals).

Once you tell them, listen carefully to their responses and reactions. If your friend says great, those are awesome goals and how can I help, then they are an advocate. If they say, you're crazy or, why would you want that or even care to try, and not offer support or help, then they are probably a detractor and a hindrance. If they say, cool, that's what I'm doing and looking to be in a few years, then that's the person you want at your core! Those first ones may be promoters, but may not have the motivation, planning, and determination that you have. The second group are most likely detractors that you should look to avoid and/or replace. The third group and responses are those individuals that you should have in your inner core circle.

Prompt: Input your core and middle 5-10 friends and confidants on the grid below and articulate based on their mindset and qualities they exhibit. Should they be in or out of the circle?

Name	Growth or Fixed Mindset	Advocate or Detractor	In/Out
1			
2			
3			
4			
5			
6			
7			
8			
9			
10			

Who should be replaced and positioned as more of an acquaintance? Anyone with bad, destructive, or toxic habits should be replaced. _____

_____

_____

"Surround yourself with people who challenge you, teach you, and push you to be your best self." — Bill Gates

Your number 1 in your inner core circle being your best friend, partner or spouse is key. As an example, my wife is a highly motivated, persistent, and confident individual. She has routines and habits that are all wellness based. She exercises regularly, prays often, reads a lot, eats extremely healthy foods (even checking sugar content), is very competitive and career orientated, and is a saver not a spender. She is a type A doer and a growth minded individual. I would suggest that a lot of this has and will continue to rub off on me living with her. These are the qualities that you should be looking for in individuals to challenge you to be your best daily and drive quality results.

Another important consideration regarding our social circle and partners is how you are going to meet and connect with these people. There is a direct correlation between expanding your circle and joining new groups, clubs, and associations to network and build a Board of Advisors and Advocates. These can be searched through online and social media platforms, besides hyper local options.

My wife and I met via the original social media method of the personals in a periodical, so you never know. You must put yourself out there to see where the chips may fall. Challenge yourself to investigate these groups and see how they may improve your development and transform your wellbeing.

You should strive to spend more time with advocates and growth minded people who are more successful than you to pull you up and not keep you down. Think of it like draft day in the majors. You're adding higher quality position players to your roster to make improvements in the overall quality and results of the team. You will seek to remove or demote those that detract from the team's overall success.

Do coaches tend to keep negative influences on the team, even if they have superior skills? Not usually for long, unless they are willing to make the necessary changes. The same applies to your inner core circle. We need to surround ourselves with individuals who can provide us with good vision, best practices, and quality assistance along the way. Seek out those who will push you instead of pull at you. Those that will sacrifice and enhance your team instead of those that create rifts, errors, and a negative tone.

Seeking out a mentor who can replace another less desirable core or key player can be a good starting point. They may be able to act as your pitcher and/or quarterback and help with several aspects of your life. They may act in the capacity of a position player that can help you focus more directly on one aspect of your game of life. Maybe this is related to your financial wellbeing and/or your physical or emotional wellbeing. Find friends who will act as an accountability confidant or a partner who shares similar visions and positive motivational beliefs that you have or are trying to build. Work with them to build similar teams of mentors and trainers for the same end goals and growth. Think of them as your "health buddy" and "money buddy" who will motivate and challenge you just like the mentors. Your goal is a high performance team environment of winners just like a gold medal team.

The next layer of your sphere of influence is your middle circle. These are the individuals in your life that you have contact with but not on a regular basis. They may have some ties to your inner core circle but have not cracked this circle yet or were in your inner core in the past. They generally begin as part of your outer circle to start where there was very little contact, but then began to connect more regularly. They may be a part of a newer group or organization or company that you have connected or contracted with; a friend of a friend or acquaintance. The more we participate in life, the more we open ourselves up to others in our outer and middle circles. Start to make an inventory or list of these middle circle contacts who may have the qualities that warrant them to be considered to be in your future inner core team.

Mentors, coaches, teachers, and other similar growth minded individuals are a good potential fit. As noted prior, it's like drafting new members of your starting team to afford benching some existing members who may have a negative impact that don't align with your vision. These are tough decisions to make, but necessary if we want to improve our chances of success with quality advocates and team players on our side.

Prompt: Who in your middle, or even outer circle, would be a good possible fit for your inner core and WHY?

1 _____
2 _____
3 _____
4 _____
5 _____
6 _____

This is a fluid and continual process for each of us. We all have people come and go in our lives; some we conflict with, some we outgrow, and some stay in our inner core. We just need to make sure that these key individuals in our inner core are there for all the right reasons, not because status quo is easier. Check to make sure you have advocates that have similar high performance expectations that surround you and draft up when necessary. Continue to network to fill your outer and middle circles for future advocates for your inner core circle. Start spending more time with those who truly care about you and your future and wellbeing.

You can use these core and middle circles to build out your Board of Advisors noted in the prior section on mentorship. A few of your buddies may be a good option, and mentors would be a great fit for your board.

If you are one that needs more moral support and finds doing things with partners better suits you, then think about who would be a good mentor for the following competencies:

An accountability partner _____

A workout buddy_____

Your food buddy _____

Your money partner_____

Career mentor _____

An emotional pal_____

A mindfulness or prayer buddy_____

An intellectual coach_____

Social skills coach_____

These are your social teammates and help make up part of your inner core.

    The reality is that those who are close to us in our inner core impact much of what we do and believe. We need to choose wisely who we let into our inner core and determine if some changes need to be made for bettering ourselves by drafting up. We should be continually looking to replace negative, toxic people exhibiting poor choices and destructive behaviors from our core and take action to distance ourselves from them.

    We will review how our social skills play an important factor in how we cultivate these core relationships and how we are perceived by others in a following section on Emotional Intelligence or EQ. Build a team that drives your growth and does not deter it. Always network for new additions to your middle and outer circle to account for future changes. Make sure those closest to you are supporters and advocates for you by creating a high performance team environment that surrounds you. Who you surround yourself with can determine a great portion of your success, wellbeing and destiny.

The Power of Gratitude

"Gratitude is the healthiest of all human emotions!"
— Zig Zigler

I was sitting in my sunroom when a bright red cardinal landed on the windowsill. His colorful red coat and the way he turned his head back and forth were enchanting. As I concentrate on my work and complete this guide, my attention strays out my window to the lilac tree that I planted many years ago and to the colorful azalea bushes in bloom. My favorite color is purple and the lilacs are at peak bloom where the white tips outline the bright purple color. My wife always cuts some for an arrangement. These are the little things in life that often get overlooked. It is our ability to be thankful and grateful for these smaller things in life that make a huge difference.

Being grateful is our self-determined ability that can be easily overshadowed and forgotten about due to the harsh realities of life and disappointments that we may face. I understand that it may be difficult to be grateful when things seem hard to deal with and you are not necessarily at a good place in your life. However, it is important to note that the benefits of being grateful can help you feel and perform better. The University of California Berkeley completed a study and found that when a randomly assigned group of people were told to write a letter of gratitude to another person, they were reported to have significantly better mental health than the other two groups.

Gratitude can be linked back to mindfulness as it takes one's self-reflection and looking at the larger picture of your life to better understand the things that you have to be grateful for. This section will focus on the positives in your life to help condition your mind to be more grateful as we reviewed in the section on emotional wellness. Some information may be redundant for good reason. It's the repetitive nature of the review and routine conditioning that will help us to be more mindful and thankful moving forward.

Personal reflection, which is one of the main tenets of this book, can increase your awareness and gratitude as it helps you to be more mindful and value these basic moments. If we can increase our awareness and mindfulness utilizing some of the tools and techniques and strategies of this guide, we should more easily recognize reasons to be grateful.

If you feel you do not have much to be grateful for, how can we work to change your perception and create quality thankful experiences? Many of us, including myself, seem to take much for granted. Oftentimes, these include: those in our lives that help shape and mentor us. We need to have days of the year devoted to reminding us to give thanks to many of these people in our lives. When was the last time you went out of your way to thank one of these key people in your life without a set day on the calendar?

Prompt: Take a moment to reflect upon who you are truly thankful for. These are the advocates, the ones who've got your back, and have helped you succeed. They do things not because they need to but because they want to. Think of those who have encouraged you to be true to you and be the best you can be. List those who fit these criteria and WHY.

1. _____
2. _____
3. _____
4. _____
5. _____
6. _____
7. _____
8. _____
9. _____
10. _____

Some of the people in your life that may not immediately come to mind are teachers, coaches, mentors, a group leader, family member, manager, coworker, or counselor. Don't discount and overlook those that have impacted you in a positive way and may have helped you during a difficult time in your life.

Prompt: The next step is to connect with these awesome people noted above and take the time to thank them. Explain the importance they hold in your life and the positive impact that they have through a phone call or sending a letter or card. These two simple words, thank you, become very powerful because they allow us to convey and underscore our gratitude. A simple action recognizing their importance and their positive actions will make you feel good or even great! This is you being generous in return and it only takes a few minutes. I encourage you to keep these simple acts of kindness or recognition in your routines as a reminder to what you have to be grateful for.

Studies consistently convey that our ability to focus on the positive and those who exude positive vibes and energy experience less stress, sleep better, and often express kindness and compassion for others. They also usually have better overall mental health and a decreased amount of depression.

Gracious and positive people attract other positive people, thus making it easier to form new connections. People want to be aligned and surrounded by positive people, not negative ones. Along with gratitude comes empathy. We are more sensitive to recognizing people's emotions when we are grateful. Grateful people also tend to exercise more and complete regular doctor's checkups to maintain their overall health. It has also been shown to improve one's self-esteem.

Adding doses of gratitude into our lives may help you to not compare yourself to others. It is tough for many of us to avoid these comparisons. If you are able to avoid it and the potential jealousy it cultivates, it can contribute to your higher self-esteem. This is accomplished by realizing what you have and what you should be grateful for, not what others may or may not have. The benefits are profound and provide for a healthier lifestyle.

There are many ways to add these doses into our daily lives. Gratitude journaling and affirmations are always a great starting point, as is volunteering. Sending a quick thank you note or visiting someone for a big hug are other options. Practice mindfulness by taking a walk, making a blessing over the bread you eat, or celebrating Thanksgiving, Pongal, Diwali, Chuseok, Erntedankfest, Kinrō Kansha no Hi, Sukkot, or Harvest Moon Festival, etc. Why have only one day a year to be thankful, why not make it every day?

Prompt: Another strategy that I added to my daily life is a gratitude jar. Find a jar or small oval candle holder, take small pieces of paper and write down things that you are grateful for. Aim for 20 gratitude affirmations in the holder. During dinner, get in the habit of having someone read an affirmation. This can act as a daily or weekly reminder and sets a great precedent and tone for our younger generation to be grateful in a time of entitlement. It's a time to think about and be mindful of the food on our plates, the roof over our heads, the clean water and air we have to breathe, the clothes on our backs, the land that we cultivate, the health that we have, the love we share, the refrigerator that keeps our food from spoiling, the dishwasher to complete the cycle! The list goes on and on.

I have provided the below affirmations as a starting point for you to fill in and potentially recite as a benefit. One of the key elements of this guide is to convey the importance of visually putting things out in front of you to serve as reminders. It's also about repetition and conditioning. I have also included in the Workbook a similar pullout page for you to place in a well trafficked area. I have a similar one on my bathroom sanctuary mirror. I recite it as my morning mantra and ritual. Try it out and see if it helps you as it does for me.

Gratitude Reminders

I am thankful for the love and affection of my _____ & family.

I am grateful for my good health and fortune.

I greatly appreciate my partner/spouse.

I am thankful for my faith, free will, and independence.

I am thankful for the roof over my head and the food and water that we are blessed with.

I begin today by being thankful for my _____ .

I appreciate the support that _____ gives me.

I am grateful that I can give back to _____ by assisting them with _____ .

I am grateful for my position and/or career.

I truly appreciate _____ for being in my life.

I challenge you to wake up daily and focus in on the things and people that you are grateful for. I like to start my day with a dose of gratitude linked as a twofer to my morning sanctuary routines.

There are several strategies, tools, and techniques that we can use to help us be more mindful and grateful. I encourage you to try some of these, incorporate them into your routines, keep them out in front of you to visualize, and continue to learn other ways to facilitate this beneficial competency. I am grateful for the opportunity to share this guide with you. Every day is a gift and not a given. Live every day like it's your last one and make sure that you thank those that have contributed to it positively over the years.

Overcoming Adversity

Helen Keller is the epitome of someone who was able to overcome multiple adversities. Most of us have read the story of how she as a young infant fell ill and became blind and deaf. At the Perkins Institute for the Blind she received help from her visually impaired mentor and teacher, and was able to learn to communicate by spelling words. She was later able to earn a Bachelor's degree and go on to become a lecturer and author. This is just one great example of how each of us has the inert ability to overcome tremendous odds and adversity.

"A man who cannot tolerate small misfortunes can never accomplish great things." — Chinese proverb

We all face challenges throughout our lives, some big and some small. Problems, rejections, and disappointments are realities of life. We cannot avoid the inevitable; it's how we deal with these issues and situations that makes the difference. Rejection and challenging situations and problems can cause us to have poor self-talk and lower self-esteem. If we replay and focus our attention on revisiting these in our head, it will only create more negative feelings and attitudes and upsetting thoughts. We need to intercept these thoughts and deflect them with more positive ones. I once heard this strategy for dealing with past rejection and disappointment, or as we call it, baggage; we need to drop it, leave it, and not look back.

This section is an attempt to examine how we can react more positively to these adversities and discuss the tools and techniques available to assist in the process regarding the many challenges that life throws our way. Reframing the problem or rejection is one option and creating a problem solving plan of action is another. Having a positive attitude can be a beneficial technique when we are faced with some of these obstacles. Your positive attitude can facilitate your ability to push through many of these difficulties.

Try this: When things go wrong or the unexpected happens, just say; plot thickens and move on.

Sometimes it is not that easy, and we will need a more formal approach. Reframing the rejection into something different and more positive will help considerably. As an advisor who continually reaches out to people to offer my expertise and services, I am constantly rejected on a daily basis. It's par for the course. I remember one day at the office when customers said no to me at least 15 times. Yet, I still got up and met someone else and picked up the phone for the next call. Overcoming these elements entails motivation, determination, and persistence. I overcame these rejections by using a strategy of saying to myself that they were not rejecting me, they were rejecting the process or the options as I reframed the rejection. Don't make it about you if you can, make it about the process, the situation or the circumstance, and take the personal element out of it. It should help by reframing the situation and its outcome and removing the personal element and pain in your thoughts, feelings and reactions.

If you feel bitterness, anger, resentment, stress, avoidance, and unfairness they are normal emotions, but are destructive. It inevitably becomes easier to blame someone else for the situation. Bum Phillips noted that; you fail all of the time; but you aren't a failure until you start blaming someone else. This is a truism.

The ability to reframe the situation and your original thoughts that surfaced are a good first step strategy. Another way you can reframe the situation is to use it as an opportunity to reevaluate what your goal is, how close you are to achieving it, and why this is your goal. Once you take a step back, you may find that the importance and outcome of this goal or circumstance is not as earth shattering as you once thought. It may afford you the ability to seek out and uncover other potential superior options.

Prompt: Describe the biggest and most recent significant obstacles in your life and your specific reactions and actions you took to deal with them. Were they positive or negative? How can you or could you have approached and reframed these differently?

1. _____

2. _____

3. _____

4. _____

5. _____

Abraham Lincoln was another great example of someone who overcame multiple setbacks and adversities. He had many family members pass away at young ages as well as several unsuccessful attempts at winning a congressional seat in addition to other significant setbacks. Lincoln overcame these and other challenges in his life and became very successful in spite of these many adversities. He was persistent and resilient with a plan and process and battled through them to overcome and triumph. We will discuss the tie in to persistence in more detail in the next chapter.

Here is a process and technique that I have used in both my personal and professional work environment to overcome challenges and problems. We need to have a better understanding of the desired outcome we are looking for to then back into the steps that are needed to be taken along the way. Without knowing this outcome, it may become unclear on how to solve the issue. Approach a potential situation or challenge by understanding or knowing what the beneficial outcome is that you desire.

Process for solving problems

Step 1 State the problem

Step 2 State all causes of the problem

Step 3 State desired outcome of the problem to solve

Step 4 Determine possible solutions to the problem

Step 5 Decide on the best solution

Step 6 Plan the action steps to take

Step 7 Schedule and provide timeframe for action steps

Step 8 Reframe and revise plan, solutions, and outcome if it becomes necessary

Charles Swindoll's piece on our reactions guides us to another potential strategy: how you react to situations is more important than what happens. You cannot change the past, but you can change how you react to situations. I challenge you to rethink how you react to these setbacks and see if there are beneficial changes you can make using the techniques available. If you can react in a deliberate more positive, constructive manner, these challenges will not prevent you from reaching your goal.

You can choose to be mindful of the situation by thinking about what outcome you want and how you can best react at that moment to get there. It can be easy to be reactionary in the moment—mad, upset and want to give up—but once you are calm again, think about the process above and the best way to handle the situation in order to move forward.

The opposite of rejection is acceptance. Be mindful to accept the situation and reframe the outcome. Rejection can bring you to a place of self-awareness by way of self-reflection in the moment. Be kind to yourself and surround yourself with positive self-talk. Think about a coach or mentor strategy to provide input about the best way to handle the situation, as well as to keep you calm. Obstacles can be opportunities to learn and evolve. Researchers and studies have concluded that if you are good at facing rejection, it is associated with not pondering on past failures and that you are aiming high and moving forward based on the goals that you set. Disappointment and rejection mean that you are that much closer to your desired outcome.

Prompt: Review the challenges and setbacks that you noted in the prior prompt and how you dealt with them. Reflect on how you might have used one of the following techniques instead to reduce the negative impact and implications to you and your psyche.

- Process problem solving steps by understanding the desired outcome and backing into it.
- Change your reaction and don't take it personally.
- Reframe the situation and your emotions, thoughts, and outcome.
- Be mindful to accept the situation and be kind through self-talk.
- Don't point fingers; use the drop it, leave it, and don't look back method.
- Replace the negative feelings and self-talk with positive ones.
- If there is no alternative, then accept it as "the plot thickens" method and move on.
- Use other emotional hygiene tools like the power of forgiveness.

1_____
2_____
3_____
4_____
5_____

Overcoming adversity is a critical and important competency because it has the ability to affect us and our psyche in so many negative ways. As we move through life, we are constantly being detoured by setbacks, problems, and adversity. How we react and settle on the process steps to take can and will greatly affect our outcome.

There are techniques that we can utilize to reframe the situation and our thoughts, and piece together a more positive result. We should try to minimize the self-doubt, negative self-talk, and internalizing these negative thoughts. We should avoid obsessing over disappointments and failures, and focus on the positive. By facing challenges and succeeding, we gain more confidence. The lessons learned and new ways to deal with adversity will prepare us for the twists and turns of taking on new risks. The most important lesson you can gain from a setback or challenge is understanding what went wrong, how you could have approached it differently, and how you can improve or change the outcome next time as you move forward. It's a lesson learned. Transform your struggles into your strengths.

CHAPTER 9

High Level Competencies

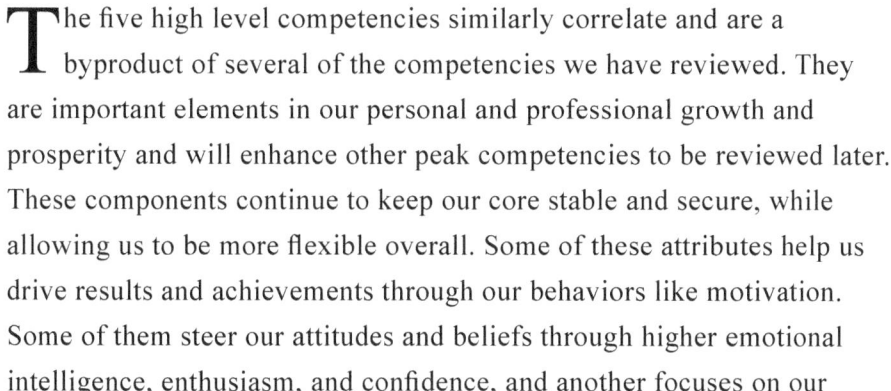

The five high level competencies similarly correlate and are a byproduct of several of the competencies we have reviewed. They are important elements in our personal and professional growth and prosperity and will enhance other peak competencies to be reviewed later. These components continue to keep our core stable and secure, while allowing us to be more flexible overall. Some of these attributes help us drive results and achievements through our behaviors like motivation. Some of them steer our attitudes and beliefs through higher emotional intelligence, enthusiasm, and confidence, and another focuses on our vision to be generous. Each plays a key role in transforming our overall growth and wellbeing.

Motivation

Motivation is a driving force behind goal achievement and success. It is what gets you moving towards your goal. When I want to clean the garden or take on the task of writing this guide, I look to my motivation to have the mindset to begin. Motivation helps start the process and creates a behavior and habit that provides the necessary momentum. Motivation grows out of a growth mindset of a participant. If motivation is lacking, it may be helpful to understand and visualize the WHY impact benefit created by completing the endeavor.

There are two types of motivation regarding psychological elements: intrinsic and extrinsic. Intrinsic motivation is most important when working towards a goal because not every goal has an external reward as extrinsic does. Intrinsic motivation is when you are curious and growth minded and want to perform and be your best for just yourself. Extrinsic motivation is working towards a goal because of the physical reward you receive at the end. It has been found that intrinsic motivation is more effective in helping people reach a goal.

We must intrinsically want a goal to find the motivation to reach the goal. How do we make ourselves want to realize the goal and then take actionable steps? How do we weigh the forces of motivation and procrastination? To me, it seems that these forces come out of having either a growth or a fixed mindset.

I am not a psychologist. For me, it's all about growing and being motivated to get new things done. The opposite is having a fixed mindset where we rationalize our status quo as being okay and then make excuses for why we can't or shouldn't do something. This also correlates to our proactive or reactive nature as similar mindsets. I have a quote on my work laptop that reads: status quo is often the symptom and procrastination is the disease. I bring this up again because it speaks to that fixed mindset.

Let's move from a fixed mindset to a growth mindset in short order. Some ways to transition include knowing and visualizing the WHY behind why you need or want to complete these tasks, plans, and/or projects. Having a strategy like the cycle of achievement will guide you through the process. Taking small actionable steps to get started is also a key initial element. Keep in mind what Confucius said related to taking small steps noted prior.

The key element is visualizing the WHY. It will help to overcome the internal self-talk and self-doubt of rationalizing that we can wait, delay, or forget about doing the task. Take a look at your vision collage, your career vision, and your goals that you jotted down in prior sections. Take a rocking chair moment and understand the impact benefit of becoming motivated to accomplish what you are setting out to do. Seeing the end result is critical to the process just as it is to at times act "as if" you already completed it or have attained what it is that you set out to accomplish.

Once you can see the benefit, create the behaviors and habits that will keep you working towards your goal. It can be difficult to sustain this motivation. So, once the initial excitement of beginning the journey toward a new goal wears off, a resilient set of routines and habits will help you stay motivated.

Do you want to get motivated to complete things you have been putting off? Then unplug your TV, put away your laptop, and only check your phone at set times you have scheduled. Start planning and taking the first small steps for the items on your vision list, and document what you want to accomplish without distractions. Pinpoint what other major distractions are consuming your free time and adjust, adjust, adjust. Every time you feel like procrastinating, think about the consequences and lack of progress and say:

Procrastination is my enemy! Repeat, repeat, repeat!

Prompt: What is/are the most important thing(s) you have been putting off that you need to accomplish? This should be something meaningful as a mid-term or long-term goal. Write down the WHY impact benefit again next to it and the timeframe to complete it. Then, write down the small first step that you will take TODAY to get started on completing it. _____

_____

_____

_____

_____

_____

_____

Stop yourself from saying, maybe later or some other time. Not later, not tomorrow, not next week, NOW! Say, I must, I will, and I have to do this NOW! I remember hearing Tony Robbins say something very fitting that applies here—The road to someday leads to a town called nowhere.

Many individuals speak of getting to a threshold that triggers them to be motivated. This is the inflection point where we realize that it is less painful to complete the task than it is to continue to procrastinate not doing it. The plan should not be to reach this threshold. We can counteract this by planning, believing, and taking small actionable steps and creating routines to complete them.

Motivation is a component that gets us started on a goal so that we can create routines and habits to provide us with momentum. Growth minded participants who are proactive have the competency already tackled, and fixed minded spectators need to better understand how to shake off the status quo and procrastination bug.

Some of the techniques and strategies we have discussed seem relevant for us to use to be successful and gain momentum. Visualizing the impact benefit of WHY you want to complete these tasks is critical.

I encourage you to revisit some of the goals and plans you documented earlier to see if you have made any progress. If not, then this is the last stop in the guide to get you motivated to start, build momentum, and complete them. You don't want to get to a place or threshold where you are in a cold sweat since you have put off the tasks you should have done prior. I know I have been there and don't want to go back, and neither should you.

Generosity

Generosity and kindness can be displayed and communicated in many forms. It can be as simple as a thank you to someone that you're grateful for or a donation to an important charity that may be part of your mission. Whatever the gesture and the size, it makes us feel good, and that is an important consideration for our wellbeing.

Most of us have been told since we were young that we should give back, volunteer, and be generous. We should explore the benefits we receive that improve our wellbeing by giving of ourselves. Research by UCLA Bedari Kindness Institute has shown that we mutually benefit from these kind acts both emotionally, as well as physiologically. Acts of kindness have a self-serving upside benefit based on these findings, and it doesn't entail getting out your checkbook.

Simple acts of kindness and recognition can ease stress and anxiety and make us healthier. Mindfulness of our gratitude or positive associations, combined with generosity, can create and sustain our wellness environment. The UCLA and a similar Stanford study confirms the increased amount of biochemical activity that may alter certain behaviors of our genes to beneficially assist in protecting us. Similar research also confirm that being generous and kind to others helps promote neurochemicals, which have the ability to stimulate our brain and elevate our mood.

We tend to think of giving in a material sense like money, gifts, or goods. These studies also show that generosity of the heart and mind can be as beneficial and transformative. We discussed forgiveness as an emotional hygiene tool earlier. Reflect on how this word includes the word "give" in the middle. If we forgive someone or avoid judging, blaming, or holding a grudge against someone it will provide a healthy benefit and outcome. Give the gift that keeps on giving and keeps you from stress and anxiety and forgive! I have had to struggle with this as situations in my early years have haunted me for decades and more recently I have been able to forgive. It has helped my mindset and wellbeing immensely.

Volunteering is closely associated with generosity. It only requires a portion of your time, and only has to be as big a part of your life as you want. Organizations that can use your help and that I have volunteered locally for include Habitat for Humanity, several local food banks, and the Girls and Boys Clubs of America. I was able to involve my children and coordinated volunteer groups from work to pitch in. Together, we helped build homes for deserving families, packaged bags for the less fortunate, and painted buildings for the groups and clubs. I align myself with these organizations because of their missions as they align with mine.

As noted earlier, my daughter volunteered regularly. Each week she would set aside a day at college to give back to her community. She helped low income families complete their tax returns, and she completed a certification course while gaining expertise in her field of study. Donating her time was the right option for her and a true benefit. Think about volunteering as a networking and skill building initiative. I met and hired an individual that happened to connect with me through one of the volunteer events that I had sponsored. I also know individuals who volunteered for an organization and ended up working for them later on.

Prompt: Think of someone or a non-profit organization that you may have ties to or coincides with your mission that could use a helping hand. Find a way to be generous with your time, kindness, energy, or donation. Write down your plans to give back with a timeline for the task and its impact benefit.

___

___

___

___

Being generous can come in many forms, some which require time, some may require money, and some may require resources. Let's segment potential generosity into three different levels: simple acts, medium sized giving, and large acts of kindness and generosity.

Simple acts of kindness can come in the form of forgiveness, offering a helping hand to a neighbor who is ill and alone, baking something for a new neighbor on your block, listening to someone who needs help, paying it forward like a cup of coffee for a first responder, thanking a veteran for his/her service, writing a letter to a veteran or someone on the holidays, and/or thanking or recognizing someone for his/her help and support.

Medium acts of generosity may include: volunteering for a few days at a local non-profit, helping someone with a project at work if they are behind, donating food to a local food bank, driving a senior who needs a ride, volunteering to coach a team or event.

Larger acts of kindness and generosity may include: volunteering regularly at an organization or school, donating regularly to an organization, becoming a trusted mentor in your field, setting up a volunteer group at your school or organization, or committing to a longer term obligation to help out. All of these acts of kindness create good will and a feeling of fulfillment. They afford us the ability to not only help others by giving, but also helping ourselves to network and meet new people, learn new skills, feel better by elevating our mood, and contribute to our overall wellbeing. That's more than a twofer!

Prompt: Think about a simple way you can be kind, a mid-sized opportunity to give back, and a larger way to be generous. Provide a timeframe for each of these acts of generosity for you to adhere to. Think about a good fit for the larger option in terms of your mission and their's, as well as their focused initiative.

Simple one in 7 Days _____

Mid-sized one over the next 60 days _____

Larger one over the next 3-6 months _____

Generosity is a great opportunity to help others and help yourself. We gain so much by cultivating relationships and connections through simple to larger acts of kindness and recognition. We should all strive to do more to help others instead of being consumed often with ourselves (and that goes for me as well).

Acts of generosity, no matter how large or small, can make us feel better and happier, can potentially assist with opportunities to network, skill-build, and promote our overall positive mindset, health, and wellbeing. I encourage you to seek out opportunities in your area and help make a difference to those in your community whose mission and initiative aligns with yours. Connect with organizations like Volunteer America, United Way, Red Cross, Salvation Army, Boys & Girls Clubs of America, Habitat for Humanity, St. Jude Hospital, local food banks, community based opportunities, sports teams, and clubs to name a few.

EQ Emotional Intelligence

Emotional intelligence (EQ) is an important skill to develop and utilize when it comes to dealing with our own emotions and helping to improve our relationships with others. It takes time and understanding to develop since it requires insight into our own unique feelings and responses and an ability to better understand others. It encompasses the ability to also have a good overall sense of awareness.

Your EQ is the level of ability you have to "read" yourself and others and have a "sixth sense" of feeling or reading what's going on without it being verbalized by others. There is a distinct difference between having social and emotional intelligence, and the well-known intellectual intelligence quotient or IQ.

There are a few elements that make up one's EQ. The first being emotional awareness or self-awareness where we recognize our emotions as they are unfolding. This is the process of tuning into or reading your own and/or other's emotions and feelings. Mindfulness techniques and the ability to evaluate your's and other's emotions plays an important role as the process to uncover these feelings.

We will review as we did in the section on beliefs and attitudes how we can use mindfulness to stretch the time between an action and our reaction. This will allow us time to react in a more positive way that aligns better with the emotions of those we are dealing with at that moment in time.

If we are able to pause and evaluate ours and other's emotions, then we can apply the techniques needed to manage them effectively. The next element of applying emotional intelligence is regulating our own emotions and our reaction to others and involves how we need to self-regulate and be empathetic to others and have self-compassion for ourselves. This strategy is completed by the continuation of emotional management skills to continue to develop and increase our EQ through good interpersonal social or "people skills."

The process begins with needing to tune into our own and other's emotions. Then we need to regulate our emotions by creating space and time between what is unfolding and our reaction to it. Lastly, we need to be able to manage and enhance these processes through learning and practice of our social skills.

In today's complex world, and especially in today's business environment, it is more critical than ever that we enhance our ability to be able to read and understand other people and coworkers' feelings, what motivates them, and how we can coexist and/or work with them effectively. We will touch on the need to have a high self-concept that includes a higher level of self-confidence and self-esteem in a later section that coincides with one's EQ.

As discussed, the ability to recognize emotions as they are happening, regulate them, and manage them utilizing mindfulness techniques is important to one's EQ success. Regulation and management of these negative emotions or difficult situations and angry confrontations comes with self-control utilizing mindfulness to stretch out the distance between the initial development and our reaction to it.

This may be accomplished by blowing off some steam on a walk, exercising, deep breathing, and other similar techniques. An ability to have empathy for others and to recognize how they feel with a sixth sense in reading someone is also an important trait. Knowing what to do and what to say to better assimilate into different group social situations is a valuable skill. These social skills will enhance our capabilities in dealing with others and groups of people including co-workers. Other interpersonal skills that we should look to enhance include communication, the ability to influence, negotiate, lead and collaborate with others. All of these help in different social situations. Many of these skills can be practiced, developed and enhanced through learning and mindfulness techniques.

There is an old Chinese proverb—He who treads lightly, goes far. Be careful not to criticize others as it will not be received well. Instead, look for common ground and understanding. Be mindful of their feelings and self-regulate your own responses and feelings.

Prompt: Mindfulness practice is a key technique and strategy that can be used with several of the competencies in the Structure and Building Blocks of Achievement and Prosperity. Practice this by taking a walk and being mindful of all that surrounds you. Then, sit on the floor in a quiet environment with no distractions and start deep breathing exercises while relaxing your jaw, arms, and legs. Mindfully focus on your breathing to relax.

When eating dinner, use your less dominant hand and be mindful of every bite while chewing slowly. This is the beginning of transitioning this routine to a social situation where you can slow down your reaction and response time as you are mindful of other people's emotions. Spend 20-30 minutes on these three activities and perform them regularly until you can become mindful and self-aware. Then, you can self-regulate your responses and reactions.

Why does emotional intelligence matter? There is a common belief that smart and hardworking individuals will be successful. However, psychologists have found that IQ only accounts for around 10% of the ingredients needed for success, while much of the rest comes from your EQ. A high EQ has also been shown to make people more innovative and have higher job satisfaction.

If you can effectively control your own emotions, while reading others to provide the best response to their emotions, you are golden. People are more likely to work with you and help you if they think you are empathetic and understanding. Possessing these qualities will help with your social skills, career, and personal development.

Do you have high EQ? Mark each with a 1 if a "yes" and you are and a 0 if "no" and you're not:

_____ Are you a good judge of character?

_____ Do you have a sixth sense to understand other people's emotions and their thoughts?

_____ Are you empathetic toward others and their situation?

_____ Are you self-confident and difficult to offend?

_____ Do you stop negative thoughts when they persist and don't get overwhelmed with your emotions?

_____ You are comfortable in group social situations.

_____ You are kind to yourself in your self-talk and have high self-esteem.

_____ You don't dwell on past problems.

_____ You watch what you say before you say it.

_____ You don't get flustered when someone says something negative about you.

_____ You don't react quickly and in kind when someone jumps down your throat.

_____ You are able to forgive and forget and not hold a grudge.

What does your score add up to? This is an informal test adapted from a longer formal test. It's a simple approach to being aware if you have high EQ and ways that you can change and adapt to increase your score in the future. My score added up to 8; I was strong on the front 7 and weak on the back 5; you be the judge.

Here are a few social skills I have learned over time:

- When you meet someone, be interested in that person and his/her story.
- Smile when you meet him/her as it leaves a good impression.

- Say the other person's name as it will help you remember it (I have a tough time with this).

- If you want to discuss someone's faults or shortcomings, provide two positive attributes or traits first, and then discuss his/her shortcomings.

- Spend time asking others about themselves. Confident people are open to learning about others and people love to talk about themselves.

I was at a wedding many years ago for my wife's coworker. We were sitting at a table with a few strangers who didn't really know many people there and neither did I. As we ate, I asked the couple next to me about themselves, where they were from, where they grew up, their family, occupation, etc. I always find it interesting to gain an understanding of where people were born and raised and how they got to where they live now (I think it's from my appraisal days). The conversation went on for some time.

The next workday, my wife came home and mentioned that her coworker and husband thought I was the nicest guy at the wedding. I kind of wondered why they thought that for some time and just passed it off as I was willing to converse with them. I think it is more based on the fact that I was genuinely interested in them and that people love to talk about themselves. I have come to use this technique in my sales role to find common ground when I meet people. It works.

Prompt: The next time you meet someone for the first time in a relaxed setting, take the time to ask them several questions about themselves. Don't dwell on you and your story. Engage them in conversation about themselves with follow-up questions and see if you build an emotional connection with them.

By utilizing some of the techniques and tips, such as mindfulness of our own and other's emotions, being interested in others, and giving others the benefit of the doubt, your emotional intelligence will grow with self-awareness, regulation, and management. Using mindfulness and breathing techniques will assist in stretching out the timeframe between any trigger event and your reaction to it by taking a step back and drawing out the timeframe between the two.

Practice these important interpersonal social skills like being empathetic to others and their situation and gaining a sixth sense about a situation and the social environment you are in. Much of our success, especially in the workplace, depends on understanding those around us and reacting appropriately based on that understanding. It is helpful to forgive and forget, not point the finger or call someone out, even though this may be difficult at the time. However, it will pay dividends later on in terms of good will.

Emotional intelligence is a competency that is important to both your personal and professional life. Being able to understand emotions as they play out is a powerful tool to have in your toolbox.

Confidence

Confidence, in its simplest form from its Latin origin, means "to trust." Therefore, having self-confidence is having trust in one's self. Confidence is a belief in yourself and your abilities. Self-confidence factors into your EQ. Psychologists have found that confidence comes from the belief that you have the ability to complete an action, reach a goal and feel that you will achieve it. Having self-confidence and high self-concept, which additionally includes having high self-esteem, puts you at or near the bullseye of the target reviewed earlier. With every new achieved vision and accomplishment comes added belief in your self-confidence to try something new and potentially something more difficult and challenging.

I have provided several emotional hygiene tools throughout the book related to enhancing your psyche, maintaining a positive vibe and demeanor. These include conditioning yourself with positive affirmations and mindfulness. Surrounding yourself with coaches, mentors, advocates, and buddies that challenge you to emotionally cleanse and confidently be your best and take on new and exciting challenges is also a step in the right direction. Having other people who help and support you should provide you with the positive reinforcement that "if other people believe in me, I believe in myself too."

There seems to be a direct correlation between confidence and courage. Having courage and fear at times are inevitable. Our ability to be courageous in light of adversity or fear with positive beliefs and faith to take small actionable steps is critical for success. Fear is the negative voice in the back of our head adding doubt to our thoughts. The stronger the belief and faith, the easier it is to meet fear head on with courage and confidence. Easier said than done.

A study on athletic teams found a direct correlation between player and coach confidence and performance of the team. When the coach and players had confidence in their ability to win, they generally did perform well. However, the results also showed that with decreases in coach and player confidence, the team subsequently did not perform as well. There is a correlation between believing you can win or achieving goals and the goals coming to fruition.

Prompt: How would you rate your self-confidence on a scale of 1-10; with 1 being having high self-confidence? _____

List some things you are most fearful of and WHY; public speaking, group situations, confrontations, competition, animals, driving over bridges... List some ways that will help you gain more confidence.

_____

_____

_____

_____

_____

If you are well informed, prepared, and motivated to achieve a goal, you will be more confident in your abilities to reach your goal. Acquiring the skills necessary and noted in the personal and career development section is one key to setting yourself up for greater self-confidence and success.

William James's strategy of, if we act as if we are confident by how we dress, stand, and present ourselves, we will feel more confident seems very relevant here. If we act in a negative way, then a lack of confidence follows.

Prompt: Stand up now for a minute. Place your legs 1-2 feet apart, push back your shoulders and chest out, place your chin up and hands in front of you with fingers touching each other, and breathe deeply and slowly. Do you feel more confident with this power pose? Remember back to the section on career development and walking into an interview with specifics on body language. It speaks volumes about you and your confidence. Take notes and practice the power stance.

When I was a market manager, I was asked by my manager to attend a meeting the next day and present an introduction to a new initiative we were implementing. I prepared enough so that I felt confident that I would represent and communicate the initiative and information well. The size of the audience was never initially discussed. When I arrived at the hotel lobby early and met the liaison, I asked how large an audience there was as I heard a large round of applause. The ballroom doors opened to a packed room of approximately a few hundred people. Without courage and confidence and proper preparation, I may have just melted on the spot. I realized then why my boss had asked me to attend in his place.

Prompt: What is a specific area of your personal or professional life where you feel you lack the most confidence and is it holding you back from your true potential? Provide the WHY and an action plan for improving this.

_____

_____

_____

_____

_____

Confidence is built on consistency and conditioning. Your growth in confidence is a byproduct of acquiring the necessary skills to improve, having a positive belief that you have the ability to achieve the goal, and putting an action plan in place. It's all in our head. I encourage you to use the prompts above while also reviewing the Workbook pullout on positive affirmations to help condition your mind.

Seek out a coach or mentor and discuss how you can make improvements. Diminishing self-doubt and negative self-talk is a huge step in retraining your mind to believe you can do anything. Preparation, preparedness, motivation, and to some degree enthusiasm, will assist with building self-confidence. Courage also plays an important role in having confidence to overcome one's fears.

William James notes that if we "act as if" we are confident and present ourselves in this way, we will be more inclined to reach this frame of mind. Self-confidence has a direct correlation to performance and success. This is an important competency to improve and master because confidence parlays into high self-concept. If you see yourself in a positive, successful light, you will be more likely to achieve your goals. I know you can get to where you want to be in your life but you need to have the confidence to take risks, stay engaged, and be motivated to achieve your goals, no matter how big the fear or how difficult the challenges may presently seem.

Enthusiasm

Enthusiasm is similar to having vitality and zest. It's approaching your life with excitement and energy and living your life like it's an adventure yet to be experienced. When we run into people who are enthusiastic, it seems like they are on cloud 9 and have a greater sense of feeling alive. By being in their presence, their enthusiasm becomes contagious.

People who are very enthusiastic seem to exude a higher level of energy and optimism about the future. They generally retain the thinking that good fortune, success, and prosperity are within their control and their grasp. It aligns with growth minded individuals who are curious and open to experiencing new things.

If you are enthusiastic about wanting to work towards your goal and are excited about what achievement and success have to offer, then you are more likely to begin those initial first steps. Having a positive attitude enhances this mindset and encourages you to be more enthusiastic toward this journey. My vision is to inspire you to ignite some enthusiasm in you to continue working and reaching for your visions. Enthusiastic individuals seem to visualize and better understand the WHY impact benefit of being the way they are, more so than the rest of us, including, to some degree, myself.

Prompt: How would you describe your overall level of enthusiasm, high or low and WHY?

_____

_____

_____

_____

_____

Enthusiasm affects those around you. I noted prior that my coworker's enthusiasm was contagious and made me feel optimistic too. Exuding enthusiasm allows you to be a leader, innovator, and naturally a person that others gravitate towards because you convey positive energy. People associate an enthusiastic person with having a solid mental and physical state and having his/her life in order. Not everyone wants to be a leader or innovator, but enthusiasm is a trait that allows you to make that possible.

Here are some techniques to generate enthusiasm:

- Vision planning by transferring your goals into writing and picture format, should get you excited about what you can accomplish.
- Conditioning your mind by following the techniques in prior sections.
- Developing a more positive attitude.
- Find the WHY to understand the impact benefit to you to set the process in motion to complete the vision. Understanding how this goal can potentially change your life and why it is important to you is critical.
- Ask for support and help from your inner core social advocates. If you can attract positive and enthusiastic people to your inner core, they will encourage you to be enthusiastic, as well as motivated.

Prompt: When you wrote down your visions and goals in the beginning of this journal, which one were you most excited about? Now that some time has passed, what can you do to continue the excitement and spark enthusiasm about this goal?

_____
_____
_____

Enthusiasm and confidence are two competencies that seem to complement each other. They can often go together because if you are enthusiastic to complete a task, you are most likely confident in your abilities. If you are enthusiastic, you will stay motivated and continue working towards your ultimate goal. Enthusiasm can also counteract procrastination. I encourage you to look at enthusiasm as a way of attracting the people you want to be surrounded by because being an enthusiastic, positive person attracts similar types of people. Enthusiasm can be and is contagious!

Your attitude and enthusiasm for the goals you are working towards are important competencies to help you develop others, such as persistence and motivation. I am enthusiastic about what you can accomplish by utilizing this guide effectively for your future and wellbeing.

CHAPTER 10

Peak Competencies

The final level in the Structure and Building Blocks of Achievement and Prosperity encompasses the peak competencies. These attributes and abilities compliment others within the lower levels. They also correlate to similar themes and techniques within these competencies and share some of the same tools and resources to allow you to improve, grow, and prosper. They inevitably help us become more flexible while providing the necessary support and structural integrity necessary. They include: taking on opportunistic timing and risk, being genuine and having integrity, developing a higher self-concept, adapting to change, and having the persistence necessary to drive the confidence and enthusiasm to succeed. They round us out and provide guidance for the future.

Opportunistic Timing and Risk

Opportunities come to those who are prepared to make a change. Preparation is a prerequisite for opportunity. One of the reasons I have stressed the importance of planning is for you to always be ready to take the next step in your life and/or career. You never know when an opportunity will arise. However, if you try and capitalize on an opportunity with no prior preparation, you will generally be less effective in making the changes that are necessary.

How do we know when the timing is right to take on these opportunities? This is a very tough question to answer. It is something that comes from your gut. If you feel that it is the right time to take advantage of the opportunity then you should do it. I note this as long as you have evaluated the situation properly and done your due diligence and understand the risks. I am also referencing back to the planning process to reintroduce a strategy that you should be utilizing to evaluate these risks and timing.

Whether you are starting a business or making a career change, bringing a product to market or buying a property, a business plan, development plan, and risk analysis are critical to your success. You want to capitalize on the timing and risk only after you have completed the planning, testing, and proper evaluation of an opportunity.

In real estate and in business, this is called a market evaluation, analysis, and appraisal. When taking on risk, one should always, at a minimum, perform a due diligence review and analysis. If you have your planning, analysis, and due diligence in place, then by the time an opportunity comes along that fits your interests and priorities, you should have a good understanding if it's a good fit based on the timing and associated risks.

Here are a few ways to move forward with an opportunity. Networking can be a way to prepare for opportunities. As reviewed in the personal and career development section, a high percentage of people receive job offers through the connections made directly through their network. Great opportunities may come to you by way of people who are in your inner core or middle circles, advisory board, or sphere of influence. Especially if those relationships are valuable and with high caliber individuals. That is why successful individuals want to connect and network with other successful individuals. Many high-level executives and political candidates play golf and join clubs to network with other successful and wealthy people.

Another suggestion is to utilize a mentor and/or coach to guide you through the process of building confidence with a growth mindset. This mindset will contribute to success because you will be in the right mental state to understand and evaluate opportunities as they arise. Many of the other competencies will also prepare you for this decision.

Risk is a calculated evaluation of the potential negative impacts or dangers of taking a certain action. Planning and evaluating the risks (and there are many) are necessary for the actionable event. There have been times when I did not assess the risk properly or due my due diligence and ended up with a poor outcome. The following is one time when I did do the analysis and due diligence and assessed it correctly and capitalized on the opportunistic timing.

Toward the end of 2008 during the depths of the financial crisis, I was working as an appraiser. Prior to this, I realized that there were significant changes happening and planned for a potential change in occupation. As the recession deepened and the appraisal workflow basically came to a trickle, I made a calculated decision about what I should do moving forward. After reviewing the current environment and analyzing the numbers and potential growth trajectory of the business, it seemed to me that the business model and career opportunity were deteriorating. As much as I enjoyed the vocation, interacting with new people, and seeing new properties daily, the associated risks and the loss of income were overwhelming. As I evaluated the overall situation and landscape, I realized a significant change needed to be made in my career. It was stressful and a tough decision to make, especially in light of having two young children and dealing with multiple adversities at the time.

The risk I took was changing my career by looking at the landscape to determine what I was able to do with my skillset. Since I was very good with numbers and followed the financial markets for decades and always thought I should have tried to work on Wall Street, I thought becoming a financial advisor was a good viable option.

I researched positions and necessary certifications and experience as I networked with my sphere of influence. I discussed this potential change with my wife, friends, and a few acquaintances I knew who were successful advisors for some time. I trained with a broker and studied for my certifications while working part-time as an appraiser and for an estate planning company. This was a seven day a week endeavor.

It was mid 2009 when the financial market began to recover, and I was coaching baseball with one of these advisors. He mentioned that his prior broker that he trained and worked for was always looking for good quality trainees, and that I should call him for an interview.

Networking through my sphere of influence as a volunteer coach landed me my first financial advisory position. My motivation, good fortune, and opportune timing subsequently helped me to become a Registered Supervisory Principal and successfully manage large teams of advisors during a great advisory career. It wasn't an easy transition, but with motivation, planning, confidence and persistence, I was able to complete my licenses and training. This is just one example of an ability to capitalize on opportunistic timing and risk. The timing was right as many advisors were exiting the business and the risk reward ratio was also favorable.

Prompt: Write down a time in your life when you took advantage of an opportunity. Maybe it was with a career option, friend group, partner, business opportunity, or investment. Were you successful or not and was the timing and risk optimal? Did you do the proper research, planning, and due diligence?

___

Prompt: What aspect of your life today could be the opportune time to make a significant change? Maybe it's a major, career, friend group, physically challenging or financial opportunity. Write down what it is, what planning and due diligence are necessary, and the pros and cons of the opportunity and risk. Do you believe you are prepared to take this on? If you are not prepared mentally, physically, and motivationally then what can you start doing today to be prepared for this calculated risk? Provide details on the WHY impact benefit, timeline, and plan.

___

Risks come with the possibility of a negative outcome and it is unsettling to think about a potential disappointing outcome. However, change is necessary but we often avoid it to keep the status quo intact. This can be with our current job or career, investing in the market, or even asking someone out on a date. We evaluate the risk versus the possible reward in our head.

Your ability to take on risk is often dependent on your confidence, motivation, and ability to overcome the adversity of a negative outcome. We need to have the confidence and mindset to take on these opportune risks if the timing is right based on our due diligence. We also need the self-confidence to bounce back if things don't go as planned.

Opportunistic timing and risk are peak competencies that are important steps in reaching your highest potential. The ability to recognize opportunities at the right time and take on the risk to seize these opportunities are skills which can prove useful.

As you can see from my example, risk is often a necessary part of our personal and professional lives. This is a calculated change or action that involves pursuing an opportunity after proper consideration, planning, due diligence, and preparation are completed. We have to prepare ourselves for the possibility of a negative outcome. As I have stressed previously, I encourage you to prepare and analyze your growth plan so that when a beneficial opportunity arises, you have the basis for effectively implementing and capitalizing on it at the right time with minimal risk on your road to success.

Genuine & Integrity

Being genuine and having integrity are directly related to having a high degree of emotional intelligence. These attributes incorporate having a strong foundational understanding of your own ethics and tie into being generous, grateful, and courageous, and being able to admit fault. Being genuine is similar to being authentic and transparent. People often need to feel that you are genuine and not superficial to be responsive and confide in you. I think it is a common misconception that being genuine is just about being kind to people as there is a lot more to consider. Integrity is speaking the truth, living by the golden rule, and presenting oneself in an authentic way. It is the ability to treat all people equally with respect and fairness without letting personal biases interfere. Those with integrity have a sense of loyalty to others and their inner social circle and groups that they are a part of.

We must find it within ourselves to embody having integrity and being genuine in order for people to truly trust us. Trust is a very important factor in our personal and professional relationships. These attributes and traits have been shown to be important leadership qualities. I encourage you to understand how these traits can improve your relationship building social skills and your influence on others.

Emotional intelligence pertains to the ability to relate to people around you and behaving in a way that takes other people's emotions into account. Without being genuine, your emotional intelligence is lowered.

Other traits that are important are being trustworthy, generous, respectful of others, and loyal. Genuine people with integrity don't pass judgement of others, aren't hypocritical and are open-minded. They use techniques and strategies like mindfulness to guide their own internal compass of beliefs, values, and attitudes. They aren't materialistic, don't worry about what others think, and don't brag about themselves as they are confident in their results and achievements. They set good examples and aren't swayed by the mob. Discussed in prior sections, they don't blame others for their situation, they are forgiving, kind, honest, and keep their word. Most of these traits are embedded in the previous discussions and competencies. The bigger challenge is bringing them together to ensure that you are genuine with your intentions and continue to exhibit integrity.

Lastly, and equally important to being genuine, is the ability to connect with people on a personal level. This is tough to quantify, and it is an X factor that also encompasses multiple underlying traits. They include: making adequate eye contact when speaking, nodding to show agreement, having big ears (as we call it in sales) and letting others speak and vent.

It's about asking others questions about themselves and not continually harping on yourself and your own situation. It's about the EQ and confidence not to judge and brag. Moreover, it's about putting your phone down when others are confiding in you. Checking your phone when others are entrusting you with their intimate feelings and emotions shows that you lack integrity and aren't genuine.

I remember when I had tried to open up to a friend regarding some important intimate details of a situation and my friend was glancing at his phone. Because of this, I lost the confidence and trust that he had my best intentions in mind. Take notice of this as it is critically important and is a difficult habit for many of us to break!

When I think of someone who is genuine and has integrity, I think of influential people like Gandhi and Martin Luther King Jr. They were of high moral character, were always true to their personal beliefs and values, and kept their word. They were influential leaders because people trusted them as they exhibited so many quality characteristics, traits, and competencies. They were generous, loyal, and led by setting a strong example of honesty and integrity.

Prompt: Think about your own moral compass and many of the characteristics and qualities noted. Which 3-5 traits do you exhibit, and which 3-5 traits do you need to focus and work on to be more genuine and have integrity? Remember the phone issue…

1 exhibited_____

2 exhibited_____

3 exhibited_____

1 to work on _____

2 to work on _____

3 to work on _____

Others _____

_____

One great mantra is to live by the golden rule and do unto others what we would have others do unto us. We should obey this rule by developing these characteristics and strive to positively influence the people around us, just as you want the people around you to positively influence you.

    My hope is that some of these recommendations will allow you to act in a way that makes people want to be around you more often. William James notes that by acting "as if" we were like this already; we will gain the feeling that we are.

    Act as if you are genuine, trustworthy, non-judgmental, kind, honest, generous, grateful, and loyal. Being genuine and having integrity can attract other similar high caliber people to you, which in turn enhances your inner core circle and makes you better emotionally fit to grow and prosper. I encourage you to look at your inner core circle and determine who among them is of high integrity and who are genuine. We examined this prior regarding other qualities. Note that we are the average of the five or so people who are closest to us. Therefore, they can have an effect on your own integrity and genuineness. We need to incorporate these qualities into our everyday lives in order to effectively embody them and gain the trust of people around us. Challenge yourself to become more genuine by better connecting with others and having integrity at all times.

High Self Concept

Self-concept in a nutshell is how I feel about who I am. It encompasses a general notion of self-awareness through self-reflection about your identity and self-image. It was first discussed and documented by William James in his book, Principles of Psychology in the chapter on "Consciousness of Self" that identified "I am me." Having high self-concept can take on different meanings but generally involves the convergence of two elements. These include: having high self-esteem with high self-efficacy, or in laymen's terms, high self-confidence.

Self-esteem is how we see ourselves overall and our evaluation of ourselves. Self-confidence is how we view our abilities or capabilities as in our level of performance. In a broader sense, your self-concept is the set of beliefs and attitudes you hold about yourself and answers the question, "who am I?" High self-concept comes from holding yourself to a higher standard with high levels of self-compassion and self-esteem. It provides the benefit of helping you journey through life with confidence. It also incorporates many of the elements of prior competencies.

Having a positive attitude about oneself is important to our perception of ourselves and our overall self-esteem. Self-concept also incorporates a subset of self-esteem directed toward our perception of our identity; both of our physical self and our social environment. Our physical identity or our image of our body plays an important factor in our self-esteem and how we assess it overall.

I know each of us continually evaluates our own body image, sometimes to a point of obsession. Our society's focus on looks, appearance, and perfect body type does not help our own self-esteem and often provides unrealistic expectations. Just as we reviewed how to take on negative triggers and challenges in prior sections on emotional wellbeing, so to do we need to counteract the unrealistic images bombarding us daily of the perfect body types. It is tough not to compare our bodies to others, but it is often self-defeating.

The use of mindfulness to help create positive self-awareness and internal dialogue or a positive inner voice is key. Positive self-concept journaling and affirmations are other techniques to utilize to counteract these negative thoughts, attitudes, and feelings. It's a battle of the mind that pits two opposing forces against each other to see who has the willpower and persistence to win.

The assistance of these techniques, your inner circle, coaches, and mentors can help move the momentum in your favor toward the bullseye and more positive self-esteem and attitudes. Not utilizing these will allow negative self-talk to fester and slowly deteriorate your cornerstones and foundation to a point of affecting your whole.

Prompt: How would you rate your overall self-esteem when it comes to evaluating yourself and how you feel about yourself? Use a scale of 1-10 with 1 being high and 10 being low. _____

Since you read the section on conditioning your mind, what tools and techniques have you incorporated into your daily routines by now to lower this score? What steps can you take to develop a more positive impact on your overall self-concept and self-image?

_____
_____
_____
_____
_____

How can you enlist the help of your inner core circle and other coaches, groups, and mentors to assist? _____

_____

Review the sections on beliefs, attitudes, conditioning mind, learning, and confidence for reinforcement of what these battlegrounds encompass and how to make a more positive impact on your thinking and mindset. It is important to set realistic goals for yourself. You must have the positive belief in your abilities to gain momentum and propel you toward a more positive and higher self-concept. A realistic action plan will help you gain the confidence needed to succeed. It's a battle of your will.

We reviewed the notion of reframing obstacles and setbacks to have a more positive outcome. Many setbacks we encounter help us become more effective and efficient to reach our goals based upon the lessons we learn. We have the ability to be more self-aware of what changes can be made to improve our self-concept. Positive self-talk and affirmations are useful techniques for higher self-concept and confidence building. It is useful to say the affirmations and visualize yourself accomplishing these goals, and the impact benefit of what your life will look like after this accomplishment. Many athletes use self-talk to put themselves in the right frame of mind before a big game.

Overcoming negative thoughts encompasses understanding what is causing these unwanted and misdirected thoughts, evaluating their validity, coming up with a solution, and implementing the solution to combat doubt. Emotional hygiene techniques like positive self-talk and journaling are great strategies for instilling a positive outlook and self-image and becoming more confident in your abilities.

We need to find ways to counter and challenge the negative thoughts we have after setbacks by identifying why the thought might not be true and potentially reframing it. We should be treating our self with self-compassion, care, and understanding that we are not perfect. The use of positive self-talk, journaling, verbalizing affirmations, reframing situations, and visualization techniques to improve confidence and self-esteem are an investment in ourselves that can afford us the ability to reassure our mind with positive thoughts, feelings, attitudes and confident abilities.

Prompt: Think of some constant negative and doubtful thoughts you have, what your inner voice is saying when they enter your mind and write them down. Maybe it's, "I'm not good enough, I won't succeed, I am not smart enough." Next, come up with 1 or 2 lines of positive self-talk or affirmations you could have said to yourself like, "I decided to tackle this positively; I am good enough, I will be successful," Meet each negative with 1 or 2 positives. Lastly, spend some time visualizing yourself successfully being or completing whatever it is that you were doubtful about and reframing the outcome. Refer to the target for additional ideas and support.

I have confidence that I will

_____

I am positive and confident that I will

_____

I will be self-assured that I can

_____

I know that is not the case since I was successful prior with

_____

I know that I am not perfect and will learn from this setback that

_____

I have decided to stop comparing myself to others as it's not healthy

_____

I think it's important to review certain considerations that parents may want to incorporate into developing self-esteem and confidence in their children. Recently, there has been a movement to help children avoid disappointment and frustration by giving praise for little or no achievement attained (the most common example is the addition of participation trophies). I have viewed firsthand how this strategy not only breeds entitlement but can have negative consequences as children will not naturally learn the necessary lessons on how to cope with certain disappointments.

We all want our children to have high self-esteem and confidence, but this comes from positive feedback that praises achieving an actual goal or overcoming a specific challenge. We should provide specific feedback based on a completed action, challenging children to work through hard times, giving realistic positive feedback, and encouraging competition. By doing so, children will be able to develop self-esteem and confidence based on their own experiences and not be rewarded for a lack of specific goal attainment.

Another strategy is to base your positive feedback on the amount of effort the child gives, and the impact of the achievement and goal reached. We should challenge them to want to overcome obstacles and better prepare them for their futures encouraging a higher level of self-concept and self-image.

Both self-esteem and self-efficacy, or self-confidence, affect our self-concept and our mindset. Beliefs, attitudes, feelings, and our inner voice all have an effect on how we carry ourselves and what characteristics we exhibit. The more positive these are the better we feel and the more capable we become with a growth mindset.

More negative thoughts and attitudes generally facilitate a fixed mindset. We need to meet each negative thought and attitude with one or more positive thought(s) or self-talk to neutralize them immediately. Reframing these thoughts and utilizing mindfulness techniques are a few ways to fight the battle and win the appropriate mindset for your overall health and wellbeing.

These thoughts and beliefs effect our intrinsic motivation to keep working, our ability to overcome obstacles, and our belief to accomplish the goals we set for ourselves. The techniques described here, and in prior chapters throughout, provide a guide and blueprint for injecting positive emotional hygiene into our daily lives to overcome obstacles, be more self-compassionate, and more self-confident. My hope is for you to identify and define your self-image in a more positive way and focus and aim closer to the bullseye of higher self-concept.

Adaptability

"The one who adapts his policy to the times, prospers."
— Niccolo Machiavelli

I began the guide by noting that it is very important but difficult for each of us to adapt and change. The older we get, the more set in our ways we seem to become. The world and our environment are always changing and triggering new events and challenges. Our ability to pivot and adapt to these changes is paramount to our success and prosperity. I have provided several examples of how we can and should make these changes and hopefully provided some resources and techniques for you to use to adapt as a starting point.

My aim and vision are to also provide specific examples of my own life where change was unwanted but necessary. In the introduction, I laid out several paradigms that are unfolding that should act as the impetus for us to make and/or incorporate some of these necessary changes into our lives. Machiavelli and Darwin both expose and document the need to adapt and change. Being adaptable is more important now than ever before due to the rapid changing environment and circumstances in our lives.

As I write this chapter in 2020, my daughter returned home from college three months early, my wife and I are both working from home indefinitely, and we are barely leaving the house due to the novel Coronavirus pandemic effecting the entire world.

Every person in this current pandemic has been forced to adapt and many may be considering changing jobs and careers because of an eminent recession, their situation, as well as these paradigms. I am hopeful we all can use some of these recent experiences and strategies to build upon becoming more adaptable regarding certain aspects of our lives.

Change can be a very daunting task for most of us. Many elements and competencies within this guide are provided to self-reflect and discuss the challenges we face and the tools and strategies to effectuate positive and lasting change. That was one of my basic goals in writing this book. We all will go through multiple changes like getting married, moving, having children, getting downsized, divorced, and becoming sick and losing loved ones.

Adapting to changes within all six wellness competencies or many of them should be beneficial to most of us. Those who have a growth mindset will be able to deal with these changes more productively than the fixed mindset individuals who are more content with their status quo. Our ability to learn, grow, adapt, and move away from this status quo comfort zone will guide us to our destination while minimizing the impact of the transition.

Prompt: During the COVID-19 pandemic, what have you learned about yourself in terms of being able to quickly adapt or not adapt to change? How has change affected you? How can you better prepare and adapt to future changes?

_____

_____

_____

_____

_____

Some of the main qualities of adaptable people include: being curious, resourceful, forward looking thinkers, open-mindedness, seeing opportunity instead of failure, and having self-confidence. Curiosity will allow you to seek out new methods of solving problems and overcoming obstacles. Resourcefulness will entail seeking out others for advice, following the examples of others, and researching alternative ways of thinking and reframing outcomes when faced with solving problems. Being open-minded is another pivotal characteristic of an adaptable person as open-minded and growth minded people are more open to suggestions from others. Having a more positive attitude will also assist in expediting change. Those individuals are more open to taking on risk, trying new solutions, and looking at a scenario from a different angle.

Prompt: Write down a time when you successfully adapted to a major change in your life. What was the strategy and steps you took to make this change? How can you use these same techniques for new future changes?

_____
_____
_____
_____
_____
_____

Prompt: If there was one thing about your life currently that you want to change what is it and WHY? What steps can you take today to help move the process along?

_____
_____
_____
_____

Being adaptable is a useful mindset for all aspects of our lives. It coincides with the ability to overcome adversity. We are all faced with challenges and setbacks, and our ability to adapt and bounce back quickly is paramount to our success and prosperity. Growth minded positive individuals are generally very adaptable and do not let obstacles keep them down. This is an important skillset to master for our personal and professional development.

Similar to overcoming challenges more quickly, someone who is adaptable won't be quick to feel overwhelmed and hopeless when faced with challenges and problems by having a plan. Creating a plan and implementing that plan is a better strategy than being reactive and negative when faced with necessary change. Adaptability of changes within our career is also important. If we are forward looking then we can more accurately predict and effectively adapt to changes in processes or our work situation. It is an important part of life if you want to be successful. I encourage you to self-reflect upon your ability to change and use the techniques and strategies provided to assist in your efforts to adapt regarding all aspects of your life.

Persistence

"Tenacity and adversity are old foes."—Chinese proverb

Persistence is all about finishing what you started and continuing the actions needed in spite of any obstacles in your way. I now realize what it means to be persistent while finishing this project. This is the last competency in the Structure and Building Blocks of Achievement and Prosperity. It has been a journey not void of setbacks and questions.

This one, including the background research needed, the outline, scope, and key elements, has been one of the largest projects in my life. For me, persistence is the ability to keep taking small routine steps in the direction you wish to travel even in light of adversity. It entails having a vision, believing that you can get there, and understanding the WHY. The Cycle of Achievement was my strategy to get to this point. My belief in this project and the potential benefits that it may provide each of you was the catalyst for my continued persistence. Our strong belief regarding certain things helps fuel our persistence to see them through. Without it, we have less drive and desire, and the project often falls into the pile of uncompleted tasks.

Being persistent is an ability to be disciplined and stick with a task. It ties in well to your motivation, enthusiasm, beliefs, habits, and your ability to overcome adversity. Persistence is an important quality in your professional life because it gives you the ability to work hard toward your goals. It is a characteristic that should be incorporated into many aspects of your life.

A great example of an individual that had great persistence is Thomas Edison. He noted that "genius is 1% inspiration and 99% perspiration." It's great to be smart and be inspired to believe, but your hard work is what helps you get the job done. Thomas Edison had very little formal education as he only attended school for a few months and was only taught basic skills by his mother. What made him stand out was his curiosity and persistence as a growth minded individual. It took Thomas Edison approximately 1,000 tries to invent the lightbulb. This is the epitome of persistence because he was motivated, goal-oriented, disciplined, enthusiastic, had strong beliefs and habits to overcome challenges to eventually discover a life altering process and outcome. His persistence and disciplined work ethic were important factors in helping him become one of the greatest inventors of all time.

Prompt: Based on this example of persistence, what goals in your life have you worked tirelessly toward? What goals do you have in mind that you want to achieve that require persistence?

_____

_____

_____

_____

_____

"I've missed more than nine thousand shots in my career. I have lost almost three hundred games. Twenty-six times I've been trusted to take the game-winning shot and missed. I have failed over and over and over again in my life. And that is why I succeed."— Michael Jordan

    I saw Michael Jordan play as a rookie in the league. It was a visual lesson and inspiration on persistence, drive, and determination. He was grace in motion on the court and purely genuine with integrity off the court. These are just a few of the qualities that he exhibits that draw us toward him and inspire us to be better. We can learn a great deal from these champion athletes and apply it to our own lives to transform, grow and prosper.

Each of you can effectively reach your goals while continuing to be persistent in your efforts. Your persistence in getting this far and following the prompts will hopefully lead to bettering yourself. My hope is that you are persistent enough to complete your guide in its entirety, revisit it often for direction, and continue to utilize it with additional pages to persistently journal and document what is most important to you.

CHAPTER 11

Congratulations! Turn the page…

Congratulations, you have made it this far!

Now it is time to turn the page of your life regarding those aspects, elements, competencies, and strategies that need to change and improve upon. It's an opportunity to invest in yourself by promoting YOU and your brand and not spending your gifted time on distractions. I am turning the page in my life to adapt to the current situation as I encourage you to do so. I began the guide discussing how hard it is for most of us to adapt and change, especially as we get older. My vision within these pages was broad and diverse; I hoped to accomplish many things.

Some of these include flushing out what success and prosperity are; what makes individuals successful; empowering each of you with strategies and building block competencies to focus on; challenging you to utilize many of these strategies as a planning resource and guide to assist in realizing your potential; inspiring you to self-reflect, dream big, and visualize your passions and interests in a rocking chair moment. It was to act as a mentoring book for my children. A type of playbook to utilize, similar to how champion athlete's and successful franchises have their playbooks, and enterprises have their business and financial plans and strategies. I wanted to provide a place for me and you to document and memorialize our true wishes, interests, visions, beliefs, parting thoughts, and important considerations. To provide an all-inclusive guide you can revisit and revise often as life changes.

Ultimately, I want to help empower you to become the designer and architect of your future and wellbeing as a growth minded participant instead of a fixed minded spectator throughout your life. Michelangelo challenges us to "set our aim high" and that each of us should aspire to try and reach our highest potential. It's your choice… so please choose wisely. The Target of Beliefs and Self-Concept were provided in the Workbook so that you can pull it out, enlarge it, and hang on your wall as a reminder of where your aim will be in the future; hopefully closer to the bullseye!

Personally, journaling evolved into a weekly exercise that allowed me the opportunity to document and memorialize my thoughts, passions, situations, challenges, and many of life's curveballs that were being thrown at me. I began to understand its value and expanded upon ways to utilize it by incorporating sections on gratitude and achievements. It began with lists and expanded into larger sections as I worked through several career changes, life defining moments, and unusual situations. More recently it morphed into a research project and work on what truly defines success, prosperity, and wellbeing.

My hope is that by reading and utilizing these strategies and prompts, you will be inspired through self-reflection to answer some important questions and transform those aspects and competencies of your life that need it most. By writing them down and documenting them, you will have the opportunity to revisit, revise, and restructure some of them. This way, when the next financial crisis comes (and it will) or the next serious crisis, you are better prepared and positioned to weather the storm and ride it out. As I self-reflect and look back on my life and specifically on my professional career, adjustments that I have made over the years seemed overwhelming at the time and were not easy adjustments to make. It seems to make it easier and simplify the process by utilizing many of the strategies and competencies to muster up the confidence and enthusiasm to turn the page.

The paradigms discussed in the beginning of the guide describe some of the significant changes and challenges coming at us that will truly affect certain aspects of our lives. This includes a highly competitive job market where more time and devotion are needed on our part to invest in our own personal branding and career development. It also includes putting more onus on our own savings, investment, and retirement plans, and our ability to be knowledgeable about the many financial options available.

It will also challenge us to be careful about how we are utilizing technology and making sure that AI in its many iterations is not controlling us, but we are controlling it. It presents additional concerns and challenges for each of us to invest in ourselves since information, advertisements, and social media apps are being hurled at us and consuming our time, focus, and money and energy! Our ability to be mindful and careful about filtering out some of this negative and useless data will be critical to our success or lack thereof. Energy flows where the focus and attention goes. If your focus and attention is dedicated to social media constantly, you will not have the time or ability to focus your energy on more pertinent competencies to cultivate, realize, and grow.

In today's chaotic world it seems critical to share these facts, and provide potential guidance especially related to a balanced WE wellness environment. Aristotle teaches us the importance of self-reflection and what prosperity and wellbeing encompass. He challenges and inspires us to self-reflect about our own situation to better understand who we are and why we are the way we are. An expanded definition of prosperity and flourishing based upon his original writings would include having balance between one's physical, emotional, intellectual, financial, social, and occupational wellbeing. This is my true definition of success.

My effort to provide some guidance on often overlooked key competencies of having positive beliefs and self-compassion by way of emotional hygiene techniques hopefully will resonate with most or all of you. Our journeys always seem to take some detours and hit some stormy weather and it's our ability to clean off these setbacks, weather these storms, and adapt in a way that boosts our confidence to continue the journey. My daily practice of gratitude, mindfulness, positive affirmations, and other thought-provoking strategies learned and realized from great thinkers and teachers like Buddha, Confuses, Aristotle, William James and Michelangelo have been shared to assist in promoting your wellbeing as they have mine.

Hopefully, you have written down all the prompts in each of the sections to help you frame your interests, passions, beliefs, habits, attitudes, and the like to name a few. Some of the chapters and sub sections may be of more or less interest to you. The guide follows the Structure and Building Blocks of Achievement and Prosperity to guide you through the most important competencies that each of us should incorporate and add as tools in our toolbox to prosper.

It begins at its base with the cornerstone competencies of visions, beliefs, and actions that anchor us and our ability to form a stable foundation from which to build upon and grow. These are the components of the Diamond Cycle of Achievement that also include the pivotal wildcard of mentors into the strategy. This is a process that I have used repeatedly. All great achievements begin with a vision. When we add in positive beliefs and taking action through behaviors and habits we see results and achievements. Utilizing the benefit of coaches and mentors helps simplify and expedite the process.

The middle sections of the blueprint include the foundational and core competencies that help create additional support as a strong and stable base. The routine of planning and journaling is a starting point. Creating a more positive attitude and productive habits daily are critical. Continually learning and gaining knowledge of all aspects and competencies of life from an early age will help grow our brand and career later on. Creating a Board of Advisors that includes mentors can be a great springboard for success.

Financial planning is key to gaining security and independence in your future. Conditioning your mind and body will focus your attention on two elements that are critical to your overall health and wellbeing and mimic the beneficial repetitive training of champion athletes and artists. Continually reading, learning, creating your brand, networking and developing your career vision and trajectory are central to your future growth and success.

The focus on our inner core social circle cannot be overlooked as we are the average of the five or so people that we are most aligned with. Consistently incorporating gratitude into my life on a daily basis has been an "ah ha" moment for me. Lastly, our ability to overcome adversities consistently being hurled at us on our journey incorporating persistence and a positive attitude in the challenging struggle is very important.

The higher and peak level competencies allow us to grow and prosper utilizing different attributes that provide flexibility and allow us to differentiate ourselves while still grounding us to our core. Motivation as growth minded individuals is a starting point to build momentum through habits and routines. Being generous by volunteering not only helps others, but is an important factor in furthering our health and wellbeing. Realizing higher EQ by way of a sixth sense to be able to read and evaluate ourselves and those around us in our personal and professional careers cannot be overstated.

Building self-confidence will be the basis for creating a higher self-concept and better self-esteem in how we view ourselves and working on our self-compassion. Enthusiasm, similar to motivation, may provide us the positive attitude to change. Taking on calculated opportunistic timing, while accounting for the risks, can be a tactical strategy for advancement. Always being genuine and exhibiting integrity will act as a magnet to attract other similar like-minded individuals to grow your network and develop your key inner core advocates. Lastly, being adaptable and persistent in seeing things through to fruition are critical elements for our continued success, prosperity, and a balanced harmonic wellbeing.

The following Journal Workbook has been provided to be a resource, directory, checklist, and organizational tool for you and your future. Portions of it can be used as tear out lists for furthering your interest toward transitioning toward the target's bullseye.

Other sections function as a directory of your personal medical and financial information and estate considerations. There is a biography and mission statement, high achievements and personal characteristics sections. The login ID and password organizer has been included for you to consolidate and keep handy as many of us tend to misplace or lose them! There is a bucket list and family tree to inspire you to connect with your elders and connect again with your inner voice. It's a catch-all to guide you along your path. Please take some time to review, document, and manage the Workbook as I am hopeful that it will be insightful and help you organize and consolidate your thoughts and some needed information moving forward.

Thank you for purchasing my work and allowing me the opportunity to come into your life hopefully in a positive, productive, and collaborative way. A portion of the proceeds will be donated to the organizations noted in the preface that have been important and valuable causes I support and are part of my mission. I am grateful for the opportunity to make a difference. I am hopeful that this work will have an impact benefit on your life.

I wish you all the best in your journey to become the architect to transform your future, destiny, and wellbeing and to reach your desired potential!

Prompt: If you knew with virtual certainty that you were going to die within the next year, what changes would you make in your life and in your planning? This is not a bucket list per say as that follows later in the Workbook. It may include things like: making amends with someone you care for, giving back in some way, donating generously, planning and getting your affairs into order using the Workbook, building or learning something new, attitude adjustment for your emotional wellbeing with some hygiene techniques, and maybe some fun things to round it out. One of mine was to learn to play guitar.

1. _____
2. _____
3. _____
4. _____
5. _____
6. _____
7. _____
8. _____
9. _____
10. _____

PART THREE

Your Journaling Workbook

An Essential Life Directory and Organizer

CHAPTER 11

Workbook Resources and Toolkit

My Life's Personal Mission Statement

My mission in life is to _____
_____
_____
_____

I accomplish this by _____
_____
_____

The benefit(s) and importance is/are_____
_____
_____

Personal Biography & Achievements

Hometowns _____

Hospital born, Town/City/State _____

Height _____ Blood type _____

Eye color _____ Hair color _____

Favorite color _____ Food _____

High School _____ Year/Decile-Ranking _____

GPA _____ SAT _____ ACT _____

Middle and elementary schools & towns _____

Favorite subject(s) _____

Parents birthplace/years and how they met (ancestors see family tree) _____
_____

Children's full names _____
_____

Siblings/family _____

Nicknames _____

Best friend(s) _____

Ancestry locations _____

Nationalities – dual _____

Religion _____

Interests, talents, and passions _____

Languages fluent _____

Memberships/Organizations _____

Artistic endeavors or instruments played _____

272 | Transform Your Future & Wellbeing

College/Universities attended & year _____

College/University Degree(s) _____

Honors and offices held _____

Fraternity/Sorority or club member and positions held _____

Jobs, career occupation, businesses _____

Companies employed _____

Honors, certifications, awards _____

Volunteer org/charities _____

Clubs, groups, sports interests _____

Wedding/honeymoon locations and date _____

My mentor or advocate _____

Pets _____

Tattoos _____

Interesting facts, interests, and hobbies _____

Horoscope sign _____

Biggest achievement(s) _____

High Achievements

My greatest moment(s) to date _____

_____

My biggest talent is _____

My greatest strength is _____

Most generous moment was helping_____

_____

My biggest adventure was _____

_____

I met my partner/spouse through _____

_____

Best planning and project effort _____

_____

Craziest ride was on _____

My greatest physical feat/most points/goals/hits was _____

Biggest beneficial change I ever made was _____

_____

Most difficult scariest moment/situation of my life _____

_____

I am/was most grateful for/when _____

_____

Most compassionate moment(s) was _____

_____

_____

Most spiritual moment was _____
_____

I was most courageous when _____

Biggest risk I took that worked out well was _____
_____

Greatest adversity that I was able to overcome was _____
_____

Biggest prize I ever won _____

Weirdest/unusual moment(s)_____
_____

Highest elevation I was at _____

Lowest elevation I was at _____

Longest walk, run or biked _____

Number of and continents visited _____
_____

Number of and countries visited _____
_____
_____

Number of and states visited _____
_____
_____

I am currently most enthusiastic about _____
_____

Proudest moment of my career was _____
_____

Best result/position of my career is/was _____

_____

Smartest career move was_____

_____

Smartest financial move was_____

_____

Net worth and date _____

Best result related to changing a bad habit was _____

_____

My persistence has allowed me to _____

_____

First car I purchased _____

First house/property purchased, location & type _____

_____

Smartest change in my inner core circle for the good was _____

_____

Continue to journal your achievements weekly at the back of the Workbook.

Part of the benefit of the journaling process is to determine your current interests, visions, characteristics and attributes noted below. However, don't let these characteristics necessarily define you, you can explore opportunities and strategies in the guide for you to make changes. Look to transform your future to realize the meaningful changes and growth opportunities in front of you.

Summary of Personal Characteristics and Traits

1. Where are you aiming; high/low/bullseye? _____
2. Are you a participant or a spectator? _____
3. I love to _____
4. What are your biggest visions from rocking chair moment? _____
   _____
   _____
5. I believe that _____
6. I landed on the Target of beliefs and self-concept at number _____
7. I am growth minded or fixed minded?_____
8. I am an optimist or a pessimist? _____
9. I am proactive or reactive? _____
10. I am ambitious or not very?_____
11. I have or have not journaled in the past and my biggest planning project realized?_____
    _____
12. I have a positive or negative general attitude?_____
13. I am an extrovert or an introvert? _____
14. My most prevalent habits other than usual ones are _____
    _____
    _____
15. I like to read books and learn or not? _____
16. I have a written budget and financial plan or don't? _____
17. I am neat or messy? _____

Chapter 11: Congratulations! Turn the page…

18. I am organized or disorganized? _____
19. I am a procrastinator or motivated doer?_____
20. I am or am not a healthy eater? _____
21. I do/don't exercise regularly? _____
22. I do/don't work on my personal branding? _____
23. I take time/don't to be grateful about life? _____
24. I do/don't look to use coaches and mentors?_____
25. I do/don't look to replace people in my inner circle? ___
26. I am/am not sensitive and emotional? _____
27. I am/am not curious? _____
28. I am observant or more oblivious to things? _____
29. The one thing I want to change about myself is and WHY _____
    _____
30. I do/don't have tattoos and piercings?_____
31. Do you know your IQ? _____
32. Do you know your EQ? _____ What was your score in the guide? _____
33. I have idiosyncrasies like_____
34. My most creative or artistic project was? _____
35. My biggest supporter, mentor, or advocate is _____
36. I am/am not intellectually fit and continue to learn new things?_____
37. I am a spender or a saver? _____
38. I am/am not financially fit and secure? _____
39. I am a conservative, moderate or aggressive investor? ___
40. I am/am not physically fit? _____
41. I am/am not emotionally fit? _____

42. I am/am not career minded? _____
43. My 3-5 year career vision is _____
44. My inner core circle includes _____
45. I am/am not sociable and personable?_____
46. I am/am not a member of clubs or groups?_____
47. I am empathetic to others?_____
48. I am self-compassionate or self-deprecating? _____
49. I am compassionate? _____
50. I have/don't have a sixth sense? _____
51. I practice or don't practice gratitude often?_____
52. The person I am most happy to be around is_____
53. My biggest challenge (s) to date are? _____
54. I am patient or impatient? _____
55. I am strict or lenient?_____
56. I am tolerant or intolerant? _____
57. I am/am not self-confident? _____
58. I am/am not courageous?_____
59. I am modest or extravagant? _____
60. I am enthusiastic or lackadaisical? _____
61. I easily forgive?_____
62. I take risks or not? _____
63. I am/am not handy? _____
64. I am/am not artistic? _____
65. I am/am not athletic? _____
66. I like/don't like to gamble? _____

67. I am generally honest or dishonest?_____
68. I am/am not genuine or put on a facade?_____
69. I have/don't have integrity and am trustworthy?_____
70. I have/have not cheated on a partner? _____
71. I am a leader or a follower?_____
72. I am courageous or shy away from things?_____
73. I am/am not religious and spiritual? _____
74. I am independent or more dependent on others?_____
75. I am politically conservative, moderate or liberal?_____
76. I am a Democrat, Independent or Republican?_____
77. I am/am not civic minded? _____
78. I have high or low self-concept? _____
79. I am funny and can make light of things?_____
80. I am generally happy? _____
81. I adapt well or don't adapt well to change?_____
82. I am/am not generous and giving?_____
83. I volunteer/don't occasionally or regularly? _____
84. I am/am not persistent? _____
85. My worst trait or characteristic? _____
86. My best trait or characteristic? _____

My Interests, Favorites, and Facts

1. Most memorable childhood moments prior to age 15 _____
_____

2. Most memorable moments after age 15 _____
_____

3. Best concert attended _____

4. Other concerts attended _____
_____
_____

5. Favorite animal and pet _____

6. Favorite snack _____ candy _____

7. Favorite drink _____

8. Favorite book _____

9. Favorite partner …. _____

10. Favorite thing to do _____

11. Favorite thing I did _____

12. Favorite place to visit, hang out _____

13. Favorite movie(s) _____

14. Favorite series _____

15. Favorite type of music _____

16. Favorite band and album _____

17. Favorite radio station _____

18. Favorite art/museum or cultural event _____

19. Favorite celebrity and WHY _____

20. Favorite sports to play _____

21. Favorite place to ski _____

22. Favorite place to vacation _____

23. Favorite beach(es) _____

24. Favorite golf courses _____

25. Family interests and favorite spots _____

26. Favorite car owned _____

27. Favorite spectator sport _____

28. Favorite sports team(s) _____

29. Favorite ice cream _____ flavor _____

30. Favorite food(s) _____

31. Favorite restaurant _____

32. Favorite takeout food _____

33. Favorite store _____

34. Favorite possession _____

Summary of Answers that Reflect and Define Who I Am

1. If I change my name it would be _____
2. What is your biggest fear? _____
3. What was the craziest, most bizarre, or scariest moment in your life or that you witnessed? _____
4. What is your fondest memory? _____
5. Have you ever broken the law? _____
6. What person do you admire most and WHY? _____ _____
7. Who in life has been your biggest supporter? _____
8. What was the event/s in your life that made you stronger? _____ _____
9. Who in your past do you wish you still had contact with? _____
10. What do you regret most in your life? _____
11. Are there any mistakes that you keep making? _____
12. What areas of your life are you not progressing? _____
13. Is there anything that consistently overwhelms you? _____
14. What are you obsessive or compulsive about? _____
15. Is there anything that you're ashamed of? _____
16. Has anyone ever broken your heart or you their's? _____
17. What apps do you use the most? _____
18. If you could bring only one thing to a deserted island that was not for life support what would it be _____
19. What one state or city do you want to live in? _____

20. What is your dream job or career? _____
21. What is your dream destination? _____
22. What is your dream car? _____
23. My dream house and location is _____
24. What tattoo/piercings would you get? _____
25. Would you rather be rich or madly in love? _____
26. If you could change the world for the better in one way, what would it be? _____
27. What's your biggest turn on? _____
28. Do you believe in heaven and hell? _____
29. Do you believe in UFO's and aliens? _____
30. Do you want to have children and # (if you don't already)? _____
31. Are you pro-life or not? _____
32. Do you support the death penalty? _____
33. What is the biggest event or change that you think may happen in the next 10 years? _____
34. What's the most embarrassing thing that has ever happened to you? ____
   _____
35. What is the biggest risk you ever took? _____
   _____

Here are two riddles… what building has the most stories?

If an analog clock reads 3:15, what is the distance measured in degrees between the small hand and the big hand? It is not zero and the answer is after the travel roadmap toward the end of the Workbook.

Pullout of Vision and Positive Affirmations and Gratitude Conditioning Resource

Vision Planning

My primary passion and goals are _____

My mission is to _____

Today I will invest in myself by _____ and

not waste my gifted time by _____ .

I will begin visualizing myself _____ .

In the next 30 days I have decided to learn more about and become adept at ___
_____ .

I will focus on more productive tasks and routines early in the day.

I have decided to become more of a participant regarding_____
_____ and will drive this activity moving forward.

My balanced health and wellbeing are critical to my success and I have determined that changing my _____ will begin today and become a routine each day for the better.

I decided that I am motivated and enthusiastic to join _____
as I intend to meet and learn and/or accomplish_____ .

I am committed to saving more, spending less on unnecessary items, and beginning a thorough investment planning strategy.

Setbacks and challenges are part of life, and I am committed to not let them get in my way.

My career vision currently is _____

Carpe Diem – seize the day!

Positive Affirmations

I have integrity and will begin to love myself more.

I will begin today by being a more positive and optimistic person.

I believe in having a positive attitude and will reject the negative.

I decided that today I will be more grateful, happier and smile more.

I decided that I am capable of loving, giving and forgiving.

I believe in my ability to grow, prosper, and create my own destiny.

I am working on being self-compassionate and _____

I am confident in my ability to be mindful of the beauty of things.

I am generous and will look to be thankful and pay it forward or volunteer.

I believe in my ability to have a positive growth mindset and become successful, healthy and well!

I won't let negative situations and problems ruin my day.

Gratitude Reminders

I am thankful for the love and affection of my _____

_____ & family.

I am grateful for my good health and fortune.

I greatly appreciate my partner/spouse.

I am thankful for my faith, free will, and independence.

I am thankful for the roof over my head and the food and water that we are blessed with.

I begin today by being thankful for my _____ .

I appreciate the support that _____ gives me.

I am grateful that I can give back to _____ by assisting them with _____ .

I am grateful for my position and/or career.

I truly appreciate _____ for being in my life.

Essential Life Directory & Organizer

- **Recommend copying many of these critical pages and keeping them in an accessible place with your important documents**

Your phone numbers _____

Spouse's/partner's contact/email _____

Children's phone/email _____

Children's phone/email _____

Children's phone/email _____

Parents' phone numbers _____

Primary Emergency contact, Guardian _____

Secondary Emergency contact _____

Other contacts: Military/Government/town/businesses/friends contact info ___

_____

_____

Hospital you prefer _____

Blood Type _____

Primary Physician contact info _____

Other Doctor's contact info: _____

_____

Eye Doctor _____

Children's Dr. _____

Children's Dr. _____

Children's Dr. _____

Dentist contact info _____

Transform Your Future & Wellbeing

Pharmacy contact info_____

Medications currently on with dosages, frequency and refill dates

_____ Dosage/frequency _____

Refill by_____

_____ Dosage/frequency _____

Refill by_____

_____ Dosage/frequency _____

Refill by_____

Health conditions _____

_____

Allergies _____

_____

Veterinarian Contact info _____

_____

Dog Chip info _____

Parents' doctors_____

Location of parents' Wills/DPOA_____

Funeral Information – see later sections.

Place a copy of above into Emergency Folder in central location: one separate for Medications.

- **Recommend adding your information into your phone Emergency and Health App/ID: allergies, medical conditions, medications, and donor information as noted in the Knowledge and Learning section.**

Emergency & Evacuation Checklist & Documents:

The purpose of this section is to provide guidance on the necessary items and documents you would need in a timely evacuation situation. Gather the following: checkbook with extra checks, cash, bonds, stock certificates, gold coins, medications and toiletries, extra set of keys for cars and all others, safety deposit box keys, credit cards, this guide, laptops, phones, pet meds, external hard drives and storage SIM cards, wedding album, jewelry, deeds, contracts, titles, estate docs, recent bank statements with no online access, important pictures/photos/DVDs with family memories and other small family heirlooms, emergency preparedness and toolkit, flashlights, gloves, batteries, radio, duct tape, towels, food, clothing and anything else that you deem necessary.

Driver's license # and expiration _____

Social Security cards location _____

Health Insurance card & contact _____

Passports/Citizenship papers _____

Birth Certificates location _____

Bonds, coins, stock, and cash location _____

Adoption papers location _____

Marriage certificate _____

Prenuptial agreement _____

Divorce or separation papers _____

Copy Emergency contact list, passwords and PINs, clear out safe.

Document Filing Organizer

Create a file folder filing system with all of your important documents including photocopies of the login IDs and passwords and information noted below. Major life events such as changing jobs, evacuations, buying a home, hospitalization, or passing of a loved one poses unique challenges. The more you are organized during these times, the more productive and faster one is able to react to the event. Having a filing system that is readily accessible is a key component to this success. The below checklists and organizer should help you get your documents, contacts, contracts, PINs and important details in order.

Central location of your files_____

Include the following with PIN numbers if necessary:

- Copy of this Workbook's important information, instructions, and guide
- Photocopies of all critical documents: DL, SS card, Medical card, passports...
- Emergency items and contacts
- Birth certificate and marriage license.
- Health insurance info, Health Savings Accounts & medical records/bills.
- Insurance contracts and records: Property, home, vehicles, other.
- Banking information: folders for checking, savings, CDs, credit cards, UTMA/UGMA, safety deposit box info, other.
- Loan file: mortgages, student & personal loans, promissory notes.
- Investment Account information: Brokerage, mutual funds, stocks, bonds, annuities.
- Retirement plans (separate): IRA/ROTH/SEP/401/403/Pension Plans, HSA's, stock options, executive comp plans, etc.

- College 529 & State Prepaid Plans (separate with multiple children).
- Life Insurance contracts including corporate group life, prepaid funeral plans.
- Long Term Care contracts, plans, and disability income plans.
- Estate documents: wills, durable power of attorney, health care directives, and trusts. May include codicils, gifting plans, funeral plans and prepaids, death certificates, cemetery plots.
- Titles, deeds and tax certificates, jewelry & real estate appraisals.
- Business, corporate, LLC registrations, TINs, certificates, filings, websites, Buy/sell/partnership agreements, etc.
- Tax Documents: at least the last 7 years of federal and state filed returns.
- Legal: other legal documents; proceedings, birth, marriage, adoption, divorce decree, expungements, name change, etc.
- Utilities: cable/internet, electric, gas, telephone, water/sewer, garbage.
- Car: Insurance, warranties, repair/oil change info, purchase contracts, lease info and payoff.
- Real Estate: property tax bills & Homeowners Association: HOA bills, information. Rental and lease agreements.
- Warranties for appliances/other, service contracts on mechanicals and instructions for home, car, animals, etc.
- Parents' wills and estate documents copies.
- Other important documents: military discharge, VA insurance docs, association affiliation, clubs, charitable organizations.

Do not leave stock certificates in a file without registering them with a transfer agent in case of loss. Same goes for Government Bonds not registered with TreasuryDirect.com where they can be registered.

If a central filing system is not established, then input location of all key documents, titles, deeds, investments, tax forms, insurance info, etc. in the individual spaces provided in each section. Most have been accounted for.

Computer, Phone, Website Login, PINs & Email Contacts:
use pencil, photocopy and keep in a safe place

Computer login screen password _____

Tablet login password _____

Other tablet password _____

Child/parent computer passcode _____

Child/parent computer passcode _____

Phone password _____

Second business phone password _____

Phone service provider password _____

Main Gmail and password login _____

Secondary email/password _____

Other email/PIN _____

Business: Phone _____

Business email & password _____

Business computer password _____

Business phone code & password_____

Cable service provider & router password _____

Cable Co. online website & password _____

House alarm code/password _____

Keyless entry-garage door opener passcode _____

Lifelock ID & password _____

Antivirus ID & password _____

Other gate-security system code/password _____

Bank online ID & passcode _____

ATM/Debit PIN number _____

Other Bank ID/passcode _____

Brokerage account ID/passcode _____

Other investment account ID/passcode _____

Other investment account ID/passcode _____

Corporate 401k ID & passcode _____

Corporate 401k ID & passcode _____

Quicken/other financial ID/passcode _____

Home/Car Insurance Company ID/passcodes _____

Life Insurance Co ID/passcode _____

Health Insurance ID/passcode _____

Prescription provider ID/passcode _____

Social Security Admin ID/passcode _____

Medicare ID & passcode _____

Apple online ID & passcode _____

Apple/other watch password _____

Amazon password _____

Facebook ID & passcode _____

Paypal password _____

College ID & password _____

College ID & password _____

State Unemployment ID & Pin _____

Linkedin ID & passcode _____

Careerbuilder/Indeed passcodes _____

Instagram ID & passcode _____

Snapchat ID & passcode _____

YouTube premium account ID/passcode _____

Twitter account ID & passcode _____

Netflix/Hulu ID & passcode _____

Ebay ID & passcode _____

AARP ID & Passcode _____

Sirius/Music ID & passcode _____

Costco/BJ/Sam's Club online ID & passcode _____

Membership ID _____

Subscription IDs _____

Dropbox – cloud ID & passcode _____

Ticketmaster ID & passcode _____

Stubhub ID & passcode _____

Storage Sandisk passcode _____

Site _____ ID/passcode _____

Site _____ ID/passcode _____

Site _____ ID/passcode _____

Site _____ ID/passcode _____

Site _____ ID/passcode _____

Site _____ ID/passcode _____
Site _____ ID/passcode _____
Site _____ ID/passcode _____
Site _____ ID/passcode _____
Site _____ ID/passcode _____
Site _____ ID/passcode _____
Site _____ ID/passcode _____
Site _____ ID/passcode _____
Site _____ ID/passcode _____
Site _____ ID/passcode _____

Finances

CPA/Accountant contact info _____

Location of last 2 years Federal/State returns _____

Broker Firm Financial Advisor info _____

Broker Firm Financial Advisor info _____

Life & Annuity Co. info _____

Life/Annuity Co. info _____

Annuity Co. info _____

Corporate retirement Plan Sponsor _____

Corporate retirement Plan Sponsor _____

Corporate retirement Plan Sponsor _____

Budget & Cash Flow Analysis	Monthly $
Housing	
Rent or Mortgage & Taxes	
Homeowners Assoc fee	
Utilities (gas, electric, water/sewer)	
Cable & Internet	
Phone	
Insurance: Homeowners or renters	
Repairs / Maintenance contracts	
Lawn, cleaning, other services	
Other - streaming services	
Auto - Transportation	
Auto Loan or Lease Payment	
Second Car payment	
Auto Insurance	
Gas	
Maintenance / oil changes	
Parking, Uber or Public Transportation	
Other	
Medical	
Medical/Dental/Eye Insurance Premiums	
Deductibles	
Presription Drugs/Pharmacy	
Life Insurance Premiums (LTC/Disability)	
Other	
Personal	
Groceries Supermarket	
Dining out/Takeout	
Entertainment	
Gym or Club memberships	
Personal Care/Hair, nails, etc.	
Clothing	
Vacations & Travel	
Gifts & Occasions	
Hobbies & recreation - other	
Child care	
Child support	
Alimony	
Loan payments - student/personal	
Charitable contributions	
Other - credit card	
Other	
Other	
Total Monthly Spending	$
Monthly After-Tax Income	$
Surplus or Shortfall	$

Monthly Income	Monthly $
Salary 1	
Salary 2	
Freelance income	
Investment income	
Dividends	
Social Security 1	
Social Security 2	
Pension 1	
Pension 2	
Annuity 1	
Annuity 2	
Alimony	
Child support	
Rental income	
Rental income	
Other	
Monthly Income	$

Net Worth Analysis: Investment Detail - Liquid Assets

Institution - Bank - Brokerage Co & Account #	Account Owner - Ind. or JT	Asset Value	APY/Avg rate %	Maturity Date & Beneficiaries; Notes
Bank cash assets: checking/savings/CD's				
Investment Brokerage - Non Retirement				
Retirement: 401/403/IRA's/Pension/HSA/ESOP				
529 - Annuities - Funds - Stock/Options - Bonds - Life Ins.				
Total Liquid Investment Assets		$		

298 | Transform Your Future & Wellbeing

Total Net Worth Analysis

Assets & Liabilities	Owners (Individual - Joint)	Market Value	Cost Basis	Other - income cash flow
Total Investment Assets (from prior page)		$		
Real Estate Holdings				
Primary Residence				
Secondary Residence				
Rental Property				
Business Property				
Other:				
Other Assets				
Vehicle				
Vehicle				
Jewelry - Art - Collectibles				
Other - Business Inventory				
Other - Business - LP's				
Total Assets Calculation		$		

Debts - Liabilities with Start Date	Owners	Outstanding Debt Owed	Interest Rate % & Term	Refinance notes
Primary Mortgage				
Home Equity Line				
Primary Mortgage - second property				
Home Equity LOC				
Auto Loan				
Auto Loan				
Student Loan				
Other loan - credit card				
Other loan - credit card				
Total Liabilities Calculation		$		
Total Net Worth Calculation (Assets - liabilities)		$		

Chapter 11: Congratulations! Turn the page…

Retirement Income - See cash flow analysis

Insurance – Health, Disability, and Long-Term Care

Health Insurance Co contact _____

Health Savings Account Co _____

HSA Login & passcode_____

Medical bills location _____

Medicare supplemental info _____

Medigap plan info_____

Prescription plan info _____

Social Security info & ID _____

Veteran's administration insurance documents_____

Disability Insurance info_____

Outpatient, assisted living & long-term care facility information _____

_____

Protection Planning Analysis

Life Insurance Company_____

Life Insurance Company_____

Work Group Life Info _____

Life Insurance Analysis

Owner/Insured & Type (Term or Permanent)	Death Benefit	Cash Value	Annual Premium - Term	Beneficiary
		$		
Total Death Benefit & Cash Value Calculation	$	$		
Total Liquid Investment & Retirement Assets	$			
Total liquid Assets	$			
Total Debt: Loans + Mortgage + College	$			
Total Income Replacement	$			
Asset Shortfall or Surplus	$			
Long Term Care & Disability Analysis				
Owner/Insured & Type	Yearly maximum benefit	Monthly maximum benefit	Annual Premium	Notes - Benefit & Elimination periods

Property/Home/Apartment

Homeowner's Property Insurance Company contact _____

Home/Car insurance Co. login ID & passcode _____

Car lease or finance company and docs _____

Homeowner's policy location _____

Property tax bill _____

Homeowner's Association Bills & contact _____

Rental and/or lease agreements _____

Mortgage documents _____

PMI/Mortgage insurance documents _____

Real Estate Deeds, other certificates/titles _____

Motor vehicle title docs _____

Appraisals of home, jewelry, cars, etc. _____

Inventory of personal effects; see following pages _____

Spare keys to house, cars, other vehicles located _____

Safety deposit boxes location _____

SD Box key location _____

Parents' safety deposit boxes _____

Safe location and code _____

Storage unit location and PIN _____

Loaned out tools & equipment _____

Legal & Estate

Attorney info & type _____

Attorney info & type _____

Current class action suits, Divorce/Adoption, or litigation in process info:___

_____

_____

_____

Estate Planning Documents:

Will location (don't leave only in safe deposit box!) _____

Durable Power of Attorney docs_____

Living Will/Health Care Directives _____

Trust documents & trustee _____

Military discharge papers _____

Business registration/LLC docs _____

Buy/sell agreements _____

Peace of mind Information: Final Wishes & Funeral requests

Location of parents' wills/DPOA _____

Cemetery plot deed location _____

I do/do not want to be cremated and location of ashes _____

Organ donation document; I do/do not want to donate_____

Prepaid funeral or expense documents _____

Spouse's or other death certificate location _____

Name & phone # of Executor _____

County Surrogate Court address, clerk contact and phone/email info:

_____

_____

Name, phone & address of Executor Funeral Director

_____

_____

Memorial services to be held at _____

Only graveside service or other _____

Memorial gifts to_____

Clergy/religious contact info_____

_____

_____

Requested Pallbearers and/or Eulogy presenters _____

_____

_____

_____

Special Requests: Music/setup/videos/hymns, donations, preference of burial and cemetery and/or ceremony information

_____
_____
_____

Public Announcements: Family members, birthplace, Resume/Bio/Education highlights, date of marriage/spouse, religious/charitable donations/social/Fraternal affiliations, businesses affiliated with and special diploma's and achievements; attach to workbook.

I was born on _____ in _____ resided in _____
_____
_____

Valuable personal property beneficiary: _____
_____
_____

_____   _____
Date   Signature

Special thoughts I would like to share with my family and friends: attach here

_____
_____
_____
_____
_____ .

Chapter 11: Congratulations! Turn the page… | 305

Family Tree

My mother's maiden name is/was _____

She was born on _____ in _____ resides/d in _____

My father name is/was _____

He was born on _____ in _____ resides/d in _____

My grandmother's maiden name is/was _____

She was born on _____ in _____ resides/d in _____

My grandfather's name is/was _____

He was born on _____ in _____ resides/d in _____

My great grandmother's maiden name is/was _____

She was born on _____ in _____ resides/d in _____

My great grandfather's name is/was _____

He was born on _____ in _____ resides/d in _____

My great grandmother's maiden name is/was _____

She was born on _____ in _____ resides/d in _____

My great grandfather's name is/was _____

He was born on _____ in _____ resides/d in _____

My great grandmother's maiden name is/was _____

She was born on _____ in _____ resides/d in _____

My great grandfather's name is/was _____

He was born on _____ in _____ resides/d in _____

My great grandmother's maiden name is/was _____

She was born on _____ in _____ resides/d in _____

My great grandfather's name is/was _____

He was born on _____ in _____ resides/d in _____

My brother's name is/was _____

He was born on _____ in _____ resides/d in _____

My brother's name is/was _____

He was born on _____ in _____ resides/d in _____

My sister's name is/was _____

She was born on _____ in _____ resides/d in _____

My sister's name is/was _____

She was born on _____ in _____ resides/d in _____

My child's name is/was _____

He/she was born on _____ in _____ resides/d in _____

My child's name is/was _____

He/she was born on _____ in _____ resides/d in _____

My child's name is/was _____

He/she was born on _____ in _____ resides/d in _____

My grandchild's name is _____

He/she was born on _____ in _____ resides/d in _____

My grandchild's name is _____

He/she was born on _____ in _____ resides/d in _____

My grandchild's name is _____

He/she was born on _____ in _____ resides/d in _____

_____
_____
_____
_____

My Bucket List

1. My greatest desire, dream, and vision are to _____
   _____
   _____

2. The road trips that I want to take are _____
   _____
   _____

3. The great books that I want to read are _____
   _____
   _____

4. The sites that I want to see are _____
   _____
   _____
   _____

5. The person(s) I want to make amends with, forgive or connect with are
   _____

6. The things I want to learn to do are _____
   _____

7. The project I have been wanting to complete is _____
   _____

8. The place I want to experience, pray, or feel enlightened is _____
   _____

9. The things I wish to touch, smell, and taste to experience are _____
   _____
   _____
   _____

10. The sunrise and sunset that I wish to experience are_____
    _____

11. The adventurous and exciting things I want to experience are _____
_____
_____
_____
_____

12. The show(s) that I want to see are _____
_____
_____
_____
_____

13. The things I want to experience with my partner are _____
_____
_____

14. The artistic endeavor I wish to learn and/or complete is _____
_____

15. The reunion I want to have happen is _____
_____

_____
_____
_____
_____
_____
_____
_____
_____

Vision Travel Roadmap

Top destinations in the US

1. Yellowstone National Park: Old Faithful
2. New York City: Statue of Liberty & Ellis Islands NY/NJ
3. The Grand Canyon, South Rim, Arizona
4. Walt Disney World, Florida
5. Yosemite National Park, Half Dome, Ca.
6. National Mall, Washington, DC
7. Niagara Falls, Maid of Mist, Buffalo, NY
8. Mount Rushmore, South Dakota
9. Las Vegas Strip, Nevada
10. French Quarter & Preservation Hall, New Orleans, LA

Honorable mention: Museums of Natural History & Modern Art, NYC; San Francisco; Gondola ride in Telluride, CO; Silverton-Durango Steam train ride; Hoover Dam; Volcanoes National Park, Hawaii; World Trade Center Tour and 9/11 Memorial; Jackson Hole, Wyoming; Mesa Verde National Park, Colorado; Whitewater rafting down the Colorado or West Virginia; Hollywood walk of fame, Times Square, Brooklyn Bridge and Golden Gate Bridge walks; every great city, park, zoo, aquarium, cavern, theme park, seashore, cathedral, grounds, seaport and byway throughout this great nation! If you're in New Jersey, visit Grounds for Sculpture in Hamilton.

Map of US

Chapter 11: Congratulations! Turn the page… | 311

International top 25 Destinations

1. Rome, Italy
2. Greece; Acropolis, Athens and heritage sites
3. New York City, United States
4. Paris, France
5. London, England
6. Jerusalem, Israel
7. The Pyramids, Giza, Egypt
8. Great Wall of China & Forbidden City, Beijing
9. Machu Picchu, Peru
10. Great Barrier Reef; Coral Sea, Australia
11. Angkor Wat, Cambodia
12. The Serengeti, Tanzania & Kenya
13. Galapagos Islands, Ecuador
14. Venice, Italy
15. Victoria Falls, Zambia
16. Prague, Czech Republic
17. Tokyo, Japan
18. Barcelona, Spain
19. Taj Mahal, India
20. Rio de Janeiro, Brazil
21. Chichen Itza; Cancun, Mexico

22. Northern lights; Canada and Iceland

23. New Zealand; South Island and 7 Mile hike

24. Germany, Octoberfest anywhere!

25. Moscow, Russia

Honorable mention: Petra, Jordan; Mount Everest, Nepal; Vienna, Austria; Amsterdam, Netherlands; Hong Kong, China; Fiji and Bora Bora; Dubai, United Arab Emirates; Vancouver Island, Canada; Singapore; Casablanca, Morocco and so many more…

Answers to riddles: Library and 7.5 degrees.

A Wellness Vision Challenge

This is a review of your rocking chair moment...

What are your greatest visions or passions and mission that you want to pursue? Document specific goals related to your future with the WHY impact benefit, small initial next steps, and associated timeframe.

1. _____

_____

Next steps & timeline _____

2. _____

_____

Timeline _____

3. _____

_____

Timeline _____

Take some time to self-reflect and review some strategies and techniques to incorporate into your planning to enhance your overall wellbeing:

Strategy(s) to benefit your emotional wellbeing include _____

_____

_____

_____

Timeline, frequency, and next steps _____

_____

Review the emotional hygiene techniques noted.

Strategy(s) to benefit your physical wellbeing include _____

_____

_____

Timeline, frequency, and next steps _____

_____

Strategy(s) to benefit your financial wellbeing include _____

_____

_____

Timeline, frequency, and next steps _____

_____

Review the financial planning section for savings and investment considerations.

Strategy(s) to benefit your intellectual wellbeing include _____

_____

_____

Timeline, frequency, and next steps _____

Strategy(s) to benefit your social wellbeing include _____

_____

_____

Timeline, frequency, and next steps _____

Think about new groups, hobbies, or volunteering you want to explore and join.

Strategy(s) to benefit your occupational wellbeing include _____

_____

_____

Timeline, frequency, and next steps _____

Review options for corporate tuition reimbursement for degrees and certifications, as well as networking and mentorship opportunities.

What are your biggest non-productive time vacuums on a daily basis?_____

_____

_____

Strategy(s) to improve your time management may include _____

_____

_____

Timeline, frequency, and next steps _____

Don't procrastinate; Carpe Diem!

What are the biggest challenges you are currently dealing with _____

_____

_____

Strategy(s) to help overcome these adversities_____

_____

_____

Timeline and next steps_____

10 Day Emotional Wellness Checkup

Day 1 – Complete the positive affirmation and self-talk pullout in the Workbook and hang it in a place where you will view it often, like a sanctuary wall or desk. Recite the list and mindfully inhale the meanings and benefit.

Day 2 – Print out Charles Swindoll's quote on Attitude and hang it up on the inside of your cabinet.

Day 3 – Call, facetime, text, or send someone who is close to you and an advocate a message or gift that you are thankful that they are in your life (and that you love and worship their partnership). Smile while talking to them!

Day 4 – Complete your achievement collage and hang it up somewhere where you can enjoy it every day!

Day 5 – Complete the gratitude jar project and at dinner, go around the table and ask everyone to say what they are grateful for.

Day 6 – Forgive someone that has wronged you and make amends if that's possible. If not, drop the baggage, leave it by forgiving, and don't ever look back!

Day 7- Start taking a walk or meditating with deep breathing daily. Be mindful of the benefits of nature's beauty or what pure silence has to offer you.

Day 8 – Volunteer to help a non-profit organization.

Day 9 – Listen to podcasts of comedians or the comedy channels on cable or satellite radio. Smiling for periods of time is infectious!

Day 10 – Find and embrace meditation, faith, prayer, and positive belief into your life through religion and/or mindfulness. Use music as a conduit.

Financial Wellness Checkup

Day 1 – Complete your budget and cash flow analysis.

Day 2 – Complete your Investment Detail and Net Worth Statement.

Day 3 – Complete your changes in your spending and savings plans by taking the first step toward a sufficient emergency fund.

Day 4 – Review higher rate money market options for your excess cash.

Day 5 – Checkup on your outstanding credit balances and your credit score. Create a new savings plan if there are balances and look to renegotiate down your high credit card rates with the bank. Review better cash reward programs online.

Day 6 – Review options to refinance higher rate student loan, car, or mortgage balances to a lower rate or potentially a shorter term to pay off loans quicker.

Day 7 - Review the buckets of money and the three options to determine if your strategy is on target.

Day 8 – Review or set up your company retirement plan, your IRA or SEP IRA accounts, and options. Make sure that you are receiving the company match and determine if you can contribute more moving forward. Set up a contribution schedule for your IRA contribution quarterly or yearly.

Day 9 – Perform portfolio reviews for all accounts for diversification, asset allocations, rebalancing, dollar cost averaging, and fees. May take longer...

Day 10 – Begin to consolidate or close out any unneeded bank accounts and old retirement accounts into your existing accounts or IRA through a direct rollover.

Day 11 – Begin reading the book, The Intelligent Asset Allocator. Create a college savings plan or open a 529 college account if you have children and have not started these.

Day 12 – Checkup and analyze your life insurance protection and death benefits and terms. Use the life insurance analysis provided and, if you are underinsured or do not have an individual non-company policy or need to reapply for a higher benefit, begin this process today. Add in any company paid life insurance benefits to your total policy benefits.

Day 13 - Review your company benefits for additional cost saving options like commuter, legal, child care, wellness credits; review your disability and long- term care options either within the plan or outside of it.

Day 14 – Review or complete all of your necessary estate planning documents.

Day 15 – Review all account beneficiary designations for possible updating on your bank accounts, investment and retirement accounts, life insurance policies, deeds and annuities, etc.

Yearly Wellness Growth and Maintenance Plan

January 2 — Spend 1-2 hours this week on your weakest area of the six wellness competencies. Review the wellness chapter and then focus on the cycle to guide you. Set some small daily and weekly goals and use the 10-minute daily refresh to reset your mindset. Input reminders on your phone or calendar for your checkups for each wellness focus noted.

Plan your year by journaling new stretch goals, classes and events, growth opportunities, connecting with coaches and mentors, and networking and volunteer options. Add weekly and monthly visions and passions to your day planner or phone reminders.

January — Emotional wellness focus; since we are entering a period of potential isolation due to the weather, implement new emotional hygiene strategies of journaling positive self-talk, putting out a gratitude bulletin or jar, or practicing mindfulness or meditation routines. Review the emotional wellness checkup.

February 1 — Social wellness focus; join a group, club, or class this year to meet new people and network.

March 1 — Physical wellness focus; review your exercise routines and nutrition intake and determine if you have a reasonable plan to realize good health. Review physical wellness checkup and begin to implement some of the healthy options. If you have already, try and improve portions of the plan. Schedule your yearly checkup for your medical and dental appointments in addition to others deemed necessary.

Complete your tax preparation; see financial planning section for potential free tax preparation options.

April 1 — Financial wellness focus; complete a financial wellness checkup of your budget, savings, and investment plans as a start. Good time to review rebalancing and dollar cost averaging strategies for your portfolio either quarterly or semi-annually depending on your strategy. If you are further along in accomplishing these, then spend time on other areas including: creating written financial plan, life insurance protection and beneficiary review, and/or portfolio asset allocation and tax efficient strategies if you have not done so already.

May 1 — Intellectual wellness focus; time to invest in your intellectual growth by signing up and attending a new class, lecture, or degree/certification curriculum. This will be the initial steps for next month's career focus. Learning more about and focusing on a new competency or building block attribute. Review summer concert, lecture and art related series locally and other free events in your local or state sites as great budgeting options.

June 1 — Branding and career wellness checkup by rating your progress over the past year; review guide section for options and locate a mentor in your focused area to connect with and gain insight and pinpoint networking and planning related resources. If you work for a larger company, review benefit plan for options on mentors, attaining degrees, certifications, designations, and networking opportunities.

July 1 — Renew physical wellness; it's summer and a great opportunity to get moving with a gardening, designing, and/or renovation project outdoors besides the usual workout routines. Join a YMCA to swim or do other simple workout routines. How about joining a hiking club or coaching youth sports to keep yourself active, interested, and engaged. On the nutritional side, search out some new cooking options and review section for other healthy elements to incorporate.

August 1 — Renew financial wellness; may be time to rebalance portfolio.

Review cash flow, savings, and potentially implement dollar cost averaging and rebalancing plan. Complete financial checkup by reworking your net worth statement, beneficiary review, investment return analysis YTD using the spreadsheets found in the Workbook. Schedule some time to review your free credit report with a financial professional to get a second opinion.

September 1 — Renew intellectual wellness; back to school is a great reminder for you to take charge of your intellectual wealth and invest by visiting the library, museums, cultural events, joining a fall class, or researching your company tuition reimbursement plan to review options.

October 1 — Renew emotional wellness; try and add other types of emotional hygiene techniques into your daily routines and volunteer to give back. Review the emotional wellness checkup to implement new gratitude, forgiveness, and mindfulness routines with a 10-minute refresh. Thanksgiving is soon to be upon us, so it's a great time to pay it forward.

November 1 — Renew occupational wellness; may be time to improve your LinkedIn profile and connect with recruiters if necessary. Review groups and organizations aligned with your occupation to join or get involved with in your area. Seek out degree, certification, or designations to add to your bio and resume. If you're a business owner, look to expand through networking, advertising, or donating to enhance visibility.

December 1 — Renew social wellness; it's family holiday time and an opportunity to reconnect with friends and loved ones. Complete a social checkup by reviewing your inner core social circle to potentially trade up by adding and rebalancing. Look to sign up for next year's groups and classes to get a head start on meeting new people.

My Daily Ritual

Most Important 30-minute Refresh of My Day Every Day!

- 10 minute morning refresh routine: includes a positive affirmation and gratitude review while getting ready; several minutes on the floor stretching/yoga, breathing exercises, and a minute or two to goal plan the most important tasks for the day.

- 10 minutes at lunch to: take a walk and be mindful of breathing and nature or listen to a wellness podcast; check on your vitals and trackers; read an article that is wellness related, or thank someone for his/her help and pay it forward. Grab a piece of fruit. An alternative is to connect with a mentor, coach, Board of Advisors, or someone within your Sphere of Influence (SOI) to review next steps or strategies.

- 10 minute pre or post dinner to: take the walk that you didn't at lunch and/or spend some time stretching, slow breathing, and meditating. Take a few minutes to review small and large achievements completed during the day and think about a few items that need to be cultivated for tomorrow. End with a few minutes of gratitude and self-confidence and compassionate self-esteem affirmations.

This is 30 minutes that you will not be distracted from any form of technology (other than wellness based) or social media. You will not allow negativity into your life, and you will create routines to bring positivity, gratitude, and generosity into your life. 30 minutes is 2% of your day! Try and make it 60 minutes.

Ten Simple Elements/Tips & Routines to Live by…

1. Act "as if" you have already accomplished what it is you desire; you're happy and enthusiastic by smiling often, laughing more, walking with a big gait and chin up with purpose!

2. Condition your body by waking up earlier and spending 10+ minutes on stretching/yoga and/or exercise. Swap out fruit for bread products.

3. Condition your mind by spending 10+ minutes on emotional hygiene by rewarding yourself with compassion being mindful of your achievements, gratitude, positive affirmations.

4. Don't spend more than you earn and save at least 5% of your income to invest.

5. Link up emotional hygiene routines with your morning personal hygiene routines in your bathroom sanctuary. Place mirror reminders to visualize.

6. Don't spend more than 1-2 hours of non-educational screen/video time daily.

7. Find ways to invest in yourself and your mission and passions.

8. Find simple ways to give of yourself and pay it forward, and forgive as it will come back to you as a benefit.

9. Hang up the vision, gratitude and positive affirmations in well trafficked areas for your continued review.

10. Live by the Golden Rule and approach each gifted day as a growth minded participant with motivation, confidence, and persistence as if it was your last.

Diamond Cycle of Achievement

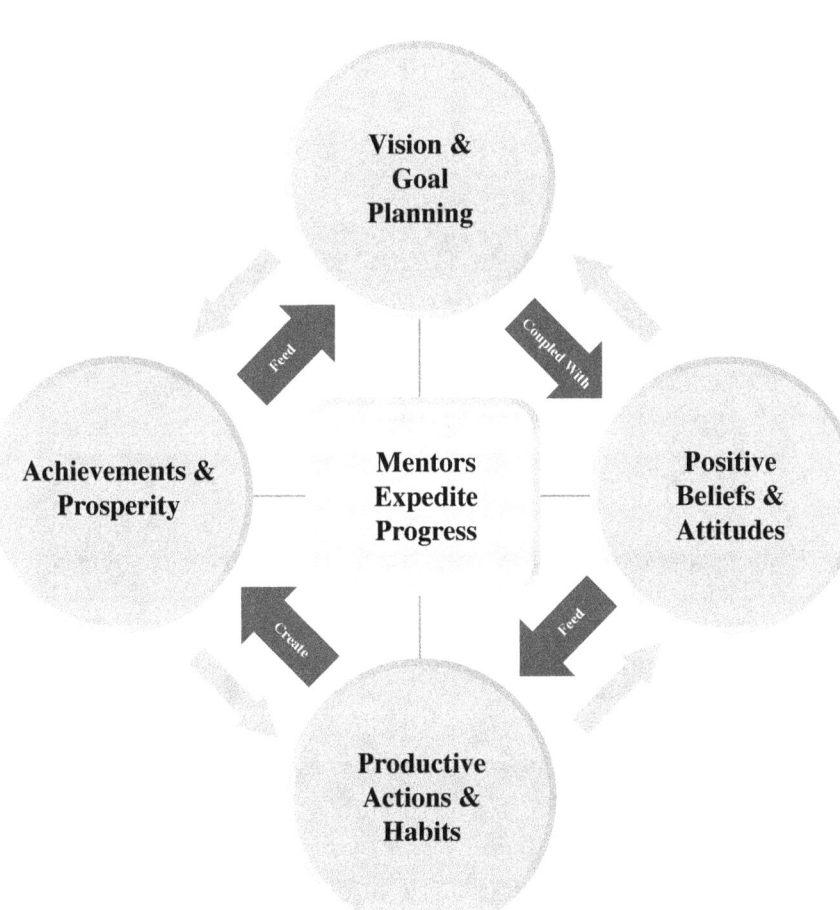

Chapter 11: Congratulations! Turn the page…

Structure & Building Blocks of Achievement & Prosperity

SUCCESS
SELF ACTUALIZATION
ACHIEVEMENT AND PROSPERITY

PEAK COMPETENCIES

| Opportunistic Timing & Risk | Genuine Integrity | High Self Concept | Adaptable | Persistent |

HIGH LEVEL COMPETENCIES

| Motivated | Generous | EQ Emotional Intelligence | Confident | Enthusiastic |

CORE COMPETENCIES

| Conditioning Mind & Body | Career & Brand Development | Core Social Cirle | Gratitude | Overcome Adversity |

FOUNDATIONAL COMPETENCIES

| Planning & Journaling | Positive Attitude | Productive Habits | Mentors | Knowledge & Learning | Financial Planning |

CORNERSTONE FOOTINGS & CYCLE OF ACHIEVEMENT

| Vision & Goals | Beliefs | Actions | Achievements |

AND FEED CREATE

© Copyright 2017 Richard S. Olin

Target of Beliefs & Self-Concept

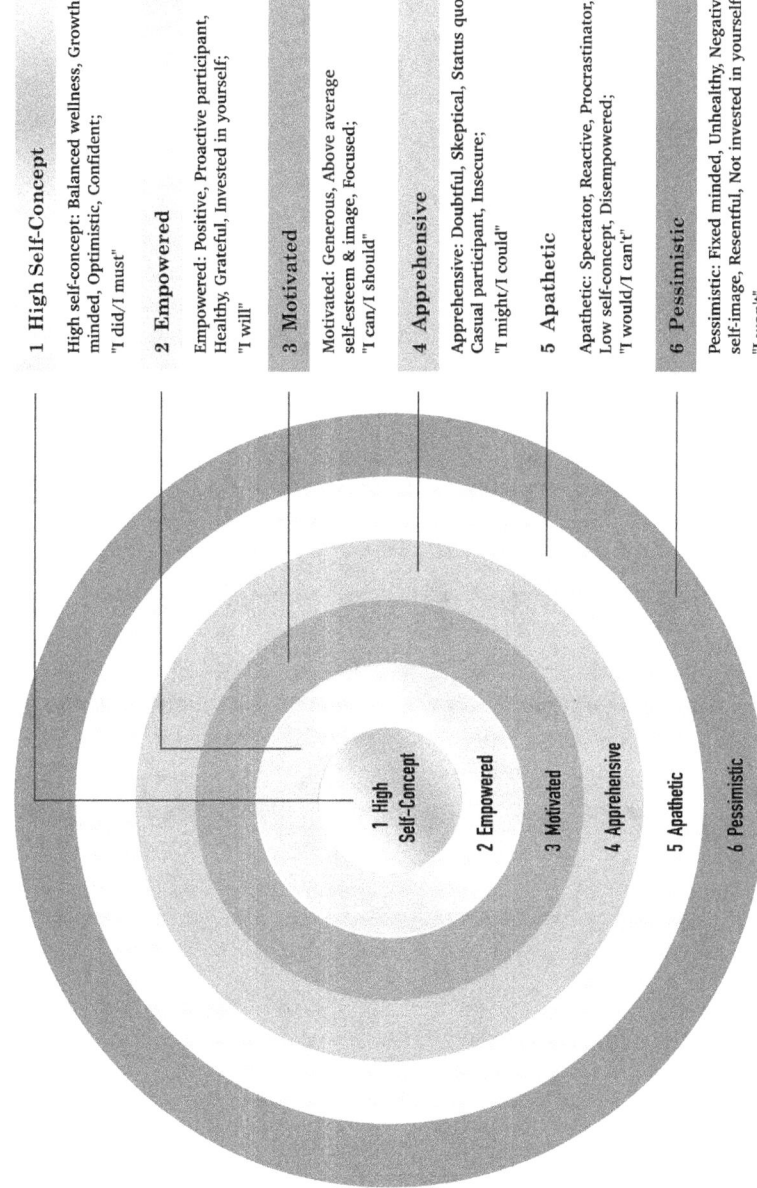

1 High Self-Concept

High self-concept: Balanced wellness, Growth minded, Optimistic, Confident;
"I did/I must"

2 Empowered

Empowered: Positive, Proactive participant, Healthy, Grateful, Invested in yourself;
"I will"

3 Motivated

Motivated: Generous, Above average self-esteem & image, Focused;
"I can/I should"

4 Apprehensive

Apprehensive: Doubtful, Skeptical, Status quo, Casual participant, Insecure;
"I might/I could"

5 Apathetic

Apathetic: Spectator, Reactive, Procrastinator, Low self-concept, Disempowered;
"I would/I can't"

6 Pessimistic

Pessimistic: Fixed minded, Unhealthy, Negative self-image, Resentful, Not invested in yourself;
"I won't"

Structure & Building Blocks of Financial Wellness

PROSPERITY

FINANCIAL WELLBEING

SECURITY & INDEPENDENCE

PEAK COMPETENCIES - DISTRIBUTION

| Alternative Investments | Tax Efficient Strategies | Philanthropic & Grateful | Complex Estate Planning | Hedging & Risk Management |

CORE COMPETENCIES - ACCUMULATION & CONSOLIDATION

| Real Estate Ownership & Income | Investment Planning | Retirement Income Planning | Debt Elimination | College 529 & State Prepaid Planning |

CORE COMPETENCIES - ACCUMULATION

| Low Cost Indexing | Asset Allocation & Diversification | Career Development | Dollar Cost Averaging & Rebalancing | Retirement Planning |

FOUNDATIONAL COMPETENCIES - PROTECTION

| Budgeting | Good Savings & Spending Habits | Emergency Fund | Insurance Planning | Basic Estate Planning |

CORNERSTONE FOOTINGS & CYCLE OF WELLNESS

| Vision & Goals | Beliefs | Actions | Financial Wellness |

AND — FEED — CREATE

© Copyright 2019 Richard S. Olin

Buckets of Money Strategy

1 $_____

Emergency Funds

6-12 months expenses

No risk liquid cash

2 $_____

Medium Term Funds

Partially protected & liquid

Moderate Risk & Return

3 $_____

Longer Term Funds

Retirement Assets 401k/IRA

Higher Risk & Return

4

Protection & Estate Plan

Insurance planning

Life, health, P&C, other.

5 $_____

Retirement Income Plan

Soc Sec + Assets + Pension =

Monthly income covers expenses

Resume Preparation Form

(make copies of sample)

Name _____

City, State _____

LinkedIn Address _____

Phone number(s) _____

Email Address _____

Professional objective and summary: _____

_____

_____

_____

Employment History – Professional Experience:

Employer _____ Dates _____ to _____

Job Title _____

Responsibilities and accomplishments:

_____

_____

_____

_____

Education: Degrees earned, Name of University or College, and State

_____

_____

Professional Development _____

_____

Technical Training _____

Honors_____

Associations/Organizations/Military _____

_____

Activities_____

_____

_____

Chapter 11: Congratulations! Turn the page…

My VISION and HOPE is that you will continue to use this guide, its prompts and the Workbook to:

- Inspire you to uncover your passions, vision, and mission and realize personal and professional success through self-reflection, planning, and implementation.

- Document through journaling prompts what is evident and important to you in your life and challenge you to adapt and overcome life's adversities.

- Motivate you to build your brand and career vision and a supportive inner core circle as a Board of Advocates and Advisors as mentors to help you.

- Motivate you to be a growth-minded participant versus a fixed-minded spectator in life and continue to learn and explore and transform routines into productive habits.

- Empower you to take control of your focus, beliefs and attitudes and utilize emotional hygiene techniques to elevate your emotional wellbeing. Help you become more positive, confident, compassionate, and build higher emotional intelligence and self-concept skills.

- Share strategies, resources, and competencies to help you plan and design a blueprint to transform your future and wellbeing. Educate you on key building blocks of achievement and prosperity.

- Empower you to invest in yourself as opposed to spending your gifted time on distractions.

- Convey the importance of continuing to search out new social connections and groups.

- Learn to create a comprehensive financial plan and take control of your cash flow, investments, and retirement strategies for your prosperity.

- Review and revise your essential life directory and organizer of all your personal, emergency and financial information, documents, passwords and login ID's, bucket list, and final wishes and more.

- Assist in planning your next steps for success related to most aspects of your life.

- Challenge you to volunteer, mentor, and give back to your community as a generous attempt to become more involved and live a more fulfilled life.

- Create a healthier, grateful, more mindful lifestyle and a balanced harmonic wellbeing.

- Help you plan well, live well, get well, adapt well, and grow well!

- Instill the importance of treating every day as a gift and not a given.

"You are the designer and architect of your future, destiny and wellbeing." — Richard S. Olin

ACKNOWLEDGMENTS

I have been very lucky throughout my life to be associated with so many gifted and genuine people. I want to first and foremost thank my wife, Paulette, for her hard work and dedication whose love, support, guidance, and friendship have allowed me the ability to search out my true passions and vision in life. She inspires me to reach for my full potential as she is the only person I know who lives a well-balanced wellness lifestyle. She has instilled in me the importance of many of the key competencies laid out in this book. I want to thank my daughter, Lauren, for assisting with several aspects of this guide including portions of the detailed research. A special thank you goes to both my son, Jonathan, and Lauren who have inspired me as a father, coach, and mentor to better understand from early on how important it is to focus on those aspects of life and be my best self. Jonathan has also acknowledged my limited ability as a musician and offered challenging and comforting words of encouragement that every aspiring musician needs. Thank you to my parents, Renee and late father, David, who were instrumental from a young age in my growth and development and providing me a stable foundation. I also want to acknowledge my sister, Jamie, and brother, Richard, and all of my friends for their continued love and support throughout my life and career.

NOTES

Introduction:

viii **Taking the time to self-reflect and take a logical approach; on wellbeing and being prosperous:** Hart, Michael H. *The 100: A Ranking of the Most Influential Persons in History.* A & W Publishers, 1978: pages 105-109.

viii **notion of true wellbeing, prosperity and "living the good life," as he called it, was that each of us should have balance between physical, emotional, intellectual, and political or social well-being:** Gilkey, Charlie. "The 3 Key Ideas from Aristotle That Will Help You Flourish." *Productive Flourishing*, 29 Feb. 2008,

viii **Additional information obtained from:** Barnes, Jonathan Edited. *The Complete Works of Aristotle.* Princeton University Press, 1984, USA www.productiveflourishing.com/aristotle-the-good-life-and-gtd/.

xvii **Millennials at jobs for 3.5 years:** Ng, Eddy. "Are Millennials More Likely to Switch Jobs and Employers?" *Psychology Today*, Sussex Publishers, 29 Mar. 2015, www.psychologytoday.com/us/blog/diverse-and-competitive/201503/are-millennials-more-likely-switch-jobs-and-employers.

Chapter 1: The Diamond Cycle of Achievement and Prosperity

7 **"emotion is the mind's perception"** James, William. "What is an Emotion". *Mind*. 1884.

7 **see a bear and run example:** Ibid. James, W.

Chapter 2: Vision Planning

12 **Studies consistently document that by writing down goals, you are much more likely to reach them, than if they're not written down:** Murphy, Mark. "Neuroscience Explains Why You Need to Write Down Your Goals If You Actually Want To Achieve Them." *Forbes*, Forbes Magazine, 15 Apr. 2018, www.forbes.com/sites/markmurphy/2018/04/15/neuroscience-explains-why-you-need-to-write-down-your-goals-if-you-actually-want-to-achieve-them/#60a878f17905.

12 **Effectiveness of writing down goals:** Cites a study by the Dominican University of California related to written goals and sharing goals. Greene, Brett. "New Tech Seattle." *New Tech Northwest*, 7 Aug. 2019, www.newtechnorthwest.com/the-psychology-of-writing-down-goals/.

Murphy, Mark. "Neuroscience Explains Why You Need to Write Down Your Goals If You Actually Want To Achieve Them." *Forbes*, Forbes Magazine, 15 Apr. 2018, www.forbes.com/sites/markmurphy/2018/04/15/neuroscience-explains-why-you-need-to-write-down-your-goals-if-you-actually-want-to-achieve-them/#60a878f17905.

16 **Michael Phelps's pre-meet visualization:** Phelps, Michael, and Brian Cazeneuve. *Michael Phelps: Beneath the Surface*. Sports Publishing, 2008.

16 **Alex Hannold visualization:** Chinn, Jimmy and Elizabeth Chai Vasarhelyi. *Free Solo*. National Geographic Documentary Films, 2018.

Chapter 3: Positive Beliefs

25 **Story of Nick Sitzman the railroad worker:** *Ekeren, Glen Van "The Speaker's Sourcebook" Englewood Cliffs, NJ: Prentice-Hall, 1988*

25 **Aristotle in 350 AD:** Hart, Michael H. *The 100: A Ranking of the Most Influential Persons in History.* A & W Publishers, 1978: page 105.

26 **"flourish as it is the proper"** Gilkey, Charlie. "Ideas from Aristotle That Will Help You Flourish." *Productive Flourishing*, 29 Feb. 2008, www.productiveflourishing.com/aristotle-the-good-life-and-gtd/.

26 **The growth mindset is based on the belief that your basic qualities and competencies can grow and develop through your efforts, learning, resources, strategies, and additional assistance from mentors and coaches: adapted from writings:** Dweck, Carol. *Mindset: The New Psychology of Success.* Ballantine Books, 2016.

27 Ibid. Dweck, Carol

30 **windshield and life metaphor adapted from:** Markel, Adam. *Pivot.* Atria Books/Simon & Schuster, Inc., 2016

33 **"a clumsy archer"** Desan, Paul and team *at The Pursuit of Happiness.* "Aristotle: Introduction: Aristotle's Definition of Happiness" www.pursuit-of-happiness.org/history-of-happiness/aristotle/

Adapted from: Aristotle, *Nicomachean Ethics* (2004), ed. Hugh Treddenick. London: Penguin.

Chapter 4: Productive Actions

39 **40% of daily routine:** Society for Personality and Social Psychology. "How We Form Habits, Change Existing Ones." *Science Daily*, 8 August 2014. www.sciencedaily.com/releases/2014/08/140808111931.

40 **8 hours of screen time per day:** Pesce, Nicole Lyn. "The Average U.S. Adult Will Spend Three Hours and 43 Minutes a Day on Mobile Devices This Year." *MarketWatch*, 6 June 2019, www.marketwatch.com/story/for-the-first-time-ever-americans-will-spend-more-time-on-mobile-devices-

than-watching-tv-2019-06-05.

40 **"A Quote by Steve Jobs."** *Goodreads*, Goodreads, www.goodreads.com/quotes/374630-your-time-is-limited-so-don-t-waste-it-living-someone.

Chapter 5: Celebrate Your Achievements

49 **"I have a choice today."** – Anonymous, not attributable to any one writer. My father shared this with me as a young man; 2010.

Chapter 6: Foundational Competencies

63 **Americans spend more time vacation:** Mitra, Mallika. "You're Not Alone If You Spend More Time Planning Your Vacation than Working on Your Finances." *CNBC*, CNBC, 2 Aug. 2019, www.cnbc.com/2019/08/02/1-in-5-people-spend-more-time-planning-vacations-than-finances-survey.html.

64 **Planning Process**: Revised from the US Army Corps of Engineers 6 step planning process. "6-Step Planning Process." *Planning Community Toolbox: Processes*, www.planning.erdc.dren.mil/toolbox/processes.cfm?Id=0&Option=6-Step%2BPlanning%2BProcess.

68 **"Life is 10% what happens"** Charles R. Swindoll Quotes (Author of The Grace Awakening)." *Goodreads*, www.goodreads.com/author/quotes/5139.Charles_R_Swindoll.

75 **Survey of AA programs:** Duhigg, Charles. *The Power of Habit.* Random House, 2012.

77 **Habits of wealthy individuals:** OK, Deji. "100 Success Habits of Self-Made Billionaires Entrepreneurs." *EliteSavvy.com*, 17 Mar. 2017, www.elitesavvy.com/2017/03/17/100-habits-self-made-billionaires/.

78 **Successful people, when surveyed, consistently rank having a mentor as being one of the most critical elements that helped make**

them successful during their growth period: Corley, Tom. "16 Rich Habits" *Success.com,* 8 Sept. 2016, www.success.com/16-rich-habits/.

85 **Studies and surveys consistently document how successful people spend a significant amount of time reading every day:** Ibid, Corley, Tom

92 **Studies document that wealthier Americans consistently rank reading, knowledge:** Ibid, Corley, Tom

94 "A Global Financial Literacy Test Finds That Just 57% Of Adults In U.S. Are Financially Literate." McGrath, Maggie. *Forbes*, Forbes Magazine, 20 Nov. 2015, www.forbes.com/sites/maggiemcgrath/2015/11/18/in-a-global-test-of-financial-literacy-the-u-s/.

95 **50% of high schools don't require personal finance:** Nova, Annie. "Financial Education Stalls, Threatening Kids' Future Economic Health." *CNBC*, 8 Feb. 2018, www.cnbc.com/2018/02/08/financial-education-stalls-threatening-kids-future-economic-health.html.

96 **63% don't have $500 for emergencies:** McGrath, Maggie. "63% Of Americans Don't Have Enough Savings to Cover A $500 Emergency." *Forbes*, 6 Jan. 2016, www.forbes.com/sites/maggiemcgrath/2016/01/06/63-of-americans-dont-have-enough-savings-to-cover-a-500-emergency/#f72d5c44e0d9.

104 **$300 in bank fees:** Bresiger, Gregory. "Most Americans Don't Realize How Much They Pay in Banking Fees." *MarketWatch*, 18 July 2016, www.marketwatch.com/story/most-americans-dont-realize-how-much-they-pay-in-banking-fees-2016-07-18.

106 **#2 Cause of Divorce:** Scott, Shelby B, et al. "Reasons for Divorce and Recollections of Premarital Intervention: Implications for Improving Relationship Education." *Couple & Family Psychology*, U.S. National Library of Medicine, June 2013, www.ncbi.nlm.nih.gov/pmc/articles/PMC4012696/.

120 **SPIVA ratio:** Liu, Berlinda. "SPIVA® U.S. Year-End 2019." *SPIVA® U.S. Year-End 2019 - S&P Dow Jones Indices*, 2 Apr. 2020, www.spglobal.com/spdji/en/spiva/article/spiva-us/.

122 **"The man who begins to speculate"** "The Man Who Begins to Speculate in Stocks with the Intention of Making a Fortune Usually Goes Broke, Whereas the Man Who Trades with a View of Getting Good Interest on His Money Sometimes Gets Rich. - Charles Dow." www.quotemaster.org/q544e5e3a46c2f3ad5e12bdf4749e217d.

137 **30% don't have a valid will:** "2020 Estate Planning and Wills Study." *Caring.com*, www.caring.com/caregivers/estate-planning/wills-survey.

Chapter 7: Balanced Harmonic WE Wellness Environment

154 **WE Wellness Environment:** Hudziak, Jim Dr. *Behavioral Change Health Studies*, University of Vermont; Larner College of Medicine, 2016

Chapter 8: Core Competencies

167 **Yoga for backpain:** Harvard Men's Health Watch/Tribune Content Agency. "Get Moving to Banish Those Aches and Pains." *The Star-Ledger, Affiliated with NJ.com*, 23 May 2019, p. H4.

167 **Mayo Clinic aerobic exercise:** Mayo Clinic Staff. "10 Great Reasons to Love Aerobic Exercise." *Mayo Clinic*, Mayo Foundation for Medical Education and Research, 5 Feb. 2020, www.mayoclinic.org/healthy-lifestyle/fitness/in-depth/aerobic-exercise/art-20045541.

169 **Australian study:** Academic Minute. Andrew Oswald, *University of Warwick* "Fruits, Vegetables and Happiness." 9 Dec. 2016, www.academicminute.org/2016/12/andrew-oswald-university-of-warwick-fruits-vegetables-and-happiness/.

170 **list of superfoods:** adapted from: Rosenbloom, Cara. "Mood Boosting

Foods." *The Star-Ledger, Affiliated with NJ.com*, 25 May 2017, p. 36. Also adapted from: Henry, Julie, RN, MPA. *NUTRITION*, BarCharts Publishing, Inc., 2016. Both of these sources had food, drinks, and supplements that dieticians have found beneficial. I adapted these recommendations to create a simplified list that I personally have seen results from.

171 **Registered dieticians:** Cohen, Deborah A, MD, MPH, and Mary Story, PHD. "Mitigating the Health Risks of Dining out: The Need for Standardized Portion Sizes in Restaurants." *American Journal of Public Health*, American Public Health Association, Apr. 2014, www.ncbi.nlm.nih.gov/pmc/articles/PMC4025680/.

172 **National Academies of Sciences, Engineering, Medicine:** "Report Sets Dietary Intake Levels for Water, Salt, and Potassium to Maintain Health and Reduce Chronic Disease Risk." *The National Academies of Sciences, Engineering, and Medicine,* 11 Feb. 2004, www.nationalacademies.org/news/2004/02/report-sets-dietary-intake-levels-for-water-salt-and-potassium-to-maintain-health-and-reduce-chronic-disease-risk.

173 **Proper laying position:** Rosario, Francesca Del. "5 Benefits of Placing A Pillow Between Legs When Sleeping." *ECOSA,* 5 June 2020, www.ecosa.com.au/blog/post/5-benefits-of-placing-a-pillow-between-legs.html.

179 **CareerBuilder Survey:** "One-Third of Workers Do Not Work in Occupations Related to Their College Major." *Press Room | Career Builder*, 14 Nov. 2013, www.press.careerbuilder.com/2013-11-13-One-Third-of-Workers-Do-Not-Work-in-Occupations-Related-to-Their-College-Major.

187 **Networking:** Morgan, Hannah. "Don't Believe These 8 Job Search Myths." *U.S. News & World Report*, 17 Sept. 2014, money.usnews.com/money/blogs/outside-voices-careers/2014/09/17/dont-believe-these-8-job-search-myths.

193 **SOAR answer to interview questions adapted:** Collamer, Nancy. "The No. 1 Way To Nail A Job Interview." *Forbes,* 2 May, 2017 www.forbes.com/sites/nextavenue/2017/05/02/the-no-1-way-to-nail-a-job-interview/#7c8159c55c29.

205 **Zig Ziglar Gratitude:** Ziglar, Tom. "The Gratitude Journey." *Ziglar Inc,* 30 Mar. 2017, www.ziglar.com/articles/the-gratitude-journey/

205 **University of California Berkeley letter of gratitude study:** Brown, Joshua and Joel Wong. "How Gratitude Changes You and Your Brain." *Greater Good,* 6 June 2017, www.greatergood.berkeley.edu/article/item/how_gratitude_changes_you_and_your_brain.

207 **They also usually have better overall mental health and a decreased amount of depression:** Source: 2012 study in Personality and Individual Differences; *Forbes.* 2012

207 **grateful people tend to exercise more:** Craig, Heather, BPsySc. "The Research on Gratitude and Its Link with Love and Happiness." *PositivePsychology.com,* 18 Mar.2020, www.positivepsychology.com/gratitude-research/.

211 **Bum Phillips:** "Bum Phillips Quote #6." *247Sports,* www.247sports.com/Coach/3616/Quotes/You-fail-all-the-time-but-you-arent-a-failure-until-you-start-bl-35961247/.

213 **Problem Solving Process:** *The Problem Solving Process.* www.gdrc.org/decision/problem-solve.html.

214 **face rejection:** OK, Deji. "100 Success Habits of Self-Made Billionaires Entrepreneurs." *EliteSavvy.com,* 17, Mar. 2017, www.elitesavvy.com/2017/03/17/100-habits-self-made-billionaires/.

Chapter 9: High Level Competencies

218 **"status-quo is often the symptom"** – not attributable to one individual; anonymous

220 **The road to someday lead's to nowhere:** Robbins, Anthony. *Personal Power 2*, Robbins Research International Inc., 1 Jan. 1996

222 **we mutually benefit from these kind acts of kindness:** Watanabe, Teresa. "Will Cultivating Kindness Make Us All Healthier?" *The Star Ledger*, 22, Dec. 2019 Study completed by UCLA Bedari Kindness Institute.

222 **increased biochemical activity:** Gerasimo, Pilar and Dallas Hartwig. "Generosity." *Experience Life*, Dec. 2019, p. 81. Stanford University Study.

222 **generosity of the heart and mind:** Ibid, Watanabe, T.

226 **self-awareness, self-regulation, management. Social skills as well:** Michael Akers & Grover Porter. "What Is Emotional Intelligence (EQ)?" *Psych Central*, 30 July 2020, www.psychcentral.com/lib/what-is-emotional-intelligence-eq.

228 **"IQ only accounts for around 10% of ingredients":** Michael Akers & Grover Porter. "What Is Emotional Intelligence (EQ)?" *Psych Central*, 30 July 2020, www.psychcentral.com/lib/what-is-emotional-intelligence-eq.

229 **EQ Test** adapted from Travis Bradberry article: I consolidated 12 leading questions in the EQ test based on Bradberry's article of 18 characteristics: Bradberry, Travis. "18 Signs You Have High Emotional Intelligence." *Business Insider*, Business Insider, 3 March 2016, www.businessinsider.com/18-signs-you-have-high-emotional-intelligence-2015-2.

232 **Psychologists have found that confidence comes from the belief:** "Learning, Remembering, Believing: Enhancing Human Performance." *National Academies Press*, 1994, www.nap.edu/read/2303/chapter/13#174.

233 **a study on athletic teams found a correlation:** Skinner, Benjiman R., "The Relationship Between Confidence and Performance Throughout a Competitive Season" (2013). All Graduate Plan B and other Reports. 285. www://digitalcommons.usu.edu/gradreports/285

Chapter 10: Peak Competencies

248 **Identifying I am me:** James, William. *Principles of Psychology*; *Consciousness of Self,* Henry Holt and Company, Vol 1, 1890 and *The Writings of William James; Comprehensive Edition*, Random House, NY 1967

257 **"Genius is 1% inspiration"** "Genius Is One Percent Inspiration and Ninety-Nine Percent; Thomas Edison Perspiration." *Dictionary.com*, Dictionary.com, www.dictionary.com/browse/genius-is-one-percent-inspiration-and-ninety-nine-percent-perspiration.

258 **"I've missed more than 9,000 shots"** Jordan, Michael. "ForbesQuotes." Forbes, Forbes Magazine, www.forbes.com/quotes/11194/.

Chapter 11: Conclusion

262 **"set our aim high"** A Quote by Michelangelo Buonarroti.

263 **Aristotle teaches us:** Gilkey, Charlie. "Ideas from Aristotle That Will Help You Flourish." *Productive Flourishing*, 29 Feb. 2008, www.productiveflourishing.com/aristotle-the-good-life-and-gtd/.

Start of weekly and/or monthly journaling

Mission, vision & goals journal & collage

_____

_____

_____

Beliefs & attitudes journal

_____

_____

_____

Actions & habits/routines journal

_____

_____

_____

Achievements journal & collage

_____

_____

_____

Mentors journal

_____

_____

_____

_____

Knowledge & intellectual journal

_____
_____
_____

Financial journal – copy spreadsheets

_____
_____
_____

Physical conditioning and food journal

_____
_____
_____

Emotional conditioning journal

_____
_____
_____

Branding & career development journal

_____
_____
_____

Social circle journal

_____
_____
_____

Gratitude journal

_____
_____
_____

Overcoming adversities journal

_____
_____
_____

Motivational journal

_____
_____
_____

Generosity journal

_____
_____
_____

Emotional intelligence EQ journal

_____
_____
_____

Self-confidence and self-esteem/image journal

_____
_____
_____

Success, self-actualization, wellness and prosperity journal

_____
_____
_____
_____
_____
_____
_____
_____
_____
_____

Dedicate some time to going backwards in time to document prior years highlighting key elements including achievements, visions, beliefs, important considerations, dates, challenges, self-reflecting thoughts, and life changing events.

_____
_____
_____
_____
_____
_____
_____
_____
_____
_____

ABOUT THE AUTHOR

Throughout his life, Richard has dedicated himself to being a devoted husband, son, and father to his two inspirational and wonderful children, Lauren and Jonathan. He strived to be a mentor and coach to them, as well as to countless associates, colleagues and employees that he has engaged, managed, and worked with. Richard is an author, advisor, speaker, musician, and adventurer who enjoys the challenge of identifying and achieving new passions and learning new disciplines to becoming well-rounded and reach his full potential.

Richard has been a lifelong volunteer donating his time and energy supporting important causes dear to him including Habitat for Humanity, Boys & Girls Clubs, Special Olympics, Multiple Sclerosis, Junior Achievement, and local food banks, and as a youth sports coach. He was a lead Regional Volunteer Champion for a division of Bank of America/Merrill Lynch during his management career with the organization where he encouraged and garnered widespread associate support for these and many other beneficial non-profit community-based initiatives.

His professional experience includes a successful career as Vice President and Market Sales Manager for Bank of America/Merrill Lynch as a

Registered Supervisory Principal managing teams of Financial Advisors, Relationship Managers and Bankers and a region of the bank's Financial Centers. Throughout his illustrious career, he has been a lead trainer for the Division and designed associated training programs.

As a tenured Financial Advisor, he has consulted with, designed, and implemented planning strategies for scores of clients regarding their financial, investment, retirement, insurance, college and estate planning needs. Prior to this, he was an Estate Planning Manager, Licensed Real Estate Appraiser and Realtor, and small business owner. He has also enjoyed working as a recruiter, mortgage consultant and bartender.

Some of his additional interests include playing guitar and harmonica, being an amateur magician, entrepreneur, adventurer, investor, gardener and collector (or as his wife calls, a hoarder). Richard's major accomplishments besides this work, his career, and family dedication, include cycling the Pyrenees Mountains, completing 110 miles of bicycling in one day, skiing some of the high peaks of North America, successfully completing several challenging career transitions and starting and managing several successful small businesses.

Richard's mission is to educate, inspire, and empower individuals to become the architect of their future and wellbeing. To encourage them to design and develop a vision and blueprint to be successful and realize their HarmonicWE or a well-balanced wellness environment and prosperous lifestyle.

He has extensive knowledge and experience as a longtime presenter, coach and trainer on topics encompassing vision and mission planning, balanced wellness, transforming your future and wellbeing, career development, financial, investment, retirement and estate planning strategies, emotional wellness, real estate valuation and sales best practice related topics.

Richard Olin is available for dynamic and entertaining musically infused presentations. As a professional speaker Richard inspires, educates and energizes audiences to develop a playbook and roadmap for reaching their full and desired potential in life. His interactive presentations motivate, challenge and empower attendees to create a personalized actionable next steps plan for success.

For further information on large quantity orders or select speaking engagements please contact us at:

Harmonicwe@gmail.com

www.Richardolin.com

www.HarmonicWE.com

www.ingramcontent.com/pod-product-compliance
Lightning Source LLC
Chambersburg PA
CBHW070300010526
44108CB00039B/1383